Living Overseas

Living Overseas

By LOUISE WINFIELD

FOREWORD BY HARLAN CLEVELAND

Public Affairs Press, Washington, D. C.

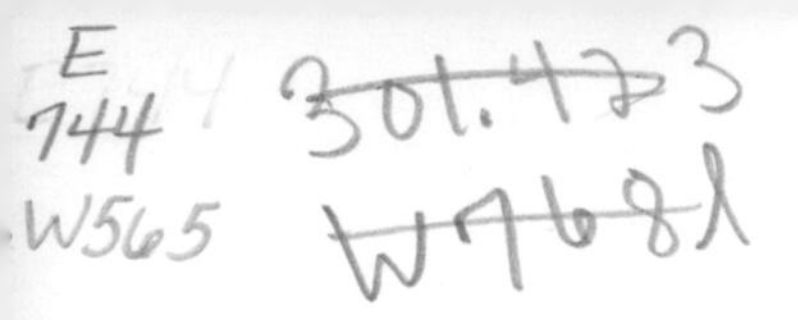

THIS IS A GUIDEBOOK FOR AMERICANS
WHO FOLLOW JOBS TO THE ENDS OF THE EARTH
AND A REPORT TO THE FOLKS AT HOME
WHO WONDER WHAT IT IS LIKE TO BE
TWENTIETH CENTURY PIONEERS

419 New Jersey Avenue, S. E., Washington 3, D. C.
Printed in the United States of America
Library of Congress Catalog Card No. 61-18155

FOREWORD

On December 1, 1961, at a home in Alexandria, Virginia, five Cabinet wives met with three Foreign Service wives and a dozen other disstaff representatives of the New Frontier. In an all day Kaffeeklatsch remarkable for sticking to the subject, they tried to decide how wives could best help their husbands while traveling. The Cabinet wives were just back from that week last autumn in which half the United States Cabinet migrated to Tokyo. On the plane coming home, the men talked about the Japanese balance of payments, but their wives were deciding that something had to be done about training American women for overseas life and work.

Unknown to them, the wife of a long-time Foreign Aid official was just finishing this book. It becomes, on publication, the best guide to overseas living in a regrettably sparse literature on the subject.

Yet the notes on that historic little meeting in Alexandria could have served as the outline for the concentrated package of wisdom you now hold in your hand or have propped up on the drainboard. For the Cabinet wives, with that excess of parentheses characteristic of female prose — but not of Louise Winfield's — covered a mighty range of relevant topics:

"Best ways to get acquainted,"

"Hostile criticism, how to deal with it,"

"Problems of climate (mildew),"

"Servants (may quarrel, may leave, communication difficult),"

"Things to avoid (like wearing red, white or black at the wrong time),"

"Rats, insects, wildcats, etc. to deal with."

The last entry is followed shortly by another, perhaps on a different subject: "Entertaining American Officials (A pleasure!)".

When it was all over the New Frontier's women agreed on a final report which Mrs. Dean Rusk submitted to the Secretary of State. The Department of State now says it is going to do something about training officials wives who go abroad, and "debriefing" them when they get home. The Department had better do so: Big Sister is watching. For the lighthearted notes on the Alexandria meeting shifted near the end to an ominous and threatening tone:

"Discussion resumed on financial limitations of the Department and the Foreign Service.

"Indignation, 1: No money for training F.S. wives, a serious mistake . . .".

Louise Winfield has produced just the text these cheerful and earnest ladies thought somebody should write. Her book is as readable as a whodunit and as useful as a cookbook. She teaches without preaching, guides without shoving. Every American going overseas, to live or to visit, should take her book along.

HARLAN CLEVELAND

Washington, D.C.

PREFACE

With approximately 1,800,000 Americans, including about 250,000 family groups, now living outside the boundaries of the United States there is a need, expressed by many, for a comprehensive yet informal volume designed to answer questions of fact and to raise for discussion questions regarding the attitudes, purposes, and practices of those who live abroad. I have undertaken to write such a book because I am so much aware of the importance of the way our citizens live in other countries. How they conduct themselves is of consequence to them, to the people among whom they live, and to all who stay at home but nonetheless are represented by those who go abroad.

Knowing well that each person must form out of the patterns and resources of his own individuality the design for his life abroad just as he must do wherever he lives, I have avoided the temptation to draw one blueprint and offer it to all readers who expect to live and work overseas. It has been my purpose, however, to discuss the kinds of problems and adjustments that most families find in many foreign communities, to give sources of information, and to suggest principles, procedures, and examples that may be applicable in a great variety of situations.

(The term 'family' has been used not just to denote parents and children but also to refer to a husband and wife without children as well as to individuals or groups of individuals who maintain their own homes.)

Throughout the book I have been writing about the why of doing this or that as well as the how-to-do-it because in most cases that matter seriously the reasons for doing are basic to the ways of doing. Without apology I have stated the values at stake as I see them because I am concerned about the implementation of values in today's world.

In deciding upon the contents and preparing the materials for the following sections, I have drawn upon our family's experiences in pre-war China and in post-war Burma as well as observations in other countries we have visited during the years since 1932 when my husband has had one or another assignment in a foreign country or has been directly related to overseas programs. I have been guided also by conversations and correspondence with many who have returned from overseas or who are now living abroad. The latter group includes a married daughter and her husband who have completed a tour of duty in Asia and are presently living with their young children in a newly independent country of Africa.

I have been in touch with people who are responsible for hiring and directing overseas employees in business, in church groups, in government, and in private philanthropies. I have asked men and women of other countries to tell me what they think Americans who live among them should keep in mind.

If I were to attempt to acknowledge all the individuals who have contributed to this enterprise I would have to go back thirty years and call the roll of friends and colleagues, of strangers and passers-by who at one time or another have inspired me, stimulated me, provoked me, or otherwise provided me with ideas and experiences out of which this material is largely drawn.

In recent months there have been numerous people in government offices; in business establishments; in foundation, mission or council offices; in libraries and in schools who have responded to my requests for specific data.

I would mention in particular Esther Cole Franklin who is the director of the course for wives offered in connection with the training program for international business executives at the School of International Service of the American University in Washington, D. C. If Dr. Franklin hadn't prodded me so relentlessly and encouraged me so heartily I might never have set myself to the task of completing a manuscript which has been writing itself in my mind for a number of years.

* * *

As recently as 1946 the movement of American families to other parts of the world was an uncommon phenomenon, limited for the most part to missionaries, to diplomats, to certain business people, and to a relatively small number of army and navy families. At the present time it would be hard to find a city neighborhood or a rural community that doesn't count among its former residents people who are now living in foreign countries.

The new frontiers of opportunity beyond the borders of our own land are attracting American men and women from a great variety of places and professions. County agents are learning that new governments, beset with old problems, are wanting men with practical experience to help them increase their yield per acre. University professors are applying for fellowships for study abroad. Engineers are reading advertisements about job openings in foreign countries. Teachers are challenged by the eager looks on the pictured faces of illiterates. Young economists are approached by firms with overseas contracts. Churchmen are being inspired to give time and talents to overseas projects. Retired professional people are realizing that their maturity and abilities are in demand in rapidly developing, and newly industrialized parts of the world. Young men and women with skill and dedication are putting aside personal plans and professional opportunities to join the Peace Corps and perform useful service in needy areas of the world.

Most of the applicants who are selected for overseas work will be successful as employees and also as personal representatives of our country. Some will be decorated by the heads of foreign governments for service distinguished and beyond the terms of a contract. Some will be members of teams which will make significant inroads on age old enemies of humanity. Some will have tear-splashed garlands placed around their necks, as devoted friends and household servants bid them farewell when their assignments overseas are completed. Many, probably unaware that they have done anything more than the jobs demanded, will have been directly responsible for steps forward in good government, in sound social planning, in professional integrity and competence, and in industrial efficiency and productivity. Some of the unassuming ones will have contributed also towards a world community in which there is more understanding and more hope.

On the other hand, some of the men and women who are now preparing to leave America will, before long, find themselves quietly—and in not a few cases sadly—packing for a premature return to the United States. Others will stay out their terms but will not have contract renewals offered to them. It isn't because these people will lack professional qualifications, or will not have worked hard at their jobs. The abandonment of an overseas career may be the result of failure to adjust to overseas living, of the inability of one or of all members of a family to take the shocks of cultural difference and the pressures of change and uncertainty. Or it may be that unwittingly or carelessly an American will have permitted himself or his family to disregard the customs and feelings of the people in the host countries

Employers are becoming very much aware of the importance of the wife's role, and of the total family impact wherever Americans are working. Whereas just a few years ago it was only the employee himself who was interviewed by a personnel director, now wives as well as husbands are often asked to be present when overseas jobs are described. Frequently, a recruiting officer calls at a prospective employee's home to better assess the intangible qualities of husband and wife and of children as well.

Church mission agencies have long been sensitive to the importance of sending abroad only those married men who have well qualified wives. They have known that just one unsuitable missionary in a non-Christian community can damage the reputation and the opportunities for useful service for all missionaries in that country.

Today the directors of firms whose stated objective in sending employees abroad is to operate economically profitable businesses want to satisfy themselves not that wives can wear clothes well and conduct themselves with poise at a dinner given by a company's president, but that the women about to be sent to New Delhi or Rio de Janerio or Accra or Beruit have such graces as humility, acceptance of other people, and teachability. The directors must know that the wives as well as their husbands can keep sober, can be responsible in unpredictable circumstances, and that they can be depended upon to demonstrate staying power in the face of either monotony or sudden crisis.

All employers who send people abroad have much at stake in their success. A business executive recently estimated that it costs his firm $50,000 to get one man on a job overseas. This includes preliminary training in this country, costs of moving a family and allowances for the establishment of a new home as well as the employee's salary during the first months when he can only be learning his way around in the new situation. "We can't afford to make a mistake," the executive commented.

Government agencies are particularly vulnerable if those they send abroad do not measure up in their day-by-day behavior. All government employees together with their wives and children are in foreign countries officially, and misconduct or blunders by any of them might complicate the workings of diplomacy and reflect upon our country's reputation.

Efforts are now being made by various organizations not only to screen and test an employee scheduled for work abroad and to give him training for the overseas job itself but also to provide guidance in the life-adjustment aspects of the assignment for him and also for his wife; in some cases for his older children as well.

The Protestant mission groups were among the first to recognize the need for special preparation on the part of families going to live in foreign countries. For more than forty years major missionary agencies have cooperated in conducting training conferences for outgoing missionaries. Wives have been expected to be present with their husbands for the sessions which now extend through six weeks. Attention has been given to the way missionaries live overseas as well as to the religions and cultures of the people among whom they work.

Several Protestant groups have recently established retreats for the families of laymen going abroad in secular positions. Currently contemplated is a coordination of such projects under the direction of the Committee on American Laymen Overseas of the National Council of Churches.

Leading commercial firms with overseas branches or affiliations have associated themselves together in the Business Council for International Understanding which for the third year is sponsoring training programs for international executives at the American University in Washington. Each session runs for four weeks with two or four additional weeks of intensive language study optional for both husbands and wives. During the third week there is a separate and comprehensive course for wives who are encouraged to join their husbands for special area study during the fourth week.

Government agencies have not in recent years been able to offer adequate training for the wives of their overseas employees because Congress did not provide the necessary legislation nor make sufficient appropriations. Wives have been generally permitted to sit-in on all but classified sessions of the general training programs, and several agencies have been able to arrange for a few hours of special briefing for wives. But the State Department's Foreign Service Institute has not been able to conduct separate training for the wives upon whose shoulders inevitable fall heavy responsibilities as they operate their households abroad under new and often difficult conditions, as they guide their families in adapting to what may be radically different cultures, and as they stand beside their husbands to represent our country in the capital cities of the world.

In September 1961 the Foreign Service Act was amended to make possible "appropriate orientation and language training" for members of families of government officers and other employees anticipating an assignment abroad. This is an encouraging development and I earnestly hope that ample funds will be made available so that not only foreign service wives but overseas-bound dependents in all agencies of government, including the armed forces, will be able to participate in orientation programs. Funds need to be supplied for travel of entire families to training centers where expanded projects should include special orientation activities for older children, and enough supervisory care for younger children so that wives can be freed to give careful attention to the extensive courses planned especially for them.

With the emergence of the Peace Corps a new emphasis on training for work abroad is merging. Orientation centers are being set up at universities and other places throughout the country to provide several months of vigorous and intensive training for the volunteers. We can be sure that the how-you-live-abroad aspect is not being overlooked.

Opportunities for learning how to live effectively and acceptably overseas are increasing. Even so, one hears again and again the observation that there ought to be more in print than is now available which people might read when they are first facing the prospects of moving away from the United States, to which they might refer as they make preparations for the trip, and about which they might think after they are settled in their new homes.

Reports describing living conditions at specific posts and in relation to definite jobs are usually made available by sending agencies. These reports are invaluable for all those fortunate enough to secure them. But of necessity they are streamlined, and are usually designed to give only matter-of-fact information. They are not prepared for the purpose of relating abstract values to actual conditions of overseas living nor to present a concept of the role of the family unit—whether it be a family of one or of ten—in the framework of the new dimensions of America's involvement in world affairs. Such a discussion could be attempted only in a book.

Other books on related subjects are available and have specialized usefulness for those going overseas. Studies about Americans abroad have been made by sociologists, by anthropologists, by political scientists, by educators, and by churchmen. Many of their findings have great merit, but they do not usually give a picture of the whole range of adjustments and opportunities which an individual American faces overseas, nor do they attempt to pull together the various threads that must be included in the fabric of living for those who leave their homeland. The travel handbooks, on the other hand, are too simplified and stay too much on the surface to be helpful to those who want to think in depth about the adventure that awaits them in a new land.

This book has been written with the hope that it will challenge Americans living in other countries to see the importance of their roles in a stronger light, that it will help them to handle their problems more confidently, and that it will to some extent make it possible for them to find the experience of living overseas to be more meaningful and rewarding.

It has been written also with the hope that the stay-at-home countrymen who read my report will have a better understanding of what is involved when their friends or relatives or unknown fellow citizens pack up and move—in family style—to far off fields where their presence could stir up trouble for them, for their new neighbors, or for all of us; but where if they care enough and if they are careful enough, they may be able to have a part in producing a kind and a quantity of good will never before available to the sons and daughters of men.

LOUISE WINFIELD

Falls Church, Virginia

CONTENTS

CHAPTER I

ON YOUR MARK

The period following a decision to go overseas is for many families characterized not only by feverish efforts to get ready to leave but also by a mixture of eagerness and apprehension.

It is, indeed, a cause for excitement that a family should find itself faced with the prospect of going halfway around the world, or that people who have long dreamed that they might see strange lands and know other peoples, find that dream suddenly taking form.

A child runs out of the house shouting, "Guess what I am going to do? I'm going to ride on a jet plane and an elephant. Guess where I am going? I'm going to Bangkok and that's in Thailand." Friends rush in exclaiming, "You lucky people."

The atmosphere becomes charged with anticipation. Older children get impatient waiting while younger children think that each overhead plane is the one they are going on and clamor to be leaving.

But the same child who has been so excited about leaving may come back into the house at bedtime asking, "Why can't Alice go with us? Alice is my best friend. Why are we going to let other people live in our house? This is our house why can't we go on living in it? Why must we go to Thailand?"

The very neighbors who expressed envy when they first heard of the proposed move raise questions, "Aren't you afraid to take the children to a part of the world where there is so much disease and poverty? How ever will you manage with servants and shopkeepers not speaking English? Don't you feel anxious leaving this country with the international situation so threatening?"

If the children didn't cling to friends and familiar places, if the pessimistic neighbors never came nor commented, a wife would, in any case, probably take a second look at the family's decision and wonder about it. The wondering may be only vague and brooding. Other times it may focus on some one doubt or insecurity and for a longer or shorter period of time it is like an acute infection. I call it 'interimitis.' Women are most commonly the victims. The men have jobs in their familiar professional areas to think about and to prepare for during the interim. But women have a hundred and one unknowns to wonder about at night and countless getting-ready-to-go tasks to wrestle with during the days which may already be loaded with housekeeping and child care.

"I have butterflies!" a friend said to me one day and I could tell from her voice that it was not an affectation but a real case of nerves. Her husband had accepted an overseas assignment and only the evening before at a neighborhood gathering she had been gayly discussing the adventure ahead of them.

"Is it the boys?" I asked her because a high school senior and a college student were staying behind.

"No, I faced that one before we decided to go. They both have what it takes to be on their own for the school months," she replied.

"Is it Judy, then?" I queried. She had obviously called me because she felt the need of talking about her anxiety, and I thought it might concern the younger child who was being pulled out of school at midyear to go into a situation where school opportunities were at best uncertain.

"Judy's going to love every minute of South America, and it will be good for her. No, it's me that I'm worried about. How do I know that I won't flounder around like a fish out of water? This new assignment means everything to Ned. What if I let him down somehow?"

The surprising thing is not that even sturdy and resourceful people like my friend become jittery while they are getting ready to move into unfamiliar territory. The thing to note is that in spite of feeling uncertain so many wives move up to the starting line with so much courage. I have seen it happen again and again. A woman is thrilled about an overseas assignment. Then she goes through a period of being frightened. In the end she pulls herself together, gets her family and their possessions organized and moves boldly into the new venture.

Sometimes time out for talk with an understanding friend can provide the shot in the arm which will put a woman back on her feet again. For most people reassurance can come only as they get specific information about the country and the particular situation to which they are going and so have a frame of reference against which they can weigh their uncertainties.

What Is It Like Over There?

After we had decided to go to Burma some years ago, we realized that we had only the foggiest picture of the place where we expected to live for two or three years. We knew the lines from Kipling about the old Moulmein pagoda and the road to Mandalay; but we did not know how much rain falls on those roads, what kind of people worship at the pagodas, what their government is like, and what their economic circumstances are. As we assembled information concerning the country to which we were moving, I felt easier about living there because with some knowledge of what it was like I could begin to plan more realistically.

General facts about a country are easy to find. We pulled out the atlas and saw exactly where Burma is in relation to other countries in Southeast Asia. In a few minutes we had learned about rivers, mountains, climate, and vegetation. After the children were in bed I read the Brittanica's section on Burma and the next morning I had interesting items to serve up to the family with breakfast. I had left the volume open so that the others could see the pictures of rice being harvested, of elephants moving teak logs, of water buffalos trampling grain, of a Buddhist priest with his begging bowl, of the Rangoon market, the modern oil wells, and the spacious harbor. The children went off to school less sad about the prospect of leaving friends because they were getting more interested in the place to which they would be going.

After school the two oldest went to the public library and came back with several books which the librarian had recommended for background reading about Burma. "Listen to this," was an expression frequently heard in our household during the succeeding weeks when one or another member of the family would bring some interesting bit of information about the country to the attention of all of us.

We were fortunate to have a library with some recent books about the country to which we were going and a librarian who was happy to help the children locate them. An appropriate place to start acquiring information about a foreign country is a library, but it sometimes takes careful searching to find the kind of books needed by those moving abroad. Books must be examined to see how up-to-date they are. Those published more than twenty five years might make interesting reading, but in order to learn what a country is like today one needs to find books that have come out in the last ten years.

A librarian whose books about foreign countries are limited is sometimes able to make inquiries and secure suitable books on loan from larger libraries. Also she might permit the inquirer to go through the library's pamphlet files which are generally not indexed but which often include useful material about foreign places.

My husband received information about Burma from the government agency which was employing him. From recommended reading lists we selected several books which seemed important enough to buy. One book, *Burmese Family,* written by a woman of the country, Mi Mi Khaing, and describing much that general books did not include about family practices and community customs was given to us by friends who had returned from Burma. It was invaluable.

If we were moving overseas with some firm or agency which did not provide book lists and country reports as the government agencies do, I would write to the embassy of the country to which we were assigned. A letter, for instance, could be addressed to The Information Officer, Embassy of India, Washington, D. C. I would tell him of our plan to live in his country, giving him the name of the city we expected to be in, and stating the name of the firm or institution with which we would be associated. I would request him to send me any material describing his country, particularly the section in which we would be living. I would ask him also for the names of books which he would recommend.

A letter to the Tourist Office of the government of the country to which a family is going (addressed care of the Tourist Bureau of the government, at the capital city) is likely to be useful if the letter is sent air mail and if there is time enough for a reply to be received. Travel bureaus, air lines with overseas services, and steamship companies have interesting and colorful pamphlets which they will mail in reply to an inquiry for information about a specific part of the world.

There is no excuse for Americans remaining uninformed about places to which they are going. Every effort should be made to get hold of dependable information and to absorb just as much of it as possible before departure.

One naturally cannot expect to learn in a few weeks, particularly weeks filled with shopping and packing and farewell parties, all that there is to know about a country, but he can learn a great deal and he can get an inkling of how much more there is to know. Even the beginning of knowledge about another country makes for a lessening of uncertainty about leaving home and will make it possible for one to be more at ease when he arrives in a new place. For those who go with eagerness and an open mind there will be endless opportunities to increase their knowledge and understanding of a land and its people.

What Shall We Take?

A friend who has returned from Cambodia tells me that when she had an attack of interimitis before leaving this country, her anxieties took the form of worry about clothes. She had no difficulty deciding what to take for two growing children—whose needs are actually more unpredictable than her own—but she kept wondering if her own clothes were all right. "As if clothes could ever make that much difference," she says now. But to a woman faced with the task of getting together a wardrobe sufficient for two years for herself, her three children, and in some cases for a you-get-what-you-think-I-need husband, clothes can seem pretty important.

It is important to have suitable and comfortable clothing overseas, but instead of worrying about one's wardrobe or rushing out to buy just anything, it is wise to consider the particular factors of the foreign situation and then to make a shopping list in accordance with those factors.

First, there is the question of climate. Will it be cold or hot, damp or dry? Are there climatic variations which require several kinds of clothes or is a year-round type of clothing indicated? Suppose you are going to live in a very damp climate, then nylon things are best because nylon dries quickly after washing. But if it is likely to be very hot in that damp place, then cotton is preferable because it is cooler and more readily absorbs perspiration. Some places which are only moderately cold in the winter are also damp and if there is no central heating in office buildings or homes then warm clothing is essential. Thank goodness it is now possible to buy insulated undies which are soft and light as well as warm, instead of being like the scratchy and bulky red flannels we had to wear thirty years ago in North China where it was dry but very cold and very windy in the winter.

Another basic factor about clothing is the nature of an employee's job and the type of social life expected to go along with it. Government officials and business executives naturally dress for their offices less casually than a technician assigned to a dam project or a Peace Corpsman who expects to ride a bicycle from one rural school to another.

The wives of the officials and executives will have many occasions to wear dinner dresses and cocktail frocks while the engineer's wife may never go to a formal party, and if the Peace Corps teacher has a wife, she too will have a full time job in a school or a clinic and the parties they attend will likely be the local counterpart of a barn dance or a community picnic.

A graduate student and his young wife about to embark with a Fulbright study grant can well be thrown into a cost-of-living tail spin if they get hold of a post report prepared for people enroute to senior diplomatic positions in the country where the student expects to go.

It is very important that the local facilities for taking care of clothes be kept in mind when selecting a wardrobe. In European cities dry cleaning may be depended upon as in this country. The same thing can be said for the more modern cities in other parts of the world. In less developed places, dry cleaning tends to be of poor quality and is likely to be more expensive than it is back home. If in doubt, select washable fabrics.

Not to be ignored by any American who has a conscience about consideration for other people is the fact that in different cultures there are different ideas about what is proper and improper, attractive and unattractive as far as dress is concerned. In some orthodox Muslim areas, for instance, women are still heavily veiled. For public appearances American women who do not want to make themselves conspicuous or, worse yet, run the risk of being mistaken for unscrupulous females, should avoid bare shoulders as well as short shorts. Slacks as well as shorts are improper attire for women in many areas. In parts of Africa a woman might be on the street with the upper part of her body completely bare, yet she would be wearing a skirt and would be horrified to see an American woman in pants. On the other hand, in areas where the Chinese culture predominates women either wear trousers or have hip hugging skirts slit up so high that generous portions of the upper legs are exposed, yet they would never have breasts or shoulders uncovered.

People of other countries do not expect foreigners to dress as they dress. Nevertheless they have a right to expect that we will not be clothed offensively while we are among them. I would emphasize here and I shall repeat many times throughout these pages that Americans are always conspicuous overseas just because they are Americans, and it is most important that they be careful not to attract adverse attention to themselves by appearing in clothes which are shocking to the sensitivities of nationals or that are so lacking in dignity that they do not fairly represent our country.

In addition to the factors of suitability I would add two other important considerations that cannot be disregarded.

One, in determining her wardrobe a woman going abroad, just as truly as a woman staying in Tower Grove, Missouri, must let her own philosophy of clothes guide her in her selections. If clothes give a woman a lift, if her spirit needs the excitement and the dramatic effect of high fashion and frequent changes—then being in another part of the world isn't going to change her nature in this regard, and within the framework of climate, circumstances, and culture she should still expect to give a good deal of attention to what she wears in order that she may go on being who she is and not feel as if she were a stranger in some uninteresting sort of clothes.

But if clothes as such have never been of special importance to a woman, then she needn't feel that because she is going to live in some foreign country—even if she is going there as the wife of the American Ambassador—that she must suddenly be a fashion plate. She should in her own way select clothes suitable for the new situation, but, like her fashion minded sister, she has every right to go on being the kind of person she is and has the very real need to feel that she is putting emphasis wherever she thinks it belongs.

The other thing to say about clothes is that people on overseas assignment are not en route to desert islands. Families going to remote areas where supplies are limited and where importations are prohibited may actually need to take enough clothes to last for the duration of their assignment. Few Americans go to such places. The majority go where local shops carry both imported garments and local items of clothing which Americans can use. In many countries competent tailors, with reasonable fees, can make quite acceptable suits, coats, or dresses. Most travelers supply themselves before they leave home with clothing adequate only for immediate needs, preferring not to be burdened with surplus supplies or with excessive debts.

An exception should be made in the case of shoes. Comfortable shoes are essential and most people find that shoes made in other countries are not as satisfactory as the shoes to which they are accustomed. So a generous supply of suitable shoes is recommended. Parents frequently arrange for a homeside shoe store to record the sizes of children's feet in order that larger sizes may be ordered at intervals.

Women are advised to provide themselves with an adequate supply of foundation garments since the ones generally available abroad are not designed for American figures. Those who sew should plan to take a portable sewing machine with a suitable transformer if it is required. A supply of basic patterns, zippers, and tapes is a good idea for the do-it-yourself folks. Women who may expect to have things made by a tailor might arrange for a fashion magazine to arrive regularly so that they can show a tailor what they want him to make.

Household Supplies

If clothing needs were the only ones that had to be considered, then an individual's or a family's preparation for departure would be relatively simple. Some (generally those without children) elect to live out an overseas assignment in hotels because they prefer not to get involved in housekeeping and household supplies. Most families would feel restless and confined in a hotel and go overseas with the expectation of establishing their own home. Here again they must make careful inquiries in advance as to the kind of housing available, and whether or not it will be supplied with basic furniture.

If furniture is not to be supplied then it becomes important to learn how much of what a family considers essential can be obtained locally, and how much must be shipped from home. Local furniture might be bought more quickly and easily and is more likely to be designed for the houses and the weather of the area (no overstuffed sofas in monsoon areas, please!). But beds, like shoes, are special; if Americans cannot be assured that local beds conform to their definition of comfort or sanitation, then they should take along at least the kind of springs and mattress they prefer.

There should be a real need for any piece of electrical equipment which is taken overseas. We Americans are so accustomed to power equipment in our homes that any one family might enter a pre-industrialized community with enough gadgets to tax the capacity of the power supply lines. One needs to ask some searching questions about this.

Are we, for instance, going to set ourselves completely apart from the local people who in some communities live in simple dwellings which are wide open to breezes and visitors alike if we install huge air conditioning units, close our doors and windows and keep the inside temperature so low that a visitor who has the temerity to knock on the door would be miserably cold once he goes inside? On the other hand, it may be that Americans who demonstrate by a high standard of living the results of scientific progress and free enterprise give to economically emerging peoples goals toward which they might work.

There is a middle ground, I think, where the modest use of modern equipment may serve the causes of efficiency and physical well-being and at the same time not establish a gap so wide that economically depressed people feel it is hopeless to try to span it, or feel resentful towards those who live on the other side.

As a matter of fact there are some real questions about whether or not it is efficient for a family to try to operate complicated equipment in places where repair service may not be available or where household servants may be unable or unwilling to shift from simpler devices. In any case, I would take overseas only those appliances which are clearly needed, making sure that the voltage was right or that we had adequate transformers.

When we come to the matter of personal effects—lamps, pictures, rugs, silver, dishes, toys—I think the main consideration is: how important is it to have certain things with us? Some people are glad of an excuse to clear away a lot of the bric-a-brac encrustations of years of living in the same place. Others report that it makes a great deal of difference to them as a family living in a strange land if they have familiar things around them; that it gives a continuity to their family experience which is worth the risks of possible damage or loss to the things themselves. This is especially important for little children, but I have known adults who might have been less restless in a foreign post if they hadn't left all the special things which symbolized home to them packed away in boxes in a fireproof, moth proof, and burglar proof storage house somewhere.

Having familiar things around may not seem essential to a family going abroad for only one assignment. Expecting to come back to the same job and the same house in two years they may easily take a holiday from all their old things. In contrast, a young couple starting out in a foreign service career and expecting to have one foreign assignment after another needs to feel that home is wherever they are, and and so they must take the makings of their home wherever they go.

Supplies for leisure time activity should be provided. A record player with a varied selection of records for children as well as adults can be much appreciated when a family gets out of reach of the homeside television and radio programs. The type of player or radio taken abroad should be determined in part by weather conditions. Either dampness or dryness might make a difference.

Books assume a new importance overseas. People frequently find that they have more time for reading in an overseas community than they have had back home. And because in most places they have limited radio or television discussion of current events and have nothing to compare with the newspapers they are accustomed to reading at home, it is necessary for them to have a generous amount of reading material available.

Relatives and friends of overseas Americans are well advised to send books as gifts. Books are easy to mail, seldom if ever cause trouble or expense at the customs barrier, and generally supply a welcome source of either relaxation or stimulation even for those who may not have had the reading habit at home.

When we went to Burma, in addition to taking old favorites from our bookselves and the new books we had been trying to get around to, we bought a great many Modern Library books which were particularly suitable for our teen-agers. The paper backs are a boon to travelers, especially those moving to climates which may be damaging to hard back or leather bound books. In a good many foreign cities the United States Information Service Library may be helpful as it was to us in Burma. The children's section of that library was outstanding and our youngsters made weekly visits to borrow and return books. Even so we took a large number of children's books overseas with us and I would advise all families to do the same.

It is worthwhile for families to have magazine subscriptions directed to an overseas address so they may keep in touch with what is being said and done back home in the various fields in which members of the family are interested. I have noticed that people going out for a second assignment generally increase the number of magazines to which they subscribe.

Sports equipment will not only be useful to the members of a family who take it along for their own exercise or entertainment, but it can also provide a good way for a family to have friendly contacts with local people. It may be difficult to get beyond formalities with the people of a host country if one only invites them to formal dinners. But if one can say, "bring the children and come over for a game of croquet," there is a better chance of getting acquainted.

A Peace Corps volunteer won't have any trouble getting on a person-to-person footing with his local colleagues during work hours if he has a soft ball to toss around when the day's work is done. Teen-age children who know only a few words of a local language can have fun on a badminton court with local young people who speak but little English.

Livestock and Apple Seeds

Many families preparing for a move abroad are faced with the necessity of making a decision about a much loved pet. This is a more difficult matter than deciding whether to take or store or give away some inanimate object. Most people decide to place cats or dogs or other pets with neighbors or friends or in an animal welfare home because the prospects of keeping a pet safe and well in a different environment are rarely good. Transportation to another country and possibly a lengthy quarantine period after arrival may prove difficult for the pet and expensive for the owners. Some countries prohibit the importation of pets. Some make exceptions according to the position or prominence of the traveler. Others have clear cut regulations. In not a few places an overseas employee finds that he has more trouble getting a little puppy across the customs barriers than he had getting his wife and children and all their baggage to the country.

Some do take their pets along and feel it is worth the effort and the cost to make the necessary arrangements. People who plan to do this are advised to ask their veterinarian to search his library for information about specific health risks for their kind of animal in the area to which they are going, and to decide for them what special protective shots should be given before leaving this country and what, if any, special precautions should be taken after arrival. This is important because different parasites and diseases exist in different countries. While good veterinary service is available some places abroad, pet owners frequently find that they are on their own after they leave this country.

Inquiries should be directed to the nearest consulate or to the embassy (in Washington, D. C.) of the country to which pets are being taken, regarding their regulations for animal entry. A representative of the airline or steamship company with which the family expects to travel should be consulted about arrangements for the transportation of pets.

It would, I suspect, be small comfort to a person who has had to decide to leave a particularly precious pet at home to tell him that he can most likely acquire another pet in the new place. But it is true that the keeping of pets is not an unusual practice, and there is always a chance that a new animal found in a new port can become, if not a substitute for an old love, at least a satisfactory companion for the duration of an overseas stay.

People for whom plant care and culture is an absorbing hobby often ask if they can take certain plants or seeds along with them to certain places. Others, uncertain as to the supply of fresh vegetables in local markets or anxious as to whether locally grown products will be safe for eating raw in an area where the dysenteries are prevalent, often think of maintaining a garden where they might grow familiar foods or where they could be sure that products were kept free from contamination during the growing period.

There is no reason why the garden minded individuals should be discouraged, but before people buy a supply of seeds or make plans to transport plants, certain factors should be considered. In the first place, it would be foolish to expect to grow in a year round summer climate plants whose life cycles require the cold of winter. Likewise, unless the facilities of a greenhouse are assured one shouldn't hope to keep tropical plants alive in a cold climate. Beyond that there is the consideration of keeping plants healthy during transport and of conforming to the export regulations of this country and the differing regulations of foreign countries about the importation of plants and seeds. Those interested may write to:

Plant Quarantine Division
Agricultural Research Service
U. S. Public Health Service
Washington 25, D. C.

An up-to-date registry is kept regarding regulations throughout the world. Letters should state explicitly the place to which one is going and indicate the kinds of agricultural materials one wants to take.

The Problems of Packing

The last time we were packing to move overseas, I envied the pioneer mothers who had just one wagon load of things to deal with. A major move for moderns who migrate requires that every single possession must be handled either physically or mentally. And what a lot of possessions we all have! Packing decisions can't be made overnight so for weeks one must live in the clutter of piles and with the tyranny of lists.

I began by going through the house, and especially the attic, to see what we should give away and to make plans to have it disposed of as soon as possible. Some people hold a white elephant auction at this point. Then comes the chore of listing big pieces and packing or piling small things for storage.

Of those things to be taken, air passengers must make careful division between things for surface transport, those for air freight, and those limited items for accompanied baggage. Even the latter must be divided into baggage that will be checked for the whole journey, into bags that would need to be available for stops en route, and those little flight bags which must be made to hold all things actually needed on the flight itself.

Packing is a much easier job for steamship travelers than for air passengers because everything including the family car can usually go along on the same ship and the weight of hand luggage need not be so carefully limited. The only trouble about this is that today men on assignment and salary are not likely to be given a long and leisurely sea voyage, but must move at jet speeds. If wives choose to go by ship it generally means a long trip alone with the full responsibility for children.

The packing burden is greatly eased if all the major packing can be turned over to one experienced packing firm. Their men come in and do the job quickly, and in such a way that safe arrival is assured. The only thing one must watch, even with reliable movers, is that there is no confusion as to what is to go abroad and what is to go into storage. A quick wave of the hand isn't an adequate form of instruction at this point. One must know with assurance that the heirloom silver inherited from Great-aunt Ellen will be delivered to the storage vaults and that the baby's crib will be sent ahead by air freight. I shall not soon forget the consternation of a mother when she saw that a trunk, with family keepsakes had been sent to Burma instead of the trunk with warm clothes for their daughter who expected to attend boarding school in the mountains of northern India.

It is a joke in our family that when we were unpacking dishes in Rangoon, a carefully wrapped bundle turned out to be the dehydrated remains of what was probably the bag of garbage accumulated after our last meal back home. Somebody must have set the paper bag down near a pile of things labeled "to go" and packers gave it the same care against breakage that the finest dishes received.

Families who by choice or necessity do all of their own packing need to learn about the conditions under which their things will move and make sure that containers are suitable. Some families report that the contents of boxes which had not been waterproof were ruined by mildew because at one stage they had several days wait on an unprotected wharf during the rainy season. There are new ways of packing which can safeguard against damage from weather or loss from theft. Large aluminum "lift vans" are frequently used to enclose smaller pieces. Families who have tried to save money by using inferior containers report that it doesn't pay in the long run.

Careful labeling of boxes and trunks as well as hand luggage is essential. The banding or roping of trunks and boxes is often required to insure against pilfering. The wives who generally supervise the unpacking are glad if the contents have been listed so that they can know where to find the essential items when they begin the unpacking job.

There must be careful planning for the air freight which can be expected to arrive about the time a family does. The contents of those steamer trunks may have to take care of the basic needs of a family for several months until the surface freight arrives. Unless a family is sure of a lengthy stay in a hotel, there should be in the air freight not only a minimum amount of clothing but also a minimum number of towels, sheets, knives and forks, perhaps a plate apiece, a stew pan, and a skillet.

Even if a homemaker expects to buy things locally she can't expect to know her way around readily enough to buy all the utensils required to feed the family the first day they are on their own in a new place. If prepared baby food is used a supply should be included unless it is known in advance that local supplies are adequate. I would add to the air freight any essential drugs, both bath and laundry soap, some cleaning rags, scouring powder, and a good spray for insects.

Americans already in residence are almost always ready to be helpful to newcomers, but this doesn't mean that they are going to be happy to hear a newcomer with five children say "Oh, by the way, could you be a dear and loan me some sheets until our freight arrives in a couple of months." Neither will the newcomers' children be happy if in a new place they have to wait several months before they have anything with which to play, any books to read or any record to listen to.

No matter how much we may downgrade the importance of things, we have no choice but to think a great deal about them while we are getting ready to leave the country, and we are under the necessity of giving possessions priority ratings of various sorts.

Everybody Gets Shot!

Don't forget that while a homemaker is shopping and packing and showing the house, she is also getting everybody to the family doctor not once but many times. Most agencies require thorough medical examinations before departure. Even if it is not a requirement, everyone in the family should have a careful check-up with both his doctor and his dentist just as soon as a trip abroad is contemplated.

In a few cases, something turns up which would make it unwise for an individual to go to a place where specialized medical care would not be available. A thorough examination might reveal the need for some corrective measure in time to get the treatment completed before departure. In every case, a doctor's evaluation of his patient's condition and his advice as to any special procedures indicated may do a great deal not only for the peace of mind of the family, but may actually prevent a major or minor health crisis from occurring overseas. It is wise to have a written statement from one's doctor if follow-up treatment of a special illness or condition is to be made by doctors abroad. Those who have a condition that might require emergency care (as a diabetic or a person allergic to an antibiotic) should consult a doctor concerning the instructions to be placed on an identification card or bracelet.

People going to areas where death rates are high and diseases of many kinds are prevalent are tempted to leave this country with a medicine kit which more nearly resembles a drug store. This is foolish.

Many drugs and antibiotics, even those sold over the counter, have specific application, others deteriorate with time or under improper storage conditions. Some of them used in too great a dosage or too often are harmful.

A pharmacy shopping list should be made with a doctor's advice. Written instructions for the use of medicines should be securely attached to the bottles or boxes. In cases where special medicines or food supplements must be taken, arrangements ought to be made with a supplier at home to make regular shipments at least until one knows whether the needful items can be obtained abroad. It is wise to take a reasonable quantity of first aid supplies—band-aids, antiseptic, and such, but exhaustive purchases are usually unnecessary. Few places do not have a chemist's shop or a hospital dispensary. If one is dependent upon glasses then an extra pair is recommended in case of loss in remote areas. A copy of the most recent prescription should be taken for emergency use in cities where a reliable optician may be found.

The reason for repeated visits to a doctor's office before departure is that all who travel abroad must have certain immunizations and those going into certain areas must have special additional immunizations. Information about immunizations is generally given by the sending agency. It is unnecessary for people going overseas independently to get themselves into a hit-or-miss kind of immunization program, sometimes taking shots not required and sometimes omitting essential ones according to the advice they have gotten from people not familiar with exact requirements for a given area. There is no call for uncertainty at this point. Those who have not been able to get accurate information regarding immunizations for a particular place may write to the

Division of Foreign Quarantine
U. S. Public Health Service
Washington 25, D. C.

Not to be overlooked in an inquiry about immunizations are the stop-over points. Yellow fever may be non-existent in the country where a family expects to work and live, but if they are planning to stop for even a few days in a country where it is prevalent then the yellow fever shots must be taken, too, not just for protection while there but because anyone coming from there might be required to show a yellow fever immunization certificate in order to enter another country.

Detailed vaccination requirements for all areas of the world are contained in a booklet "Immunization Information for International

Travel" for sale by the Superintendent of Documents, Government Printing Office, Washington 25, D. C., at twenty-five cents a copy.

All immunizations for travel abroad must be recorded in a folder approved by the World Health Organization. This folder entitled "International Certificates of Vaccination" is furnished to a traveler at the time he applies for his passport. It may also be obtained from the Superintendent of Documents at five cents a copy. Entries must be made at the time the inoculation or vaccination is given and should be signed and dated by the doctor. A separate folder is required for each member of a family including small babies. These folders should be kept with the family passports at all times. A certificate of health is required for entrance into certain South American countries. The need for this should be checked with the foreign embassy in Washington before departure if a sending agency has not supplied the information.

In countries where smallpox vaccination certificates are required it is important to make sure that an old vaccination is renewed if it is out of date and that a first vaccination has been given at least eight days before arrival at a foreign port. Airline agents sometimes must reject a passenger at the last minute because his vaccination certificate is not in order.

Since small children living abroad will have many occasions for being "shot" by a doctor or a nurse, it is important to help them learn to accept the process without anxiety or undue resistance. Our procedure with young children has been to let them know what is coming and then to encourage them to "cry only while it hurts." Since the pain of the needle is of such a brief duration even small children may soon reach the place where it doesn't seem worth the effort to cry at all.

For certain malaria areas, anti-malaria tablets are to be taken weekly by everyone in the family beginning several weeks before arrival in the area. Fortunately, malaria irradication programs are making so much progress that the number of places in the world where the regular taking of drugs to prevent malaria is required is becoming smaller and smaller. Our daughter and her family live in one of the places where malaria is still a serious risk. Before they left, I overheard our five year old grandson explain to a neighbor:

"Did you know that I take fighting pills every Sunday? When a malaria mosquito bites me then my fighting pills will be right there in my blood waiting to kill those old malaria animals so they can't make me sick."

One doesn't want young children to become preoccupied with thoughts of illness but accurate and matter-of-fact explanations can make possible the kind of cooperation which is essential both before departure and all during the stay in a foreign country if a family is to keep well.

PASSPORTS

An American traveling outside his own country might give his money to feed the poor and he might, without a qualm, permit baggage to be tossed out to lighten the load of a troubled aircraft, but, come what may, he clings to his passport because while he is away from his homeland this is the certificate of his citizenship and the most certain mark of his personal identification. It is a valid credential which guarantees to a citizen "safe passage, lawful aid, and protection in case of need." No one may leave our shores to reside overseas without possessing a passport and no one may enter another country to become a resident without satisfying the inspectors that he is, in fact, the person pictured and described in the passport and that he has stamped in it a visa for entry into the particular country (unless in certain countries the need for a visa has been waived). An essential first step for departure from this country is to initiate steps to secure a passport. The head of each family preparing to go abroad should write to:

The Passport Office
Department of State
Washington 25, D. C.

He will receive *Information For Passport Applicants* an up-to-date circular which clearly describes everything that must be done to get a passport. Every word of this information needs to be read, and no one should discard without carefully reading the two accompanying leaflets *Getting Along Abroad* and *Do's and Don'ts for Travelers.*

One thing needed at the time of initial passport application is a birth certificate for each member of the family. In some states photostatic copies of the certificates must be secured. Since this sometimes takes time there should be no delay in making the necessary requests. If people who were born as long ago as I was, in a state where births were then not registered, want to get a passport, they must begin fairly early to take legal steps to have their place of birth and parentage verified.

Unless one is traveling on official government business and has a diplomatic or official passport issued to him, he must pay the designated fee for his passport. For a family with six children and two parents this might amount to as much as eighty dollars for separate passports. For this reason families are sometimes inclined to have joint passports issued, with a mother and at least the younger children together on the theory that they are likely to always travel jointly. But a family can't be sure that occasions will not arise when for special reasons individual members of a family may need to travel separately—a mother rushed home for an emergency operation, a teen-ager sent across a border to a boarding school. When occasions like this arise, families wish that they had spent the extra money for each person to have his own passport because unless certain time consuming steps are taken, a passport may not be carried by one member of a joint passport unless the other member or members are also traveling.

When a family is deciding before departure on the disposition of all other things, it should also be decided just where and by whom the passports and immunization cards are to be carried. Even though children may understandably be proud of their passports and want to carry them themselves it is more sensible for the head of the family to have them, both because there is less risk of loss and also because it is far more convenient for them to be presented together when the need to show them arises. This means that a brief case or shoulder strap camera case or a small overnight case which can be securely fastened and always carried personally should be provided. Passports in family quantity are too bulky for suit pockets.

A wife's handbag may seem to be just the place for passports because it is always handy and is generally so voluminous. But whose husband wants to stand around awkwardly while his lady searches through innumerable recesses and finally dumps the entire contents of her bag on the counter before a dignified immigration official? I noticed that on the second time out our son-in-law diplomatically kept the five passports for which he is responsible.

Reservations

The people who have reservations made for them by a travel branch of an agency are lucky because that is a time consuming chore from which they are relieved. Even with some one else to make the arrangements, a family generally has a certain degree of choice regarding route, stop overs, and type of carrier preferred.

Those who must make their own travel arrangements have to spend more time on it, but in compensation they enjoy the fun of studying the attractive folders and schedules which they will receive from as many airlines or steamship companies or tourist bureaus as they care to consult. An airline or steamship company will set up reservations for a whole trip even though it might not all be taken on their carriers. They can be helpful also in arranging hotel accommodations for stop overs en route. This is important because there are places where satisfactory accommodations are limited and families with small children particularly cannot afford to leave it to chance that they will have a suitable place to stay during a stop.

Airlines must of necessity impose more restrictions upon the weight and contents of baggage than steamship companies must do. It is sometimes prohibited, for instance, for passenger's baggage to contain chemical kits or compressed gases (such as hair sprays and insecticide bombs). Such restrictions are for the safety of passengers whose lives could be endangered by a significant explosion or whose clothing could be injured if at high altitude a small explosion occurred within a suitcase. With special arrangements certain articles may be carried in the pressurized passenger cabin which might not safely be carried in the unpressurized baggage compartment of the plane. However, those things acceptable in a pressurized cabin on a large aircraft might prove to be unacceptable later on in the journey when a passenger transfers to a small unpressurized plane. He would then be under the necessity of making some other arrangements for the transport of the unacceptable items.

Those planning to travel by air should read carefully the literature which spells out in detail the various regulations. This should be done early enough so that there isn't a last minute scramble to pull out of air-destined cases articles which should have been included in surface freight already en route. Ordinary bathroom scales serve very well to weigh baggage and this should always be done unless a family is prepared to discard things at the last minute or to pay cheerfully the rates for excess pounds. The happy traveler is the one who has done his homework in advance and is then ready to settle in comfortably and let the airline staff take over.

Chapter II

THE GREAT DIVIDE

Yesterday they may have been in Silver Springs, Maryland. The day after tomorrow they will be in Karachi, in Quito, in Seoul, in Accra or in any one of many faraway places. Their former neighbors speeding to work on a super highway, buying inspected meat in super-markets, pushing thermostats up and down to suit their convenience, swearing by or at television programs, subscribing to more magazines than they can read, mowing their own lawns, electing their own school board, and drinking water just as it comes from the tap, will call out to one another, "Guess Tom and Enda and the kids are about there now."

Someone will surely say, "Wonderful, isn't it, what the jet age has done for transportation?"

"It may be marvelous, but just the same the thought of doing it so fast makes me dizzy," a young mother may observe. Her off-hand observation pinpoints a significant aspect of the migration of American families to other parts of the world. Anyway you look at it, it is a breathtaking experience to leave one culture and to find yourself suddenly immersed in another culture. If it happens at jet speeds it is the more likely to leave a family confused.

Most families have reason to be dizzy before they start their journey just from the lack of sufficient sleep and the incessant driving that seems to be an inevitable part of getting off for around-the-world travel. There are so many chores that can't be delegated to outsiders, so many friends to see, so much to decide.

Frequently, there are unexpected delays or the threat of delay. A cable arrives saying that housing isn't yet available. An airline reports that it hasn't received confirmation of the flight from Paris to Beirut. Passports don't arrive in time because the holy days of some country have kept the Washington embassy closed and visas from that country cannot be secured on schedule. To say the least, this doesn't add up to a peaceful frame of mind.

People struggling against a deadline to leave are relieved to have any kind of a reprieve, yet being keyed up to go they are thrown in a state of suspension. Then suddenly something gives. An apartment has been located. Flight 309 at 19:00 Paris time has been confirmed for six Smiths. A helpful junior consular officer has obligingly gone down to the deserted embassy to stamp the visas. So the departure time is fixed. The word is passed around the family and shouted around the neighborhood, and, obliged to make up for the lost motion of the days of suspension, the pace becomes more feverish than ever.

Leave Taking

On top of this, good-byes must be said. No matter how nonchalant Americans may be nor how mobile they may have become within this country, few families escape feeling some pangs when the hour of departure arrives. Children may be grief-stricken at the thought of leaving playmates and play places and pets. People like me are likely to be found out in the backyard having a last look at the rose garden (in the dead of winter!) when everyone else and all the bags are loaded in a neighbor's car with the head of the house anxious for the show to get on the road. Parents with not-quite-grown children staying behind for college may have moments of forgetting that it is for just such a step into maturity that they have all along been preparing their youngsters. Adults with elderly parents are understandably reluctant to put thousands of miles between themselves and those loved ones whose years are numbered. It may be only fifteen jet hours from Texarkana to Tokyo but it is easily a fifteen hundred dollar round trip flight, and everyone concerned knows that fifteen hundred dollars is fifteen hundred dollars.

There is the problem of reassuring the people who stay behind. How well I remember the many reasons there were for my parents to worry about us when Jerry and I, starry-eyed and with his brand new graduate degree, started out for Peking, China, in 1932. There was honest-to-goodness war developing a few miles to the north of Peking. There was flood and famine south of Peking in the province to which, after a year of language study, we would be assigned. There were epidemics. There was polluted water. The "miracle" drugs hadn't yet been developed. There were sand storms, and air conditioning was unheard of. I can see Jerry now as he sat with his arm around my mother speaking with great authority about the statistical chances that we would be safer in North China than they would be owning an automobile in the United States, and solemnly promising her that if she and my father would not worry about us, we would try not to worry about them. Through the years they have followed our migrations with interest and always with a full measure of acceptance and support. Even so,

I never start for some far off place without wishing that I could spare them some of the cost of our going.

Adjustments Enroute

We may have faced certain hazards thirty years ago when we went to China which modern globe trotters are spared, but traveling as we did by slow boat, the adjustments of moving from one part of the world to another were in some regards easier for us than they are for those who move so fast today.

The thing I remember most appreciatively is that there was a blessed chance to rest after the getting ready to leave period and before the settling in process sure to characterize arrival at any new place. One could sleep in private quarters all night and if he desired might doze or read or play on deck all day. Meals could, for the first time in weeks, be eaten in a leisurely fashion.

Now if he is airborne, a traveler may find himself here today and there tomorrow; pillowed down through the night, yes, but without any chance to catch up with himself and his own tranquility, with no time to become accustomed gradually to the idea of going from one culture to another.

Time itself is out of kilter. Dinner is served on a jet flight from Philadelphia and before the dessert course has been finished and the tray carried away, dawn is lightening the sky and it is morning and the plane is approaching London. Just a few hours later but many miles farther east it would be night for those who caught the next plane out of London. Those who are proceeding to a distant point without stop-overs may find themselves increasingly bleary eyed as the clock keeps being set forward into tomorrow (or reversed into yesterday depending on which direction you are going) and there may be no one lap of the flight long enough to provide the equivalent of even a short night's undisturbed sleep. At some stops all passengers must disembark while the craft is being serviced. Young travelers may find it disconcerting that they have to walk around when they are sleepy and are supposed to sleep when the clock inside them is still set for being awake.

Let me not give the impression that I'm advocating a return to the good old days. There is much to be said for our speeded up transportation systems. Air travel provides quick transit in an age when speed is often essential. It is economical considering the value of an employee's time. Planes are equipped to meet the special needs of children and to reduce to a minimum the number of days when they need to be traveling. Air travelers are generally able to complete a journey without a change of clothes. A sweater for each member of the family, a reasonable number of diapers for a baby, and a clean thing or two for a young child is all that is necessary. There is no need for huge laundry bags nor for laundry to be drying in a stateroom.

There are practical things which families can do to assure that the journey into a new situation be made pleasantly and with a minimum of tension.

In the first place, it helps tremendously if passengers can think of themselves as guests of the air line with whom they may be traveling, accepting graciously the efforts of its staff to make them as comfortable as possible but not feeling at liberty to be demanding of special service or expecting that regular routines be changed to satisfy personal whims or in response to outraged criticism. The traveler who lets himself sound off at 30,000 feet is getting himself and the other members of his family in the mood to enjoy nothing about a flight and is inexcusably making other passengers uncomfortable.

The same attitude of courteous acceptance of delays which sometimes occur along the way is in order, too. The pilot doesn't plan to have an airfield fog bound, a flight engineer doesn't arrange to have instruments malfunction. No good end is served by fretting under such circumstances. Families who say "thank you very much" when the best available accommodations are provided for them by the local representative are then free to let the unplanned stop-over become the unexpected adventure it frequently proves to be.

This art of rolling with the situation is the secret of traveling without trauma. Adults may find that they need to make deliberate efforts to acquire the rhythm of air adaptability just as the seafaring travelers of other years had to learn to stay erect and keep the queasiness and sometimes the boredom under control on a long and stormy sea voyage. If parents are even partially successful in keeping their sense of humor awake throughout a long journey, then something fundamental is communicated to the youngsters and they are much more likely to go on to sleep, to eat what is available, or to amuse themselves without being *personae non grata* for the duration of the trip.

It helps to have available a few carefully chosen toys and books for little children and suitable games or puzzles or reading materials for older youngsters. It helps most if parents plan not to be otherwise too pre-occupied and can just relax with their children and with one another. (Leave the thank-you notes a while longer and let the papers in that important looking brief case stay where they are!) Life today offers too few chances for families to look together at stars or clouds or wide expanses of space, or to converse without the competition of commercials or the telephone. What does it matter what time it is when your Daddy has time to hold you on his lap and tell you about light years, or your wife has time to sit quietly and listen to your dreams?

Cultural Shock

Much of cultural difference is subtle and intangible but there is something definitely physical about leaving wet winter weather one Friday evening and stepping out of a plane at 3 a.m. on a Sunday morning and having hot dry air hit you in the face. This kind of shock happens everyday to air borne travelers, and it is not unrelated to shock at other levels. A person whose body chemistry hasn't had time to make a radical climatic adjustment may not be as ready as he would like to be to take other surprises in his stride. The surprises don't wait for him to be ready; they pop out immediately and everywhere.

There are new—and because they are new we call them strange—sights to see. Some of them may be very ordinary parts of local landscape but to unaccustomed eyes they are fascinating and newcomers exclaim or stare or take a picture. Some of the sights also common to the local people, may seem repulsive and the foreigner withdraws or protests or hastens to make mental notes of how the situation ought to be changed.

Some of the things which look so unpleasant (men sleeping on the sidewalk of a big city, pot-bellied children playing in a village, a leper begging by the roadside) may all be evidence of the tremendous problems with which a new government is coping. Haggard looking refugees huddled near a soup kitchen may be the reminder of a recent catastrophe like a flood or a tidal wave. Women carrying heavy loads of bricks at the construction site of a new power plant and little children working in a match factory may be an indication of the fact that a community is in a hurry to complete the transition into the age of industry.

There are new sounds in new communities. First of all the sound of people talking is different. It may be only a different way of pronouncing English or more likely it is the sound of a completely unfamiliar language which begins to build up tension from the first day one arrives in a foreign land. In places where normal speech is louder than a newcomer is accustomed to, he may feel that angry arguments are going on all around him. Also since he doesn't understand the words he hears he may tend to be suspicious of the people who are talking. On the other hand he may just find it frustrating to be isolated by his inability to ask or answer questions.

Some of the new sounds seem quaint and delightful; pagoda bells tinkling with the breezes, the far off sound of a flute, even the chop-chop of a cleaver cutting meat and vegetables. But other sounds are frightening.

No one had told us that it was the practice, in the suburban neighborhood to which we had been taken directly from the Rangoon airport after our 2 a.m. arrival, for the night watchmen to beat out the hours of the night on a gong. Exhausted, from sleeplessness and heat, we had all fallen into a dead sleep when in our yard and in all the compounds for miles around a ghastly din of noise set in. We had been told that dacoits (bandit gangs) roamed the countryside (this was before complete stability had been restored after World War II), and so when our watchman made an especially loud effort to let the new tenants know that he was properly awake at three o'clock, and watchmen at neighboring houses made similar noises—though not with synchronized watches—we all jumped up and assembled in the living room as if the hour of doom was upon us.

New smells are a part of cultural shock, too. As long as I live I shall remember with nostalgia and delight the smell of chestnuts roasting in charcoal at street-side mobile restaurants on cold winter evenings in North China and the captivating smell of jasmine in the gardens of tropical Asia.

But smells are not all ambrosial. Earthy is too mild a word for the fertilizer cakes drying in the Shantung countryside, for the smell of industrial waste in a country so much in a hurry to produce that it hasn't taken time to figure out what to do with quantities of residue, or for the animal heat and garlic odors generated when sweaty workers are crowded together in a public bus designed for a third the number who use it.

Then there are the different ways of doing things which surprise and sometimes alarm people. It is a bit disconcerting to have a taxi driver go headlong into traffic on what one thinks is the wrong side of the street. Adults react to this more than children do.

"We are so proud of our car," a little American pre-schooler confided to me one morning in Rangoon. "It has been trained to go on the right side of the road but now it is going on the left side just like all the other cars."

A housewife seeing her cook peeling a potato in a new way is inclined to say "But Fan, you are doing it backwards. Here let me show you," as if Fan were her little boy instead of a proud and highly skilled man. Her husband seeing his local clerk making calculations on an abacus is likely to take one quick look and conclude that business procedures are inefficient when as a matter of fact it has been demonstrated that abacus reckoning is often as speedy as modern calculating machines.

These various kinds of new experiences, some profound and some trivial, may call forth responses of uneasiness, feelings of isolation, an inclination to criticize, an urge to assume a derogatory attitude towards the people of the new country, and a tendency to cling to an exaggerated idea of the perfection of the homeland; all of which add up to a pattern of symptoms that indicates cultural shock.

Shock Absorbers

Single people who go overseas to work must be on their own to find ways of meeting cultural shock, but in a family it is generally the wife who has both the opportunity and the responsibility to provide the shock absorbers.

To make a slow start in a new situation is the best way I know to keep from being overwhelmed by newness. If it is tropical sun after a temperate climate then no all day beach party on the first Saturday. If it is a high altitude after a lifetime of sea-level living, then no extended hiking tours until blood has had time for adjustment. If one has always eaten bland food, then one should only gradually ease into a regular diet of hot curries. Without suppressing her family's eagerness to do all the special things that there are to do in the new community, a mother needs to manage the daily schedule so that for the first weeks, at least, everyone gets enough rest and a bit-by-bit exposure to whatever in the physical environment is likely to prove to be most taxing. All of which is quite different from deciding that one's children are never to eat this or never never to do that. It is just that "easy does it" when one is learning how to get along in a new place.

It is equally important to move slowly as one reacts to the more subtle factors in a new environment. It is not safe to judge from a first glance at people of another country or race what they are like as individuals or as a group. It is possible to spend just an hour at a local market, a day in a local village, a few minutes at a crowded fair, or to peep inside a place of worship and then return home giving a report based on superficial observations ("These people are all dirty—they are all dishonest—they have such queer ideas—they are all superstitious—.") Someone in the family must encourage the others to look, to listen, and to withhold judgment.

The slow start is helpful also as a family considers to what degree it should conform to local living patterns. If the practices of the local people are different from the accustomed ones then a family (or a single person living alone) has to try them out for size to determine how well they fit the family's image of itself and how adequately they express its own needs and values. No American family can expect to become a carbon copy of the local family next door. Nevertheless, many practices which people of a country have developed through centuries of living in their particular environment may well be useful to the newcomers.

Americans should examine the pace of life of their neighbors as it relates to climate and physical efficiency. They should observe the daily schedule of the people around them not only in order that they might better fit into it but so that they might learn as their neighbors have how to take advantage of the best times to sleep and eat and work in that particular environment. What the neighbors do for relaxation, how they handle the problems of dampness or dryness, how they prepare their foods—all this and much more if absorbed gradually and if adapted wisely may be of great value to the American homemakers.

Another way for Americans abroad to deal with differences is to find local eyes and ears so they may learn to see what local people see and to hear what local people mean. I once knew a couple overseas who proclaimed loudly that they were identifying themselves with the people of the country. But until the day when a delegation of nationals politely saw them off at the airport at the end of their assignment, they didn't know that they had never known what the people of the country were really like. They went through the motions of identifying with what they had decided was indigenous without looking deeply and listening carefully to what local people were, in fact, like.

Just as an overseas employee must find a dependable national counterpart, who can interpret meaning as well as words, so a homemaker abroad must find people to guide her and her family into an understanding of the intricacies of the society in which she and her family are guests. Not just any acquaintance can do this for a family, not even every good friend. But if there has been sincerity in a relationship and if that elusive quality we call empathy emerges, then there can be honesty and mutual willingness to interpret fully and frankly.

Such insight may come to a family through a co-worker. It may happen as a result of a random social contact. It may happen in part because of the special quality of a relationship with an articulate servant. It may happen through the natural friendship of children. When it does happen then a family is on the way to being able to grow in understanding and appreciation of a foreign culture.

Not to be overlooked in a discussion of shock absorbers is the importance of learning the language of the country. A new place seems less strange to foreigners who are able to understand what is being said. Those who learn even a little of the language are at a great advantage in being able more effectively to express an interest in the people and an appreciation of their country. The most fortunate people are the ones who have been able to study the new language before leaving home. But those who haven't been able to do that or who have only been able to begin a language study program can equip themselves before departure with language study materials.

Any who feel the need for advice regarding the specific language most useful in a given area, about centers for language study in this country, and particularly about useful study materials for self instruction may write to:

The Center for Applied Linguistics
1346 Connecticut Avenue, N.W.
Washington 6, D. C.

The Center for Applied Linguistics is a non-profit, professional organization established in 1959 as a unit of the Modern Language Association of America to act as a clearing house and informal coordinating body in the application of linguistic science to practical language problems. With a center like this able and willing to advise him, no overseas American should stumble along as an illiterate because he didn't know before he left home which language he should study or what kind of study materials to use.

Families who secure language study records before leaving this country may only have time to expose family members to the sound of the language and to a few elementary phrases; even this much is a help. The course can then be studied systematically and diligently after arriving in the country where the reasons for such study are more pressing. The best of the recorded courses have been prepared with a variety of native voices and after a great deal of research concerning the best steps in presenting a new language.

After arrival in the new community, nothing can take the place of a good tutor. One might consult the cultural attache of the American Embassy or the director of the department of language studies in a local university as to where to look for a class or a private teacher. It doesn't follow that because a man speaks his language correctly he would know how to go about teaching it to a foreigner. It pays to choose one's language tutor carefully, but at the same time it is helpful also to listen to anyone who is speaking the local language and to learn informally from all kinds of people. Little children speak with clarity and simplicity and it is especially helpful to listen to them.

Other Americans in a foreign community may provide shock absorbers for a newly arrived family. Some who go abroad have gotten the idea from critical reports about the "ruthless Americans" that no American who has proceeded them into the foreign country has ever cared about or succeed in understanding the local people. This attitude is too bad because it represents a conceit of loneliness which is itself crippling. It also prompts the newcomer to shun contacts with all Americans whereas if he made an unbiased approach to them he might find among his compatriots people with considerable insight regarding the nationals, with a wealth of information about the country, and with a wide association of local friends to whom they might introduce him.

On the other hand it doesn't follow automatically that because another American has been living in a foreign country that he is therefore sure to know or to care about its people. If, without selection, newcomers let themselves get pulled into an absorbing whirl of activities with just any group of Americans then they could be getting into bad company as far as their understanding of and friendship with nationals is concerned.

It is advisable to avoid both extremes and usually it is possible to find perceptive Americans with whom one can share the adventures of cross cultural understanding. With kindred spirits of one's own country a person can safely pop off when he feels baffled or downright annoyed by things in the local scene. This is particularly true when he may be provoked or worried by something going on within the American group. I'm not advocating a heart-on-your-sleeve club, but there are occasionally times when only a countryman could or should be the confidant, and when those times come it is good to know where to find him.

Another important shock absorbing device is to form the habit of viewing with perspective the problems of the country in which one is living.

People were not living in unsanitary and fire threatening conditions in the crowded mat huts that lined the main streets of the capital city of Burma when we arrived there in 1951 because they wanted to live that way or because the city or federal governments were willing to let them do it. Seeing the huts, newly arriving Americans were sometimes horrified. But for those who saw the housing crisis as a result of the war in which along with Greece and England, Burma had the greatest amount of destruction, the little hot and inadequate homes became symbols of the courage of refugees who were too proud to just give up and die. They became, also, reminders of the overwhelming number of urgent problems with which the two-year-old government was having to deal. Gradually during the three years we were there, the huts began to come down and there emerged in the suburbs an ingeniously designed transition community for refugees who were displaced when their huts were torn down to make way for one or another of the splendid new housing developments that are now a tribute to a government that didn't give up in the face of prodigious problems.

No aspect of a country's problems can be seen with understanding unless it is seen within the framework of national history and of the play of world forces in which the country may be caught. It becomes Americans who are guests in a country to seek out newspaper editors, history professors, public administrators, and all others who can fill in pieces of information about a country.

Coupled with the need for perspective is the need to remember that difference doesn't necessarily mean inferiority. Technicians have had to learn this. There is the example of American agricultural workers who insisted upon introducing a *better* strain of cotton. The farmers took the new seeds the first year and grew the cotton which had proved its superiority in America. But after that they reverted to their old variety. Because they preferred the inferior strain? To the contrary, because they had seen the demonstration that for their purposes the old strain was superior. The new strains produced more lint to be sure, but the new cotton had such short and weak stalks that it was not useful as a source of building and fuel material. The extension agents had to find a solution to the building material problem before they could introduce the better cotton.

When judging the whole range of cultural patterns and practices of the local people, Americans need to discipline themselves to inquire carefully before they make qualitative judgments about differences.

It may be a homespun suggestion that the person who is feeling lost overseas should get busy helping other people find their way around. But on more than one occasion I have had opportunity to observe that those who are having a difficult reaction to a new community or are dragging their feet about cultural adjustments, come out of shock when they join the welcome committee to greet new arrivals. Somehow the need to help a new teacher or secretary or a new family settle into what may have begun to seem like a stranger and stranger place, puts a woman on her mettle to find the not-so-strange places and ways to do things to show the newcomers. Also, chances are when she starts taking the new arrivals around and answering their questions about how to do this and that, she may realize with surprise that she is more at home in the community than she realized. With this new bit of self-confidence she may then venture further from home than she had been willing to do before and so begin to find for herself, and bring back to her family, the feeling of belonging which can make such a difference in their overseas experience.

In many places American wives (frequently those whose husbands are related to technical service missions but sometimes a representative group from the whole American community) have prepared brochures about a foreign city for the benefit of newcomers. Some are simple handbooks. Others are exceptionally articulate guides for those who would explore and understand a new community. (If you are going to a foreign capital inquire at the American Embassy to see if such a report is available there.) I once watched the preparation of a manual for new arrivals and I was fascinated to see, not only how much good material could be assembled by a group of people who had never worked together before, but also how the individuals themselves relaxed as they worked creatively to make it easier for someone else to feel at home.

Writing letters is in the same way a kind of anti-shock therapy. Most people try to reassure the folks at home and enjoy passing on to them descriptions of things they see and do in a foreign land. In the process of putting on paper both vivid first impressions and overall evaluations, one may stand on the new terrain with some objectivity and poise and with a growing realization that those differences which at first may have seemed like such a great divide, are not in fact, insurmountable.

Chapter III

A HOME AWAY FROM HOME

"I guess we shall have to call you Princess Julia," I said to a wide-eyed little American girl who had just arrived at the Rangoon airport with her mother and father, "because you are going to be living in a palace."

I knew that for a while the child beside me and her parents, who had come on a contract to produce some films for the Burmese government, could be happy in the comfortable and attractive hotel to which we were taking them—"The Kambawza Palace" named for a Shan prince who used to live in it. But I suspected that after a few weeks, her parents, like most other American couples who live overseas for a year or more, would tire of hotel arrangements and would want to find a place of their own. In some foreign cities the hotels available are not as comfortable as those in Rangoon, and so the desire to find their own residence becomes more pressing for an American family.

Almost the first question a man asks when he is being approached to work overseas is "What are the housing possibilities?" These men, and their wives for whom the housing concerns are even more important, are usually not looking for fabulous castles nor are they demanding the split-level ramblers or the all-electric apartments to which they are accustomed. They do want to be sure that in a strange land there will be a place to which they can retreat as if it were their castle. They hope that it will at lease be safe and clean.

In many cases, employees are assured in advance that a place to live is waiting for them in a church mission compound, on company property, in houses rented by a foundation, at an army post. For these people, the housing question is relatively simple. They find out in advance what the house is like, what is supplied and what isn't. When they arrive they have only to move in and set about to make it their home away from home.

For the many Americans who, with or without a housing allowance, are on their own to find and rent a dwelling, the move is a bit more complicated. Here are some suggestions:

To Find A Home

Every effort should be made before leaving the States to find out from the sending agency, from the sponsoring university, from the foreign employer, or from families recently returned from the same foreign community to which the new family is going, what the housing situation is going to be. If no other source of information is available a letter of inquiry about housing might be sent to the American Embassy in the capital city of the destination country. If there is a house waiting and ready, a family is more lucky than they may realize.

If a house is to be ready later on it is essential to find out what temporary accommodations are available. A family with four children and eighteen pieces of hand luggage doesn't just start out for Outlandia and expect to walk into a hotel and register. There may not be a hotel, but if there is, it may be full. In the face of grave uncertainty, it may be necessary to decide that the husband should go first to scout out the housing situation, with the rest of the family to follow as soon as he has found a suitable place for them to live.

When it is known that temporary quarters are to be needed, reservations should be made in advance with confirmation requested. Airline or steamship representatives can sometimes assume responsibility for recommending hotels or hostels and for making the reservations. Travel agency representatives are also in a position to do this. Even when a house is available immediately, it isn't a bad idea to have another stopping place for a few days to give time for freight to be delivered and time for the homemaker to take some first steps towards setting up her own kitchen or for finding servants.

People who must locate their own dwelling after arrival in a foreign place need to get some on-the-spot information even if they already have suggestions or names of possible landlords. They need to have their information confirmed by someone who knows the locale and the immediate situation. Neighborhoods may have changed. Laws about real estate procedures may have changed. Inquiries could be made at the American Embassy or Consulate. Lacking the presence of one of these, an English speaking bank official or the executive of a Chamber of Commerce might be consulted.

Frequently the help of a middle-man may be needed for the transactions related to leasing or renting a dwelling. He must be chosen carefully and his reputation verified by responsible people. In many countries bargaining is a part of the process of arriving at terms and the middle-man who has the interest of the American at heart can be useful in keeping the rents reasonable. Also, he could be helpful in the working out of differences that might arise later between the landlord and his tenant. The fee required by an agent may be more than saved by his services.

It is imperative to make sure that a transaction is legal. The services of a local lawyer might be needed. There can be no end of trouble if an American has entered into an arrangement which in a given country is unlawful or if he has overlooked the fine print which binds him in ways he cannot afford to be bound.

To Start Housekeeping

We have discussed in an earlier section the importance of taking to a new home in a foreign country some things from the old home in order that a family might have a sense of continuity. But to the something old there will surely be added much that is new as a house is furnished overseas.

In many places people find that local type furniture is more suitable to the climate than furniture brought from home would be. The same can be said of basic kitchen equipment. If a local charcoal stove is to be used, for instance, then the kind of cooking utensils designed for and commonly used on charcoal stoves are best at least for top-of-the-stove cooking.

Locally available equipment generally has the advantage of being less ostentatious than imported items, and frequently is more easily used by local servants. These two factors alone would seem to throw the weight of judgment about household furnishing in the direction of local supplies. Yet, it must be pointed out that while some servants want to use their own kind of tools, others are very much conscious of the status symbols of modern equipment, and would feel that they were losing face with their fellow domestics if they went to work in a home that wasn't equipped with imported items.

By the same token, western trained professional co-workers are often struggling to acquire the things which have come to them to be the outward signs of modernity and progress, and sometimes these local people are not at all impressed by the American who tries *not* to show that he can afford the things for which they are working so hard.

If the trend of this discussion leaves the reader in a quandary as to just where the emphasis should be put when it comes to decisions that are essentially related to standards of living, it can only be said that the maintenance of the questioning point of view is perhaps the most important factor.

There are no easy answers. It is required of a conscientious American homemaker who moves into a foreign community that she keep ever aware of the varied and at times conflicting forces with which she must reckon. Surely it is good for American families to identify themselves somehow with the masses who have so little. Is it not also good to show the elite of a country as well as the emerging middle classes that it is possible to work for and to possess a certain number of useful and attractive things without being possessed by them?

We have observed that if nationals see in an American a genuine liking and respect for them then they are not bothered by the fact that he has a great quantity of expensive things. But if his attitude towards nationals makes them feel that he thinks they are backward or inferior, then they will begrudge him even the modest things that are different from theirs.

The essential thing is that Americans should be truly humble as they establish and maintain their homes in the midst of an alien culture.

It is beneficial to bring a certain number of local art pieces into our living rooms overseas in order that we may learn to enjoy them and so that local guests may see that we appreciate them. I met a man recently who had returned from a quick trip to Japan where there are so many exquisite art objects. His comment was that when he went into an American home in Tokyo he felt as if he were still in Arlington, Virginia where he lives. He saw nothing in the living room which gave any hint that the family was in Japan. The house he saw is surely an exceptional one but his point is a good one: people might as well stay at home if they are going to isolate themselves completely from the culture around them.

It is particularly important to buy cautiously any pieces of local art that are to be used in a house overseas. In the first place, unless an American is living in one of the European countries with whose art most of us are generally familiar, it is possible that something which attracts his attention at first may not seem, after he has become more familiar with the art forms, to be as pleasing or of as good quality as he may have thought at first. Local people may not be happy to have art objects of their country displayed which are not good according to their standards.

The other thing about art objects is that while a few nice pieces attractively placed may add gracefully to the personality of a home, too many pieces can cause a house to lose its personal identity and come to be like a museum. I have seen not a few American living rooms in foreign countries that were on the way to needing a curator!

Homemakers might be wise to have an out of the way corner where most of the things they buy to take home to friends and relatives can be stored.

People of the country are sometimes amused at the assortment of local artifacts some Americans display so prominently in their homes. They are embarrassed rather than amused at other times.

"When you take a crude pottery teapot and give it a place of honor in your fine home" an Indian friend once said to me, "you embarrass our people because this is a reminder to us that the masses of our countrymen still can afford nothing better. We may not realize that you like it because it is primitive. We only know that you take this utilitarian thing which you bought for a few pennies and put it in your most important room. We feel that you are in some way laughing at us and we are uncomfortable."

Another Asian friend once warned me that Americans should be careful how they display religious objects. There are no valid generalizations except the flat statement that it is never wise to display an object of a religion other than one's own unless one is sure that the adherents of the religion to which it is related would be happy about its display by a non-believer and would approve of the way in which it is done. Americans, for instance, have a way of putting curios down on low coffee tables or of tucking them in with books on a low shelf. Any place below the height of the head of man is considered by Buddhists, for instance, as being a place too lowly for an object used in religious observance. The exquisite jade statue of Buddha on a coffee table may indicate to visiting Buddhists not that we have high regard for the craftsmen of their country but only that we are lacking in respect for their religious traditions.

Sometimes Americans are attracted by the color or design or workmanship of objects they see in local bazaars and buy them not knowing or caring what they are used for. If they take them home and display them before they learn their identity, they run the risk of inappropriately exhibiting some object used only in a bridal chamber, carried only at a funeral, or perchance used in the ritual of witchcraft. "If Americans would only stop putting our porcelain spittoons on their mantels as flower vases!" an exasperated Chinese scholar once protested.

To Feed A Family

However absorbed a homemaker may get in the process of furnishing her house and selecting its adornments, she must at the same time give thought to the fact that family members get hungry about three times a day overseas just as they did back home. Those families who live in hotels or those single people who by assignment or by choice are billeted in hostels or with a local family have only to turn up at meal time, but for all others a homemaker must see to it that appetizing and nutritious meals are ready.

The sources of supply are of prime consideration. If a family expected to eat exactly the kind of food the local people eat, then a homemaker could expect to get almost everything she would need wherever her local neighbors buy their food supplies. Few Americans want to do this because food habits are deep seated in all of us and food tolerance is not always a suddenly acquired characteristic. Americans who live in a foreign country for a good many years frequently learn to eat local food exclusively, to like it and, if it is nutritiously well balanced, to thrive on it, but such adaptation comes slowly. New arrivals may find the food of the new country too bulky, too greasy, too spicy, too rich, perchance too bland to be satisfying or sustaining on a daily basis. So the homemaker usually has the task of finding in the local markets or of securing from outside sources the things needed for an Americanized menu for most of the meals.

The staples are the supplies that might differ most from the supplies used by the national families. It may be another American as well as the local neighbor who needs to be consulted about where the staples commonly used in our kitchens can be secured. In most foreign communities where any considerable number of Westerners are living there is likely to be a food shop handling imported items like flour, sugar, baking powder, coffee, and the like. One generally hears the complaint that items bought in these shops are frightfully expensive. If it were taken into consideration that the merchants have a limited clientele and so must allow for loss or spoilage, and that the costs of transportation and of import duty must be paid by the customer, the charges might not seem out of line. Women with a flair for food planning frequently explore the local markets for suitable substitutes for hard to find or expensive items.

In Burma, for instance, palm sugar could be processed into a very satisfactory substitute for the imported brown sugar; used with a few drops of maple flavoring it was an acceptable substitute for maple syrup. Similar possibilities for food adaptations exist in every country.

Non-government Americans abroad are likely to interrupt at this point and say, "But, of course the Embassy people don't have to worry about where their brown sugar or cranberry jelly or washing powder is coming from. They have the American Co-op (or the commissary or the PX as the case may be)." I sometimes think that misunderstanding and hard feelings about this one aspect of life abroad is a most disconcerting factor for many Americans. A fact so seldom known is that where homeside food supplies are available for certain government personnel, it has not been sent there by our government as a special favor for its own employees while other citizens are denied the same favor. The presence of an American supplies center is at the courtesy of the foreign government. A similar arrangement is operating for their personnel on a reciprocal basis in the United States. Articles may come into the center duty free because the host government has waived duty, again as a matter of diplomatic courtesy. Transportation costs are not carried by either government but by the consumers.

The privileged consumers are not the ones who decide that all other Americans shall be barred from buying directly or indirectly the supplies on the commissary shelves. It is the host government which decides what categories of official Americans may shop at a commissary or participate in a "Co-op." It is the local official who determines that it is strictly unlawful for either undesignated Americans or for any local citizens to buy or receive goods from an embassy or armed forces shopping depot.

The cause of intra-American goodwill might be served if all supermarket establishments for our officials were discontinued in foreign countries. On the other hand, there would be no need for such a drastic step if Americans aboard would all act less like jealous children. The privileged ones should receive their largesse with less fanfare. There is no need for them to do so much shopping at one time that traffic is tied up in two directions while the supplies are conspicuously loaded into conspicuously American cars. There is no need for them to be talking with people outside the official fraternity about the beautiful frozen turkeys or similar homeside things just arrived. Likewise there is no reason why other Americans shouldn't accept the facts of diplomatic life as they are and not go around with a discrimination complex warping them.

"After all," the wife of an American business executive in South America said recently, "why should we let such a small matter come between us and the Embassy families. Any job has its fringe benefits, but there are precious few for government employees. They can't accept any sort of a gift that amounts to anything. Foreign Service people can't even accept a citation or decoration from the country where they work. I say, let them have their Florida lettuce and let them enjoy it."

The executive's wife might have added that all government employees living abroad have federal income tax withheld from their salaries. Other Americans living overseas for more than eighteen months need not file a federal tax return for money earned while working in a foreign country. Many non-government people take advantage of this, sometimes vacationing abroad an extra few months in order to achieve the minimum time for exemption. Their economic gain far outweighs any amount of savings which government people have because of their duty free purchases.

Local markets generally can supply fresh fruit and fresh vegetables in season and some kinds of meat or fish. A later section will deal with health factors as related to fresh foods in certain areas. The important point to make just now is that Americans seldom need to rely on imported canned fruits or frozen vegetables or tinned meat because, though local products may be unfamiliar they are not necessarily unsuitable for use in our kind of food, and families who develop an open minded curiosity about new foods often have happy surprises in store for them. It is not uncommon for the practice of having a local meal (local products prepared in the local fashion) as a once-a-week special, like a Sunday lunch or a Saturday supper, become the favorite meal of the week.

To Be Safe And Secure

Another aspect of establishing a household overseas is to make sure that it is going to be a safe as well as a satisfying haven. It is wise at the very beginning to take a careful look at the new establishment and to anticipate even remote hazards so that adequate safeguards can be set up. The dangers may be the same as the ones back home—poisons or medicines in reach of small children, uncovered wells or drainage ditches, traffic risks outside the house and faulty wiring inside. But there may be additional risks related to the local situation. If modern fire fighting equipment is not close at hand, for instance, then small extinguishers are indicated and routine inspection of the premises needs to be made to see that fire threatening conditions are corrected.

It is our experience that if precautions are routinely taken in small matters a family can move securely through the days without serious mishap and without anxiety. This can be true even in so called danger zones. If an area is definitely not safe for residents and particularly for foreign residents, then the Americans are always informed, by their own officials and by the local officials who generally lean over backwards to prevent an incident involving a foreign resident. It is only foolhardy to ignore the advice of those in authority. The stubborn Americans who refuse to budge when danger is real not only take unnecessary personal risks, but may also embarrass the American officials and complicate matters for the local authorities. When dangers are more imagined than real then a quiet waiting-out-the-storm period may be in order.

"Shall I take a gun?" people sometimes ask as they prepare to move overseas. My answer is that if a situation ever gets bad enough for guns to be needed then it is a situation in which a foreign civilian does not belong, and he ought to get out. As for a gun in the bureau drawer in case of thieves or bandits, I contend that an American in a foreign country where conditions are unstable is far safer if he hires a local night watchman and doesn't even own a gun. Television histrionics are all right on television. There is no place for them when we are living on foreign soil.

(This does not apply to the taking of hunting guns. In many parts of the world Americans enjoy hunting as a sport and do quite reasonably have the guns they need for that.)

To Make A Home

The time should come for any homemaker overseas when she is able to write to a relative or a friend, "We're feeling pretty well established now." She or he will be reporting that a house or an apartment or perchance a room has been found—that it has been equipped with the needful things and that a pattern of living is beginning to take shape within it and around it. In essence, she will be saying that a place which at first may have seemed like either an impossible or a delightful house has come to be a home with which family members are personally identified and in which they feel at ease with themselves. The achievement of this at-homeness in a foreign land is dependent, not on the house itself, nor on the furnishings that are put in it, important as they are for comfort, efficiency, and esthetic expression. It isn't even dependent on the security situation of the area in which it is located. It depends primarily on whether or not a family has a sense of what is vital for its existence and meaningful for its maintenance—and whether or not this criterion has been brought along and applied or adapted with imagination and insight.

Chapter IV

COMPLETE WITH STAFF

Stay-at-home Americans frequently express the opinion that it would be worth going overseas "just to have all those servants." On the other hand, I have heard wives at pre-departure orientation sessions ask almost desperately, "*Must* we have servants?"

The thought of a nurse to live in with babies, a man or woman to cook all the meals, a maid or a houseboy to keep things in order, and a gardener to take over the outside drudgery sounds like heaven to a harassed mother or to the head of a household who has to cut grass when he would rather sit in a contour chair and watch a ball game. It sounds like a dream come true, and Americans are great ones to dream; but when it comes down to it, most of us live with our feet on the ground and like it that way. The actual prospect of being surrounded by a staff of servants is frightening to some, and seems a bit out of line with the American way of life to others.

One woman about to leave for overseas said, "Why I just wouldn't know how to go about managing a lot of servants."

"What are the people in foreign countries going to think of us if we talk about democracy and then live like kings?" is another common question.

"How can we afford to hire people to do everything?" some ask.

Servants Are Optional

It is time that the stereotype of the American overseas having a whole retinue of servants be replaced with a more accurate picture. The fact is that many Americans living abroad never have domestic help. "I just don't need help," reports a wife who lives in a modern apartment on Copacabana Beach in Rio de Janerio. "Help is as hard to find in Bonn as it is in Washington, and in both places it is too expensive for us," another wife reports.

In contrast to the places where many American women do their own household chores just as they did back home, there are some places still so close to primitive conditions and still so far away from industrial development that if an American woman didn't have helpers she would be working from dawn to sunset struggling to maintain what we have come to think of as just a survival standard of living. But in either of these extreme situations and in all the places that fall between, the need for help differs according to the location within a country. Even in an underdeveloped country bread might be bought in a city whereas everything may have to be prepared at home in a village. In some places labor saving devices which are the servant substitute in America can be used, but in other parts of the same country electrical power might be so limited or so undependable that all work would need to be done the slow and hard way.

The number of servants employed depends upon the culture of the country and also upon the social patterns of the American family. In European and South American countries it is generally possible to find a maid who will take on a variety of chores. In the countries of Asia, Africa, and the Middle-East there is more likely to be a custom imposed division of labor which makes it impossible for one servant to do all the things that must be done. In India the caste system is changing, but it will be a long time before any one but an untouchable will be willing to sweep floors or clean bathrooms. In Vietnam a gardener knows how to be a gardener and doesn't know how to double as a cook or a chauffeur.

I wish that the Very Important People who make overnight stops in out of the way places and then come back criticizing the Americans abroad for surrounding themselves with innumerable servants would learn more about the social framework within which the Americans are living.

It is true, however, that the cultural traditions themselves change, and Americans should be alert to move as fast and as far away as possible from what may seem to young nationals as well as to visiting dignitaries to be a carry-over of colonialism.

The type of job a man has and the kinds of social responsibilities he carries have a great deal to do with determining how many servants might be needed in his household. When we were in Burma we needed to have guests in for meals several times a week and sometimes daily (my husband came home for lunch and the luncheon conference guests came with him). Frequently it was our job to entertain some of the "VIPs" who came through Rangoon.

I remember one Washington visitor who wanted to meet the local officials who were responsible for the public welfare programs and also the United Nations welfare specialists and the American technicians who were working on public health or related problems. It was our turn to do the honors. On short notice we arranged an informal

Sunday afternoon garden party for about a hundred people with arrival times staggered so that there could be a chance for the guests to converse with the American official and his wife. As I remember it we served only iced tea with cucumber sandwiches and home made (and home grated) coconut macaroons. How could I have managed even such a simple affair for so many people and at the same time have been on duty as hostess to introduce the wife of the visiting official if I hadn't had a cook in the kitchen and a bearer to keep food and dishes moving?

Some people in Rangoon whose social responsibilities were similar to ours had even more help than we had because their way of living and of entertaining was by preference more elaborate than ours. Others whose work carried little or no entertaining responsibilities and whose personal tastes were simple managed to get along quite comfortably with only one servant or with none.

It is so often assumed that anywhere overseas servants may be hired for a song. This is no longer true in most places, and more and more Americans are having to let the number of servants they hire be limited by their economic resources.

Servants Can Be Helpful

When women are worried about the need to have servants I remind them that in many situations servants may help a house wife achieve some of the worth while goals she holds for herself. She wants to establish and maintain for her husband and children—and for herself if she is a lone professional woman—a clean and comfortable home. This is hard to do if one is living where there are few household aids like vacuum cleaners or automatic washers or water heaters, where there are few public services like garbage collection and water purification, and where prepared foods—bread, ice cream, cookies, and mayonnaise are not available.

I shall always remember the comment of an Indian woman to a young American who wondered why she would need help in India. "You wouldn't need it, perhaps, if you could take your old uncle along to chop the vegetables, your mother to mind your baby, and your widowed sister's oldest daughter to do the washing and pressing."

She went on to say that American women are so well educated and have so much to offer in their adopted countries that it would seem to her a shame if, where help is easily available, they didn't use it in order to free themselves to make a useful contribution to the community.

Another way in which servants may be helpful is to give the children the care and security which they need. Baby sitting is an American institution. If a mother is ever to leave her children in most foreign countries she must have a full time nurse, *amah, aiya,* or maid available even though she may prefer to look after the youngsters most of the time herself.

She cannot leave them on their own as early as she would in her own country. As a matter of fact, I would be just as concerned to have a woman attendant at home with teen-age girls in most foreign countries as I would to have little children attended, even though I might permit the same teen-agers to go out at night in America to do baby sitting for someone else. In places where local young women are carefully chaperoned, local people, including the men servants of a household, might misunderstand or take advantage of parental carelessness. Also, in a situation where parents may find themselves being away from home a great deal more than they were in America, the children, being left without their parents, and frequently without television or even a telephone, may get very lonely. I shall always be grateful for the help of the Burmese *nanny* who took over with the junior members of our household when I was away from home. She seemed to enjoy tucking her sarong-like skirt up and playing war with a pre-schooler during the day, and then she was just as eager for card games with a sub-teen girl at night when her father and I were off to official functions.

Servants may be helpful also as cultural go-betweens. They frequently bring to members of the household where they work an intimate understanding of the country and its people. They recount the folklore. They describe ceremonies. They reveal religious beliefs and they express aspirations. It works the other way, too. Servants who have learned in an American home about modern health precautions, about child care practices, about holiday customs, pass on the things they learn to the people in their home communities.

How To Select Servants

There are certain European countries where it is possible to find domestic workers through the classified columns of a newspaper or by calling an employment agency, but in most of the places where Americans will be needing household help the grapevine telegraph system is more likely to be used. Word gets out that a new family is looking for help. Then people begin to turn up who want work or, more commonly, who want to speak for someone else who wants work.

The middle man may be a key person in the servant selection process, and a homemaker is wise to ask "Who sent you?" to a would-be servant who applies without appointment. If she knows the third person or knows for whom he works then she is in a better position to evaluate the applicant's credentials. She can't afford not to check on the papers shown to her because in countries where poverty is widespread it would be surprising if credentials were not sometimes borrowed or forged.

It is my experience that servants recommended by the servants of another Western family whose household standards are similar to one's own are likely to be good risks. If my friend's cook enjoys a good reputation in the community then he will be most reluctant to recommend another cook unless he is sure that the one he names can measure up both in skill and in character. The established cook would lose face if a man (or woman) he vouched for proved to be stupid or dishonest. I have had one of my own trusted servants come to me and say "If Madam would speak a word for my sister's husband to the new Americans down the road. This brother-in-law is young. He has yet to learn much about the dishes Americans like to eat, but I will teach him during my rest time, and I will see that he behaves properly."

If there is to be more than one servant then it is important to select men—or women—who will be able to get on together. This is not easy because a Westerner has a hard enough time making a decision like this in a work situation in his own country. Given cultural differences, he is at a loss to know what kind of inter-personal factors might affect negatively or positively the harmony of the household. My preference is to select carefully and personally the one servant whose position is recognized by servants in a particular community as the top position. In Burma it was the bearer (the house boy or butler in the English tradition). In some places it is the cook who is thought of as Number One. After I had employed the head servant I would ask him—or her—to help me find the others. I would see them myself, of course, and I might see those recommended from others sources. But I would rely on his judgment. He would know what religious or sectional prejudices might prove divisive and what personal attributes might be helpful or annoying. In addition to being able to sort out these kinds of factors, he would be very anxious to choose a person who could do good work because he would feel that a poor performance would bring discredit to him in our eyes. Also if I demonstrated my confidence in him by deferring to him for guidance in this important matter then he would feel honored and would most likely express his gratitude by giving us the most valuable thing a servant can ever give his employer, steadfast loyalty.

The one servant who might be chosen separately would be a children's nurse whose position in the family is generally somewhat different from other servants—particularly if the others are men. I would employ her separately and would expect her to be responsible to me directly. In many ways she is closer to the famliy than the other helpers—perhaps sleeping in or near a child's room—having meals with the children on occasions. Even so, she is necessarily in close contact with the other servants, too, and it is important to get the happiest combination possible. A fortunate arrangement exists if in a two-servant situation a husband and wife team can be found.

Qualifications

In selecting any servant or any combination of servants there are several qualifications to look for. First, employers need to be sure that an applicant has good character references, that he is held in honorable esteem by his own people and that according to our standards, he is likely to be trustworthy.

It is a help to find an experienced servant already familiar with Westerners and their household practices, but it isn't always possible to do this, and some homemakers prefer to take a willing worker and teach him how to do things. In some ways this is easier than changing the habits of a servant who had been long in service with a family whose patterns were more formal or more casual, or what have you, than those of the new family.

The language factor is an important one. Unless an American has some prior knowledge of the local language or has reason to believe she can learn it quickly then she needs to try to find a servant who can speak at least a little English. It isn't necessary that all servants be English speaking where there are more than one. If the head servant knows English, then he can pass on instructions or recipes or solicitous inquiries about a sick grandmother. It is very important to learn the language limits of a servant before employing him. His references may say that he knows English, and he may say that he does, but his grasp of English might be very limited and unless this is known it could result in some ludicrous or even dangerous mistakes.

A clean bill of health is one of the most fundamental qualifications to be considered when selecting a servant. One might take health risks with a gardener who will have little close contact with members of the family, and one might take risks with household help in most European communities, but any servant who is to work inside the house in the less developed places must be known to be free from infectious diseases, or from being a carrier of them. A previous employer's comment about this is helpful, but the only dependable record is an up to date report from a doctor or a clinic. If a servant is otherwise acceptable, then a new employer is wise to send him to a doctor and wait for the report before coming to any final agreement about employment.

The thoroughness of the examination should be determined by the local health situation. In general, it is important to have a blood test (for syphilis), a chest X-ray (tuberculosis), and a stool examination (for fecal borne diseases such as dysentery and typhoid). Such an examination should be at the employer's expense. Americans should never begrudge the cost of medical examinations of prospective servants even though they might have to pay fees for several people before finding one who is acceptable. They not only protect themselves in this way, but at the same time they make it possible for those who are examined to know about physically threatening conditions and to learn how they can take steps to get them corrected.

We once had to reject a servant who was found to have active tuberculosis. Since we had young children we felt we couldn't hire him, but we were able to arrange treatment for him and for several months we gave financial assistance to his family so that he could rest and get maximum benefit from his treatment. Later he was well enough to take work with another family and we have the satisfaction of knowing that he is alive today and is able to support his family.

What to Expect of Servants

It is important that from the beginning there be a clear understanding of what is expected of servants and of what they may expect of their employers. Later, after a servant is established in a household both he and his employer may use indirect personality-protecting devices in their discussions, but before he is hired both may speak boldly. An employer may ask bluntly, "Will you be willing to do this or that?" A servant may ask, "Who will pay for my uniform?" Each needs to pry deeply to make sure that there is a mutual understanding about the arrangements.

When both parties seem to be satisfied with the prospects in theory, then it is wise to get agreement on a first month trial period when the servant's suitability can be given a practical test. It can be pointed out to a servant at this stage that the trial period will give him a chance to see if he will be happy working with the American family just as it will give the family members a chance to see if he can do the things they need to have done.

In a few places (Germany, for instance) there are laws for the protection of domestic workers which make it difficult or expensive to dismiss an unsatisfactory servant, and in those cases the trial period before a servant is formally employed is essential. I have always operated on the basis that it is best, in any case, to be critical and careful during the preliminary period, and then after that to concentrate on making a servant arrangement work out well instead of continuing in a frame of mind which assumes that if a servant displeases you, you can always let him go and find someone else.

A servant who works for a diffident mistress is going to be ill at ease and wary. A homemaker who fires a succession of servants is going to get a hard-to-please mark on her gate and only incompetent or unprincipled workers will apply. So it behooves a homemaker to make her selections carefully in the first place and then to be reasonable and sympathetic with those who help her.

A servant's willingness to do various tasks is determined in larger part by taboos and practices in his own cultural background. Sometimes the taboos are just an outgrowth of economic necessity. Long before labor unions were operating in the western world, there had grown up in China a division of labor which protected workers in a given kind of activity. This operated very efficiently in relation to the Westerners who were all thought to be wealthy.

At one time it seemed to my husband and me that it was not only expensive but immodest for us to have two men employed to do the things which one man might easily have done in our home on the university campus. So we said to a cook one day when we were in need of a new table boy that we thought he might take on the extra chore himself and that we would be willing to increase his wages considerably if he would. He turned to my husband with terror in his eyes. "But Master, the other servants would beat me off the campus!"

There are in many parts of the world different cultural groups within a community. Burma, for instance, is largely Buddhist, but there are many Indians who may be Muslim or Hindu. There are sizeable groups of Christians. Servants drawn from any of these groups would all have, to some extent, a Burmese background which would condition them in their thinking about what a servant ought or ought not to do. In addition each would have the sanctions or prohibitions of his religious traditions effecting his sense of the fitness of things. No amount of cajoling can change this.

An Indian bearer we once had was upper class Hindu. It was inappropriate for him to sweep floors though he was a tireless worker and would get down on his knees and wax furniture to a mirror finish. I never asked him to clean the floor but was careful to say to him, "The children have scattered cracker crumbs all over the living room. Please ask the sweeper to tidy the floor before the guests arrive."

If I asked him to get the sweeper he knew that I knew it was the sweeper's kind of work and he respected me for my understanding at this point. Even so, if no one else were around and if the sweeper were off duty, the bearer would be likely to fetch a broom and a dust pan and actually do the job himself.

It was a different matter if guests were present. A plate of food might be spilled on the floor. The bearer would see it, might put a stool in front of it so that guests wouldn't stumble onto it but he would walk with dignity out of the room to get the sweeper to come and clear it away. If the sweeper were absent then the bearer would bring his own young son and would supervise him while he did the work. He wouldn't embarrass me in front of my guests by behaving as if he didn't know the proper way for a respectful Hindu man to act. If there were guests I wouldn't embarrass the butler by doing the job myself as any American housewife would be inclined to do.

The division of labor enters between mistress or master and servant just as it does between servants. This is a troublesome thing for most Americans. The few lazy ones say, "Musn't make these folks lose face by doing their work." So they hand a brief case to a driver to carry ten feet or leave clothes on the bedroom floor for a maid to hang. A disgusting rationalization, I think, and this is an admission that I belong, as I think many of my compatriots do, to the dignity-of-labor and every-body-do-his-share-of-the-work school. For people not of our school there is no real problem. They just get lazier and lazier and love it. But many wives who are used to doing housework, and who want their children (and their husbands) not to lose helpful habits are often perturbed. They have heard that they will lose face in the eyes of the servants if they do menial tasks. They have heard that servants will be offended if the mistress does any kind of household work. They feel trapped.

This is an unfortunate and quite an unnecessary dilemma. Division of labor and cultural differences notwithstanding, a homemaker is and must be the manager of her own house. Servants are employed to help and not to run the place. The servants themselves will be happier if the mistress is not intimidated. They will be relieved and not offended if the children put away their toys and the master hangs up his own pajamas.

The important thing is for the homemaker who wants to take over responsibility for some phase of the housekeeping, or wants her children to perform certain chores, to let the servant in charge know about it at the outset so that he isn't surprised to see her watering the house plants or so that he (or a maid) doesn't make over the beds which children have in their clumsy way already made. If a homemaker wants to do some one thing occasionally, she should make an explanation to the servant so that he won't think that her doing it implies criticism of him.

Take the business of cooking. Many American women enjoy cooking and would be reluctant to turn over the kitchen to someone else even though they would welcome kitchen help. Some of them just say flatly, "I will do the cooking myself," and servants are employed only to do other work. Others will say at the outset, "Cooking is a special hobby of mine—occasionally I will want to fix a meal or do some special baking." Good sense and good manners both would dictate that the lady of the house not go barging into the kitchen to stir up a batch of fudge when the cook is busy with the last-minute rush of a company dinner for which he is responsible.

There is no reason why a homemaker should refrain from telling a servant how she would like to have things done. Certainly she, rather than he, would decide if food is to be placed on the table family style and passed as it may have been done at home, or if it is to be kept on a buffet and served in a more formal fashion.

To guide a servant in improving his technique requires finesse, but there isn't anything obscure about it. The homemaker who has a reasonable amount of patience and a generous amount of respect for people will succeed; a callous and impatient person may not. It always has seemed important to me to avoid correcting a servant's conduct in the presence of anyone else. If he is making a mistake like bringing the chocolate sauce with the meat course, I would whisper to him, "Let's keep this for the ice cream and have the apple sauce now."

If it is necessary to check a servant about slovenliness in appearance or carelessness in cleaning one should speak constructively. A homemaker might say to a bearer, for instance, "Our guests always appreciate your courteous service, but I think they would like to see you in a clean shirt when you are serving. You should take time to bathe and put on fresh clothes each night before dinner."

To a sweeper one could say, "Perhaps you should put the light on when you clean the bathroom then it will be easier for you to see the mildew which is collecting on the tiles."

Sometimes a servant might be more than careless. Then it is necessary to drop the face-saving suggestions and come directly to the point: "We cannot have your friends drinking and shouting in our kitchen. You must see that it doesn't happen again."

Some women prefer to have their husbands step into a serious situation with servants on the theory that they will more readily pay attention to a man. I'm inclined to feel that if a relationship has deteriorated to the place where a servant will hear only a louder voice of authority, then it is time the relationship were dissolved. However, I am sure that servants everywhere have a special regard for the master of the household, and I think it is good for them to be noticed by the husband. On many occasions my husband has handed servants their wages and has at the same time thanked them for the things they were doing to take care of us and has made specific inquiries about their welfare.

It frequently bothers Americans to see servants doing a job the hard way or going at it in a way that to us would seem inefficient. Sometimes a suggestion as to an easier or a more effective procedure will be accepted and appreciated. Many times it falls on deaf ears. Chances are a servant has worked out his own way of doing things, and unless his practices are risky from a health viewpoint I think that in the long run it pays to let him follow his own habits. After all, he is probably not programmed as we are for speed and short cuts.

Housewives whose servants do marketing or conduct other financial transactions for them should expect to have a regular accounting given. In Burma where our bearer was skilled in both the reading and writing of English, he kept the record book and I generally went over it with him carefully only once a week. I would give him an advance and he would keep an itemized record of what the cook spent at the market, what he paid the laundry man, the egg man, and others. He took pride at the end of each month in presenting a summary of household expenditures.

It was different thirty years ago in China. Our old cook who was an artist with a pastry tube couldn't write in either Chinese or English. So every evening he told me what he had spent that day and I wrote it down in the account book. I would use that time to tell him about any special items I would like him to buy the next day. If I went out in the kitchen later in the evening I might see a duck feather or a lemon rind or some other odd thing which he had laid out to remind himself before he left for the market the next morning of items he needed to remember.

If I sometimes had reason to believe that our Chinese cook was boosting the price of something beyond the accepted ten per cent commission, I would remind him that my book showed that the same item was lower only a few days ago, or I would ask him why the price had gone up at a season when the product was in such good supply. He might stick to his quotation for that particular day, and I would let him, but two days later that item would come in for the usual or even a lower amount and he would tell me how by getting to market early and bargaining skillfully he had been able to get a better price than on that recent day when the apricots which we liked so very much had been available only for the higher figure I had remarked about.

This was a kind of game we played. He reasoned, no doubt, that he would be a fool if he didn't try now and then to get the better of me. He concluded that I wasn't a fool if I checked him before he went too far. The winner was the one who never let himself be too foolish.

It is an old game and men the world over still play it in a great variety of situations. But Americans often forget that there are checks and balances written into the rules of the game and they sometimes get alarmed and think about dishonesty and corruption and untrustworthiness if they hear that a neighbor's cook bought oranges for less than their man or woman did. They forget that their own oranges just might have been bigger or better, and if this is the case, a frontal attack profits them nothing except a loss of prestige. Servants respect you if they know that you are keeping a watchful eye on their stewardship, but if you display an unreasonably suspicious nature than they will lose regard for you and may set about to take advantage of you at every turn.

One often hears a newly arrived American ask how far he should trust a servant. It is my conviction that we have no choice but to trust them and should make it clear to them from the beginning that we do. If I expected to keep valuables in the house I would show a servant where they were, would say to him how precious these particular spoons or rings or coins are to us and would ask him to see to their safety. Then he would know that I knew that he knew the valuables were there, and not being able to deny knowledge of their existence he couldn't take them or permit them to be taken innocently. More important than this, my confidences in his honesty would be the best safeguard against his possible vulnerability to temptation.

In Burma I gave our head servant the keys to the pantry where supplies were stored, and he was the one who kept it locked against outside prowlers. I checked the stores with him from time to time in order to know what was needed, and I never found evidence that even a small item was missing. He did such a good job of looking after our supplies that late one night when our teen-agers decided to take friends to the pantry to raid the refrigerator they found the room was fastened so securely that they couldn't even get an ice cube. After that we persuaded the bearer to leave the refrigerator available to us, but I discovered that before he would leave the small room where it was kept unlocked he had moved all surplus supplies out of it and into a separate store room which he locked whenever he left the house for his own quarters.

Americans cannot afford to be the suppliers for black market or thieves market operations, of course, so if a servant proves to be a freebooter, he has to be dismissed straightaway. But if a man or woman helper takes only some sugar for his tea or coffee to offer to visiting friends, it seems to me that the most effective procedure is for the homemaker to let the offending one know that she is aware of his actions; perhaps setting aside a certain amount of the special items for his or her use. I would take steps only if a servant continued to appropriate things or began to take in sizeable amounts family supplies not expected to be furnished for him. If a nursemaid takes a pretty handkerchief when she is doing the ironing, I would give her two or three nice hankies of her own.

I have frequently suggested to relatives of people overseas that it is a thoughtful and helpful gesture if they include in Christmas packages small items like printed handkerchiefs, bars of toilet soap, or ball-point pens gift-wrapped and labeled for family servants. I have observed in many situations that servants who are given small things from time to time are much less likely to steal things at any time.

I wouldn't have servants at all if I felt I had to watch them every minute, to dole out the eggs before breakfast every morning, or walk around my house with a bunch of keys dangling at my waist!

Wages and Fringe Benefits

Determining the wages for servants is a knotty problem. Americans who are everywhere reported to be rich and who are never poor as working people in many countries are, cannot expect to pay servants as little as they might get in the homes of well-to-do local people or even in the homes of other Westerners. On the other hand, aside from the fact that few Americans abroad are rolling in wealth, they can't afford to upset the local wage scale by giving too far above it. It is well to make inquiries from others before coming to terms on wages.

The fringe benefits must be taken into account in fixing a wage. In a local household a servant might be given his food or at least the basic items like rice or beans or millet as a part of his wages. In an American establishment he may more likely be given the money instead so that he can buy and eat the food of his choice. If a servant lives in or has quarters supplied he would not need as much money as if he were paying rent elsewhere. However, if he alone lives in furnished quarters and must maintain a house for his family outside then he would need a higher wage.

There is always a question as to whether the employer should pay for all medical expenses as well as the initial and annual examination. If the medical bills are picked up for the servant, will the same be true for his wife and children? Some think that it is a worthwhile protection to finance modern medical care for servants and their families. Others, hoping to encourage economic responsibility will offer to share the cost for medical care, sometimes helping the servant to establish a small saving fund for emergencies.

If an employer requires uniforms then it is only fair that he should pay for them and, considering the fact that in underdeveloped areas, good soap is such an expensive item, should perhaps have them washed with the family laundry. Even if uniforms are not used, Americans generally want their servants to be clean and neatly dressed and they may need to make an annual clothing allowance.

Help with the education of servants' children is sometimes given. An efficient servant is likely to be an ambitious person. If he is a young man he may want to take adult education courses so that he may improve his education and increase his skills, but even though he may not expect to advance his own station in life, he may be very anxious to give his children a chance to be better prepared for modern living. In the absence of a free public school it may mean a great deal to him if his employer shares the cost of tuition or books at the nearest private school.

Scarcely anyone who has employed servants in a foreign country has not been faced with a request for an advance on wages or a loan to meet the costs of an emergency of some kind. One cannot respond hastily to such requests. To give financial help too easily is to encourage people to live beyond their means and to make them less able to manage their own affairs after the generous employer has gone home. But to deny assistance is sometimes to break the bonds of mutuality which are so often found in good relationships between servants and their foreign family. Sometimes a refusal could mean that in order to bury a father or marry a daughter a servant might be thrown into the hands of a loan shark who would charge him from thirty-six to one hundred per cent interest per year.

There is a special kind of wisdom needed at this point as in many particulars in the relationship with one's servants abroad. It is not unlike the judicious weighing of all the factors which is required of a parent with an adolescent child.

Within the Framework of Democracy

It would be a travesty of values if Americans abroad hired servants just for the purpose of impressing local people with their superior status or because they were laboring under the notion that without servants they would lose prestige in the community. Such people need to take a second look at themselves and at their concept of what it means to be an American in the world today.

On the other hand, those who want to live unpretentiously need not refrain from hiring servants they need to operate their households. From the point of view of democratic values, the important thing is not whether an American family has or doesn't have servants. It is important in the first place that they are hired for reasons of real need and not for reasons of pride. In the second place it is important that they be treated according to the best traditions of the democratic society which Americans represent.

An American living in whatever culture has the obligation to treat every man with courtesy and so far as he has jurisdiction to permit him to maintain his dignity and self-respect. This isn't just a mouthing of platitudes. It is basic to what this book is all about.

Some who read these pages are going to find themselves in societies where the observance of courtesy depends upon social class and where men without economic or political or religious prestige may sometimes be subjected to indignities and humiliations. Certainly we have too much of this in our own country where a democratic philosophy and Judeo-Christian ethics have been upheld for nearly two hundred years. It is not for us to judge those of other nations who may treat servants as hirelings. But it certainly is incumbent upon us to remember that the men and women who perform the most menial tasks in our homes are human beings with personal worth and the right to be respected. We don't have to run around looking for some list of rules about how to treat servants. We only need to accept them as people and treat them with the same kind of consideration and fairness we accord to others, plus that extra bit of personal interest which those who share a common roof generally give to one another.

This has always meant for our family that servants are addressed politely ("Sundarun, will you please move this settee out to the garden?") It has meant that we recognize them with a courteous greeting when they appear each morning and say "good night" to them when their day's work for us is finished. Our children have never been permitted to treat servants as private possessions but have been taught to ask politely for their assistance and to acknowledge service with an expression of gratitude.

When servants have lived in our house or on our grounds we have always made a point of looking into their quarters to see that they were adequate for their needs and in good repair. But we have respected their need for privacy and unless their habits proved a threat to our health or safety or seriously disturbed us in other ways, we have made no efforts to control their way of life. We have worked with them to arrange schedules which allowed for their meal times and rest periods and we have been careful not to call on them except at the times when they expected to be on call. We have taken over ourselves if necessary in order that they have regular days off duty. We have looked after a sick servant and we have taken time to talk with the son of a servant who wanted to know how he might become an engineer.

People have said to us as they have said to other Americans who treat their servants with respect, "You'll spoil them." I remind those who talk that way that respect genuinely given is never a demoralizing agent but is the stuff out of which responsibility and self confidence are born.

Having proclaimed this, I must hasten to say as a corollary that while I think servants should be treated with consideration as people, I feel they should also be treated objectively as workers with jobs to do, and should not be permitted to work haphazardly. Holding a reasonably high standard of performance for servants is as much a part of fairness as is a living wage and comfortable quarters. Servants may make more money when they work for Americans; they generally work harder, too. This effort to hold them to good workmanship is another way of contributing to their personal growth, provided of course we are not holding an unrealistic standard of achievement.

One aspect of the servant question which needs clarification is closely related to the regard for servants as individuals. When we respect a servant as an individual this doesn't mean that we should act towards him as if we thought he weren't a servant. Some well motivated Americans feel that 'servants' and 'slaves' are synonymous terms and therefore both are unacceptable for modern people. They hire servants to do the work of servants and then they try to create some new category for them and pretend that they are bosom friends or business partners or assume that some other sort of equalitarian relationship has been artificially created. Their intentions are to assure a servant that they do not look down upon him. The result may be that the servant looks down upon them with disgust and embarrassment because they have robbed him of the dignity of status in a society where class divisions are so much more pronounced than they are in our country.

He thinks of himself as a servant. He does the kind of work other servants do. His social contacts continue to be with other servants. His position in his culture is determined by his work. He is thrown into confusion if he is treated as if he were not a servant.

I watched this happen once. An American woman told her servant to call her Gladys ("as all my friends do"). She jumped in beside him when he drove her car. She offered him cookies when he was serving tea to her guests. At first it seemed to please him as flattery might please the unsuspecting child. Then it corrupted him and he became cheeky and demanding. Finally, and fortunately, his own self respect came to his rescue and he literally ran away from the job.

It is our responsibility in any part of the world to treat an individual man according to the highest dictates of our own conscience and according to the best traditions of our society. But it cannot be our mission to re-form the cultural patterns of another country. We can elevate the work a man does not by changing its name or category but by recognizing the important contribution it makes and the special skill it requires.

Particularly in societies where jobs and social status are so closely related, we cannot wave a wand of words and say that a man isn't what he knows he is. We can show him in a much more profound way that we respect him as we act respectfully towards him even though he belongs to a class different from our own according to the mores of his world. It is by our attitude towards our servants as individuals, and by our appreciation of the work they do, that Americans can most clearly demonstrate our understanding of the dignity of labor and the personal worth of all men.

Many rewarding experiences may come to Americans while they are living overseas but surely none are more tenderly recalled than those growing out of a mutually satisfying relationship between a family and its servants.

I remember the last Christmas we spent in Rangoon. With the exception of a Karen Nanny and a Roman Catholic driver, our servants were not Christians, but they all knew that the holiday has special significance for us. We sent word through the bearer that we would like all of them and their wives and children to be our guests at a party on Christmas Eve. They knew that we knew that normally they did not break bread together. The Hindu bearer and the untouchable sweeper and the Muslim night watchman could not, because of religious restrictions, cook food at the same fire. If we invited them all to come in and have food with us it was a different matter and, under the circumstance, I guess they could all grant special dispensations to themselves. In any case, eagerly and without embarrassment but with dignity commensurate with the occasion they all appeared in our living room in their best clothes.

We had arranged to show some entertaining movies and had some music. The children and I served refreshments, passing cookies we had made ourselves. Then my husband made a little speech to say "Merry Christmas" and after we had passed personally labeled toys and bags of sweets to the children and a skirt length of cloth to each of the women, my husband handed an envelope with a gift of money to each man, shaking hands with him as is our American custom. With informal smiles on their faces they all bowed formally as is their custom and even the littlest child said in carefully memorized English as he left us, "Merry Christmas, Master. Merry Christmas, Madam," and a "Merry Christmas" was said to each of our children.

Six months later when our living room was dismantled and our trunks were waiting in the foyer, these servants came again to greet us. This time the greeting was, "Goodbye, Master," "Goodbye, Mistress," "Goodbye, Miss Harriet, Miss Nancy, goodbye, Master Ted." The few who spoke more than a memorized phrase of English asked that we take greetings to "Miss Margaret" who had gone home to college a year ahead of us.

This time we were not the gift givers. The servants brought gifts of fresh and fragrant flower garlands and draped them over our heads. Some petals on mine became wilted by the warmth and salt of tears.

Chapter V

VERY WELL, THANK YOU

When a neighbor in Mamaroneck, New York once expressed to us her fears about the health risks of an overseas assignment she voiced a concern common to most Americans who are thinking about leaving a country where health standards are as high as they are in the United States today. It was actually no more than sixty years ago that vast numbers of New Yorkers were dying of typhoid fever, that many Southerners were enduring recurring attacks of malaria, that countless American children were fighting a losing battle with diphtheria. Yet in the first half of this century such spectacular strides have been made in scientific research, in public health education, and in applied medicine that the average American not only lives as close as his telephone to excellent medical care, but he also lives so far away from an environment where smallpox, dysentery, cholera, or yellow fever might flare up that he is likely to forget their existence. Abroad he is likely to be either carelessly indifferent to such killers or neurotically fearful of them.

I have seen both kinds of Americans overseas. There was the couple in Indo-China who thought that all the fuss about sterilizing raw vegetables and boiling water was silly, until their young child had a near fatal bout with bacillary dysentery, that gastro-intestinal, food-or-water-borne disease which is still widespread in Asia, Africa, and Latin America. Until certain of the miracle drugs recently appeared on the scene bacillary dysentery could very quickly bring death by dehydration, particularly to a young child.

On the other hand, there was a couple in Taiwan who so constantly admonished their children to wash before eating, to get into slippers as soon as they got out of bed, to refuse all food offered them by local people, to be careful about this and cautious about something else that before many months had passed they had a child ill, not from a tropical infection, but from a nervous breakdown. They need not have been so anxious about their children because almost without exception modern medicine has developed either an effective immunizing agent or a wonder drug for treatment. The exception of note is infectious hepatitis, but even for this a new vaccine has been announced.

Somewhere in between carelessness and anxiety there is a safe and sane position where those working in the less developed areas of the world may live with their families, assuming reasonable risks and at the same time managing to maintain good health.

Preventive Measures

The most important factors affecting the health of a person in any part of the world are those of a preventive nature. In the United States many protective measures are taken for us by the public health authorities and by the large number of health minded persons in our neighborhoods. Our water has been treated. Our milk has been inspected. There are pure food laws. School authorities require certain immunizations. The list could go on and on as could a listing of the ways in which people who are informed about sanitation are careful to keep themselves well and their neighbors protected from unnecessary exposure to diseases or infections. Such preventive measures do not necessarily surround those who go to countries where officials are only in the beginning stages of country-wide health programs, where modern doctors and hospitals are scarce, and where the masses of people may still be ignorant of even the most rudimentary fact about sanitation.

It becomes necessary for the individual American living abroad to assume a great deal more responsibility for his physical well being than he has been accustomed to doing at home. This is not difficult because so much information is available, so many diseases may now be controlled by immunizations or preventive drugs, and the routine health precautions required in the most disease ridden parts of the world are not difficult or seriously inconvenient.

That Americans abroad can and do take measures to keep themselves well is evidenced by the fact that in the U. S. Government Foreign Service *Health Handbook* it is reported that statistical evidence shows that less sick leave is taken by foreign service personnel abroad than by the average civil service employee in Washington.

Prevention begins with information, and a first step would be to secure from reliable sources a knowledge of the sanitary conditions and the health risks in a given locality. The *given* locality is important. Because there is a disease called African sleeping sickness, it doesn't follow that all who go to Africa should fear this disease.

In addition to the Government Printing Office booklet *Immunization Information for International Travel* mentioned in our discussion about getting ready to go abroad, those who live overseas might profitably take with them *The World Traveler's Medical Guide* by R. T. Atkins and J. M. Atkins (Simon and Schuster), and also Colter Rule's *A Traveler's Guide to Good Health* (Doubleday). *Health Hints for the Tropics,* a detailed and readable booklet prepared by the American Society of Tropical Medicine and Hygiene (Waverly Press, Baltimore, Maryland), is a most useful document for those going to tropical areas. *The Red Cross First Aid Manual* is indispensable for people everywhere.

Doctors in this country can find and supply useful information about health conditions in specific overseas areas, and medical people in the new country can be consulted after arrival. Doctors, both Westerners and nationals, in mission hospitals are likely to be well trained and familiar with the health situation in the immediate locality. In some places American army doctors who are acquainted with local conditions can advise American civilians even if they might not be free to treat them. Many American embassies have a medical officer or a nurse to whom any American citizen might turn for information. Our government's Agency for International Development has some forty health missions overseas with staffs of experienced health officers.

Americans should arrive overseas with the preventive immunization program already underway or completed. If any necessary shots have been delayed or omitted, no time should be lost in finding the local place where they may be taken. Some one member of the family should then become responsible to see that the immunizations are kept up to date. If an epidemic (cholera, for instance) should occur extra booster shots might be recommended by the local health authorities.

We referred in an earlier discussion to the fact that malaria irradication programs have now considerably reduced the incidence of that serious disease. There are still some areas of the world where malaria is prevalent, but in such places it is now possible to avoid the disease by the regular use of malaria suppressive medication. The small capsules may be taken by mouth easily and safely even by young children. Wherever they are needed the weekly dosage should never be missed.

It is a wise precaution to locate in the new community both a doctor and a hospital before either are specifically needed. Americans frequently turn to a western doctor, and this is generally a wise thing to do. But it is not always the best course. An English or an American doctor who has been long away from his homeland and has not kept up with medical literature or modern medical developments might in some cases be less competent than a national doctor recently trained in a modern institution and alert to new information and procedures. I would make inquiries before I selected a family doctor or decided which hospital or nursing home I would turn to in an emergency. In addition to asking other Americans for opinions, a newcomer could well visit hospitals and ask to be shown around, in order that he might see for himself what the facilities are like. Many times they are much better than you expect them to be!

Regular medical examinations are as much in order overseas as they are at home, and sometimes even more important. The person who prefers to wait until he can go back to his home town doctor may miss the early detection of some disorder which any qualified doctor overseas could spot.

Preventive measures related to climatic adjustments are sometimes needed. Those who go from a low altitude to an altitude of 7,000 feet or more above sea level are advised not to eat or drink excessively or to perform strenuous physical exercise for a few weeks while they are making an adjustment to the upper air's reduced oxygen content. Most people make this adjustment easily, but it is safer not to assume the first day after arrival that you are one of the fortunate majority.

Those who are moving into an unusually cold climate must not only dress appropriately but may need to avoid prolonged exposure which might interfere with the body's circulatory system.

In the tropics a family will need to work out practices and rules which take into consideration the health hazards related to heat and sun. Some families try to encourage naps or at least require that children play inside during the hottest part of the day. Exposure to the direct rays of the sun needs to be carefully supervised for children and taken gradually and in small doses by adults.

In hot places it is important to see that the members of a family drink plenty of water and eat plenty of salt. No one should start out on an extended expedition in an area where the purity of the publicly available water is uncertain without an adequate supply of safe water. A teen-ager who has been permitted to start on a hike without his canteen of water may find thirst driving him to a polluted spring or to a wayside stand where bottled drinks of uncertain origin are sold. Salt tablets may be needed when physical activity is likely to bring about excessive perspiration. Those who are on a salt free diet should consult a doctor as to special precautions they should take in places where others would be using extra salt.

It has been said that a climate is not in itself good or bad from a health point of view. If it is a radically different one from the one to which a person is accustomed then it will require a period of adjustment and may necessitate certain changes in habits. It is more likely that psychological factors make it hard for certain individuals to get along in some places.

It was probably not the monsoon rains themselves which made a woman so ill in Burma that her husband decided to bring her home. It may have been for reasons related to her own emotional history that rains depressed her. When they didn't let up for days and days her ability to cope with things in general was reduced and even her physical reserves became depleted. Emotional well-being becomes even more important to one's health in a new and different environment than it is in familiar surroundings.

Parents overseas need to give special thought to their children's state of mind, and to help them feel secure and happy, not only because this is important to the personality development of the youngsters, but also because it is so closely related to their physical health. It may be boredom which is causing a child to wilt in the heat. Instead of restricting his activity it might be important to explore new possibilities for social contacts and vigorous exercise.

Adults as well as children must see that they are getting enough exercise and can find interesting diversions in overseas posts if they expect to keep well. Readers of the Foreign Service *Health Handbook* are warned not to take the "alcohol route" as a way to avoid the tedium of some climatic manifestation. (During a dry season I have heard people say, "If it would only stop being such everlastingly cloudless weather!") "Maladjustment will not be overcome by alcohol consumption," the handbook states, "instead its consumption will exaggerate the condition and make the individual less able to cope with the problems."

Regular and sufficient sleep is essential, especially in hot and humid countries. It isn't always easy to get enough sleep in places where the local pace is slow and dinners frequently are served after ten o'clock. Sometimes Americans who for business or official reasons need to attend functions night after night must keep state-side office hours which require them to be at desks early and make no provision for an afternoon siesta which local people enjoy. The answer may be a nap before dinner and a bit more discipline about leaving parties as soon as one, politely, can.

Things That Go Swish

The crawling and flying creatures in a new environment often make people feel uneasy and are sometimes related to health. The first time a lizzard, commonly called the *tacktu,* appeared inside our doorway in Rangoon and let out a piercing "tack-tu, tack-tu," all six Winfields found themselves waking up on their feet and rushing together for protection. We soon learned that the wrinkled old fellow was harmless and was considered by the local people to be an omen of good luck for any household blessed with his presence. We never came to feel blessed when he put his vocal cords to work in the middle of the night, but at least we were no longer worried when we heard him. We became rather fond of the small lizzards that skitted around our walls eating flies and mosquitoes.

The flies and mosquitoes themselves never became acceptable to us. We knew that flies coming from uncovered latrines could bring to our food the causative agents of diarrheas or dysenteries. Mosquitoes in our neighborhood were unlikely to be carrying malaria because it was not prevalent there, but the malaria carrying species were present and if a case of malaria or a malaria carrier should turn up in flight range of us, then we would be endangered because not being in an established malarial area we were not taking preventive drugs. Also, we weren't about to welcome even the so called harmless mosquitoes because they disturbed our sleep and their bites could become itchy and, if scratched, might become infected.

Our first step was to see that the house was screened. It had been occupied previously by Britishers who had the un-American idea that screens in hot places cut down on the much needed flow of air. We decided that even if their reasoning about air were correct, we would rather take our chances with overhead fans and cut down on the flow of insects. (I noticed that the British friends with whom we had great fun arguing about things like screens and hot tea to cool you off, et cetera, were delighted to come to our house during the weeks preceding the rainy reason when insects of all sorts were swarming in great profusion, except in air-deficient screened houses.)

The old house we were in was not, even with screens, completely mosquito-tight so we also installed nets over each bed. The nets hung down from the inside of an overhead frame. They were tucked around the mattresses just before dark and then were folded and laid over the frame each morning. A flashlight check just before retiring quickly picked up a stray mosquito that might have been caught inside.

The screens were most effective in keeping out flies—especially after we installed a fan for the cook as a bribe to persuade him not to keep the kitchen screen door propped open.

It is still a joke in our family that our son took such an interest in fly prevention in Burma. He was about five when he came in one day to tell me proudly that, knowing how anxious I was to get rid of flies, he had invented a fly trap. At his insistence I went to the veranda to see it. The "trap" consisted of six over-ripe mangos smashed to a rotten pulp on the porch. It worked splendidly—hundreds of flies had been attracted.

"See, I figured out the trap, Mommy. Now you can figure out how to kill the flies." It didn't take me long to find the D.D.T. spray gun! Travelers to areas where insects are likely to appear (even without the inducement of a mango trap) should be prepared with an insect spray.

A frequent inspection of one's premises is needed to make sure that old cans, gutters, flower vases, or standing jars of water are not left to provide breeding places for mosquitoes. It is also important to see that vents to septic tanks are screened, and that garbage is not left in uncovered containers or dumped into open pits where it will attract flies. Garbage which must be disposed of at home should be buried or burned.

Unappealing as they were to us the huge spiders that made their way into our home in Burma were considered harmless and were no doubt actually useful because they caught flies and mosquitoes in their webs. Those who encounter the poisonous black widow spider overseas should remember that the group to which that spider belongs is as common in the United States as it is in any other country.

The sting of a scorpion is not harmless, and when they appeared on our grounds and even on the ground floor of our house, it became necessary for us to call the children's attention to them and warn them to be watchful in the dry season lest they step on one while barefooted. When a scorpion was spotted the children were expected to call a servant who generally came with chop sticks or tongs to carry the offender away to be drowned. The belief was that if a scorpion were smashed to death its mate would follow the scent and so would be attracted to the same place.

(The reference to our barefooted children should be accompanied by a statement to the effect that doctors feel there are many areas of the world where children should not be permitted to go without shoes except indoors and on concrete patios because of the presence of so many hookworms and strongyloides which are skin penetrating parasites that are damaging to the body.)

Another creature we had to look out for, as people in tropical areas must, was the poisonous snake. No one in the family was worried about snakes but it became a habit with us to check an outdoor bench or a stone before sitting down and to glance at tree limbs under which we might be sitting. When a banded krait was spotted by a night watchman just outside a door near where a child was sleeping, we were grateful for an alert watchman and glad all over again that the house was screened, because if the screen door hadn't been there the snake could have gone right into the bedroom. My husband discovered soon after we moved in that there were open drains on the floors of the bathrooms. These were covered securely with heavy screen so we had no reason to awaken and wonder what threatening reptile might be swishing around in the dark.

It seemed an extravagance to me when we moved into that beautiful tropical place that we should keep a full time gardener. When I saw how quickly, during the rainy season, the grounds could revert to jungle unless the growth was chopped back repeatedly, and then, when everything was parched during the dry season, I saw how easily snakes could go undetected if the gardener didn't regularly sweep the grounds with his bamboo broom, I decided the gardener was a sensible investment.

Each country, including our own, has some undesirable escapees from the box of Pandora. It makes sense to determine which ones are harmful and to take steps to eliminate or to control them.

Diets: Liquid And Solid

I suppose that even Frenchmen who have such delectable wines on their tables must on occasion drink the earthy beverage we call water. Surely for all people it is the most essential requirement for survival. Until the irrigation prospects are greatly expanded and the sea water potential more widely developed, people are likely to go on living only where water is somehow generally available. Unfortunately, the man who crawls the desert miles to find it and the maiden who walks to the well to fetch it and even the apartment dweller who turns the tap to release it, is not always about to drink water with assurance that it is safe.

In many parts of the world, drinking water is polluted by the nearness of latrines, by the habits of public bathers, or by bacteria carried into it on the feet of animals or from the sides of a dirty bucket or pitcher. An impressive looking water filter in a kitchen may catch straw but not germs. A modern pipe may bring clean looking water but unless it has been purified and protected it could be as dangerous as the muddy looking water from a river. People living abroad must always inquire about the water.

If there is not authoritative evidence that untreated water is safe, then water must be boiled, and boiled water must be stored in sterile containers and covered. *No if's or ands or buts!*

The common diarrheas, amoebic and bacillary dysentery, typhoid and para-typhoid fever (the vaccine provides a relative but not absolute protection) and in some areas cholera, schistosomiasis, and guinia worm infections are not diseases with which one takes chances. They are all diseases which may result from drinking untreated water, or from eating raw fruits or vegetables that have been sprinkled with or soaked in unsafe water or from swimming or bathing in polluted pools or bays or streams.

Boiling is the safest purification procedure, and it can easily be accomplished with heat, a large kettle and sterilized jars or bottles. If water is debris laden, it should be filtered before and not after boiling. Ice which is to be used in drinks should be made only from the boiled water (Sorry, old timer, it is only a myth that the alcohol into which the frozen rocks are dropped will kill the bacteria which can survive freezing).

Travelers can carry a small bottle of water purification tablets ("Halazone" or "Globaline") and use them according to directions on the bottle. In parts of the world where tea is a common beverage, the water poured over the tea leaves will have been boiling hot and the tea can be drunk safely. Uncarbonated soft drinks may be unsafe and ordinary carbonation does not make the water or beverage safe to drink. Beer is considered safe, as is coffee which has been "perked" or made with boiling water.

Milk might likewise be suspected as a carrier of disease unless the cows have been tested and shown to be free from tuberculosis and undulant fever and unless the milk is put into sterile containers and is never at any stage exposed to contamination. In some places where inspection is not rigid, a dairyman, concerned most of all to out-do his competitors, has been known to install and to advertise a modern pasteurization plant and then to add to the pasteurized milk carefully measured amounts of untreated water to stretch the supply of his product. However, the number of places where modern dairies produce reliable pasteurized milk is steadily increasing. Where fresh milk is not dependable, most people boil local milk or use powdered, canned, or condensed milk. If the supply of milk is limited or unduly expensive, calcium tablets, vitamins and fats should be considered as dietary supplements and used as advised by a physician.

Good nutrition is essential to good health, and with knowledge and care it can be provided wherever one may live, and generally without resorting to costly or imported items. When our two oldest children were born in North China we could not always get fresh oranges. We had no frozen or canned orange juice, and we didn't have synthetic ascorbic acid. But cabbage which is a good source of vitamin C was the most common of vegetables in Shantung province and Dr. Annie Scott told me how to bring cabbage to a boil and then to simmer it before straining off the water for the baby's breakfast. Now in many countries nutrition experts are at work to determine the mineral, vitamin, and protein content of local products.

A homemaker who feels that some one item is lacking in the family diet because a food she is accustomed to depend upon isn't available might write to the country's agricultural extension service and ask for the names of local foods which might supply the missing elements in the diet. Diet studies are being made by United Nations experts in various regions and American wives trained in nutrition research practices might offer their assistance to specialists at work in the area where they are living.

Most Americans who employ cooks continue to do overall planning in relation to meals though they may let their cooks decide according to market supplies just which meat or fruit or vegetable will be served on a given day. It is not difficult to teach a cook to balance an individual meal and to see that the meals in any one day add up to a healthful whole.

I have yet to hear of an American family living overseas that was underfed because enough food could not be found. Some are undernourished, as some families in America are, because meals are planned without knowledge or concern for good nutrition. Many have suffered ill effects from overeating. This is particularly true in areas where local diets have a high starch content and Americans, not doing as much physical work as they usually do at home, let themselves eat too much rice or too many noodles.

Solid food, like a liquid, can be harmful if it is contaminated with bacteria, viruses, or parasites. As with water, heat is the purifying agent for questionable food. Any food which is not poisonous or spoiled may be made safe for eating by thorough cooking or, as in the case of vegetables or fruits commonly eaten raw, by being immersed in boiling water and then, if desired, plunged into chilled boiled water.

Vegetables or fruits which have thick unbroken skins may be eaten raw without the boiling water bath if they are well washed and peeled or skinned by oneself or by a food handler who is healthy and scrupulously observes good hygiene habits.

The "pink water" (permanganate-solution) used so widely as a food wash in many places does not receive the seal of approval of the Tropical Medicine Society as being an effective substitute for boiling water for the treatment of suspicious fruits and vegetables.

The source of contamination of foods may be from the use of human excrement as fertilizer or from the use of contaminated water to keep produce fresh during marketing. We discovered in China that ingenious (but hygienically illiterate) farmers were using hypodermic needles to inject extra water into watermelons to increase their weight. The water used was not sterile. After we learned about that trick we sent the cook to the country to pick a melon off the vine if we decided we wanted to eat one.

Cooked or sterilized or home grown food will not be safe if it is prepared in or if it is served on contaminated dishes.

In hot climates refrigeration is essential to prevent food spoilage. If an automatic refrigerator (electric, gas, or kerosene) is not available, locally purchased ice must be kept in a compartment separate from food unless it is known to be made of safe water.

Local or imported canned foods which show signs of swelling should be discarded because the internal pressure could indicate the presence of deadly botulinus toxin.

Adults as well as children who are living in an area where there are health risks need to form the habit of washing hands with soap before meals. This can become so routine that it is never overlooked, but it is generally necessary to supervise young children so that they learn to do it thoroughly. It can be done so matter of factly that no anxieties about illness are encouraged. Children need to be told that they should always say a polite "No, thank you" when strangers offer food to them. Their nurses sometimes need to be instructed to see that small children do not eat food which has fallen to the floor or on the street, and then must also be reminded from time to time that the youngsters are not to be given food along the street or at the bazaars.

Americans are frequently worried about eating away from home in the less developed areas. Having meals with local people and in local restaurants is the kind of experience which many overseas Americans enjoy very much. It can be done without undue health risks and without offending one's host. In many cases a host will be sophisticated and his wife will follow modern practices in her kitchen, but if there is doubt at this point then it is a safe rule to eat generously of those dishes which are served hot and to avoid the raw vegetables or cold hors d'oeuvres. It is safe to take hot drinks but wise to avoid water if it is likely to be contaminated. All of us who have lived overseas have taken reasonable risks from time to time because a social good seemed to conflict with a health risk. The most important thing is to see that the day after day risks are controlled and that the exceptional ones are kept to a minimum.

Kitchen Care

A housewife who is concerned about the health of her family, or a single person abroad who wants to stay well, must set up clearly defined sanitary standards for the kitchen and must see that they are consistently observed.

The most important thing is that all food handlers (the cook, the person who washes dishes, the one who serves the table, anyone who handles the food after it reaches the house) are regularly given medical examinations to make sure that they are not disease carriers. Those who handle food must be instructed to keep themselves and their clothes clean, and this instruction usually needs to include the supplying of washable clothing, a place to wash, and soap and clean towels. Servants should be told explicitly that they must wash their hands with soap whenever they have used the toilet.

If water is to be boiled then a suitable kettle must be provided and the servant who performs this task should be shown how to sterilize the funnel used for pouring and the bottles used for storing.

An arrangement for washing dishes with hot water is needed. Providing a place where hot dishes can dry themselves is safer than using a tea towel which is not clean. A place needs to be provided for the temporary storage of foods too hot to go into the refrigerator or for any prepared foods not suitable for refrigeration. A screened cupboard called a meat safe is used in many places. Ours always had its legs sitting in containers of water to stop the migration of ants.

Insect poisons should be used with extreme caution. If a residual spray is to be put on the walls or if a contact spray for roaches or ants is to be used, all food and food containers should be removed from the kitchen or should be completely covered before the spraying operation is undertaken.

Instructions related to foods and sanitation need to be as simple as possible and definitely explicit. An American reporting on her experiences abroad relates a story about discussing a company meal with a cook. "Let's have a big baked fish" she instructed him. Then thinking to herself that fish odors in the home might not be pleasant she added to her previous sentence, "And be sure and use Air Wick." When the fish came to the table it looked very exotic with a bright green liquid floating around it on the platter.

I would never set up a fixed inspection time. I would let it be known at the outset that I might visit the kitchen at any time. I wouldn't, however, choose the busiest time in the cook's day to point out his deficiencies or to set up some new routine.

It is good to explain why we are careful in the ways we are, but to people completely unschooled in the principles of health and hygiene our explanations may not readily make sense, and because they don't the people who work in our kitchens may frequently revert to old ways. We must have patience and persistence more enduring than the oldest of old habits.

When reasonable precautions have been taken and healthful practices have been initiated, it is important to relax and not to be constantly worrying about germs or disease. One time or another an American overseas may have to face illness or accident. If that happens he can be thankful that modern medicine has so many answers and that modern transportation can so quickly get a patient to a doctor who knows how to handle his case.

If I were a betting woman, I would bet that an American moving into the depths of underdevelopment with his thick medical manual, his new thermometer, his first aid kit, his snake bite kit, his Halazone tablets, his calcium tablets, and his vitamin pills, will wake up some morning with all the symptoms of an ordinary, aggravating, every-day-variety, common cold.

Chapter VI

THE PERSONAL EQUATION

I shall never forget the young American couple who had to grab their baby from his crib and duck flat down on the floor behind a heavy refrigerator when bullets whizzed for a whole night through their quarters at a North Burma agricultural experiment station. That was in 1952. An isolated border clash had moved inland and the opposing troops just happened to settle down for an eight-hour skirmish across a strip of land where their house was situated. The Americans were rushed to safety the next day, and without any fanfare an efficient mother organized a hotel room into a suitable nursery. Her husband used the time to catch up on professional paper work and they waited calmly for the government's "all clear" signal which sent them right back to their bullet-riddled bungalow.

This is an unusual report only because few American families living overseas find themselves caught in the line of battle fire. Yet I think it illustrates quite well the way in which the vast majority of Americans abroad take whatever happens. They do it with such apparent ease and make so little noise about it that frequently, as in the case of the young family in Burma, only a few people close at hand hear about it at all.

The ones whom the local people readily hear about and whom American novelists sometimes choose to write about are the ones who fail to measure up to the demands of a situation.

Failure may be related to special factors in a local community, but in most cases it is a reflection of a personal shortcoming. In a foreign environment a person's deficiencies show up more clearly than they might have appeared back in the home territory.

One woman we knew overseas had grown into adulthood with finicky food habits. She had, no doubt, been able to humor herself more or less harmlessly in an American community where a great variety of food choices are available. When she lived in a place where fish and fowl were almost the only meats obtainable her stubborn insistence that she couldn't eat fish, and her oft repeated announcement that she hated chicken and duck and couldn't look an egg in the face, not only made her an unpopular dinner guest, it kept her from getting as much protein as she needed. Milk products were scarce also and being skittish about new foods she wouldn't try the soy bean cheeses used by the local people. In a few months her physical reserves became depleted and her constant complaining about food put her in the mood to complain about other things in the new environment. Her husband, an able and much needed technician resigned to take her back to her childhood home.

If a man is a cad in Kansas, chances are the people he knows there ignore his unpleasant behavior or perchance indulge him in it. In either case he gets away with his boorishness. Not so, overseas. The Americans are the first to spot an ill-mannered countryman and to regret the fact that he is being obnoxious. His conduct is important to them when it might not have been back home. Being members of the same minority group Americans in a foreign country are all conspicuous, and all are likely to be judged by the actions of any other one. More than one American overseas has had written into his evaluation file a complaint about his out-of-office conduct (or even the conduct of his wife or teen-age children) by co-workers who would never think of censoring a man in the United States for his personal or family behavior away from the job.

Restraints Are Missing

The other side of this story is that while some discover that overseas they can't get away with mediocre behavior that may have gone unnoticed at home, others who have always conducted themselves honorably in an American community seem to feel that once they are outside the borders of the United States the bars are down and they can have themselves a fling.

The wife of a highly placed consultant overseas, would, I am sure, never go into the Chase Manhattan Bank in New York City wearing floppy sandals, short shorts and a halter, yet she did that kind of thing repeatedly in the capital city of a foreign land, disregarding the sensitivities of the people of the country and surely disregarding her own sense of the appropriateness of things. It was as if she thought the two years away from home were just time out for a carefree lark.

We have seen both men and women who would never think of embarking on irresponsible escapades at home get mixed up in unfortunate sex adventures overseas. We have known people accustomed to sensible social drinking gradually slip into being notorious drunkards in a foreign land. I suppose that this letting down of restraints in another country is like a child playing with matches when mother is not at home. Children who haven't been reared to be self-directed and responsible cannot be trusted. Adults who behave according to rules and not reasons have a tendency to defy the rules when the controls are not there.

I think that in some few cases the lowering of behavior standards demonstrates the corrupting force of money and power. A family accustomed to live modestly on an average income back home may find themselves with a relatively increased salary in a country where living costs are low and the masses of people are poor. Perhaps without realizing what is happening they begin to think of themselves as rich.

They buy things they don't need and they set a stage for high-style roles they are ill prepared to play. But they go through the movements of playing them and admire themselves in the parts. It is just one step from feeling pretty proud of themselves to feeling superior to others. This can lead to a condescending kind of charity which even a hungry man will hate. It can lead also to their being caught pathetically in a web of conceit. It goes something like this: I am better than you because I have more than you, therefore in all things I am better. When such a self-important attitude crops out in an alien culture it can provoke a kind of bitterness which may smolder for years.

The same thing happens occasionally when a man or woman who has been carrying on creditably in an inconspicuous job in his homeland is placed in a position of prominence or power overseas. He may start to throw his weight around. In one case a man so elevated shifted easily into an office marked "director" but his wife lost her sense of values and actually sent a notice to inform the lesser ladies that it would be fitting for them to stand whenever she came into a room.

There are also situations where a superficial understanding of the local culture leads an American into careless or dishonorable conduct. He observes or hears about some kind of corruption in the community and accepts it as a norm. For instance, he knows that local Mr. A bribed local Mr. Z in order to get a contract. He concludes that this is the way the people there do business so he too accepts and gives bribes. What he doesn't appreciate is that the responsible citizens of the country are trying hard to put down the very practices he supports, and that even if they weren't they would not approve of an American stooping to what they know he knows is corrupt.

This misjudging of a cultural pattern may account for some of the arrogance which is displayed by a few Americans and has sometimes unfairly been attributed to most. Coming as he does from a country which prides itself on being a classless society, an American has been used to accepting as his personal equal the barber who cuts his hair, the teller who cashes his checks, and the cabbie who converses with him about the state of the union. He moves into a country where there is a clear-cut social stratification and he falls into what he thinks is the local habit for the educated and well-to-do to feel superior to the common herd. This may be a new experience for him and if his ego needs bolstering he may take advantage of his privileged position. He yells "boy" when he wants service. He berates a workman for slowness or inefficiency. He makes blunt and unreasonable criticisms of his subordinates. In short, he imitates, but overdoes his imitation, of the behavior of the local upper class.

In addition, he is likely to miss completely the fact that even a caste-bound system has within it subtle compensations that ease the edge of difference. Generally, not using the local language, he doesn't know the polite ways of addressing an inferior, nor the inflections and particular expressions that convey consideration even across lines of status difference. He may not be aware that there are face saving processes that operate to smooth relationships in even the most casual transactions. He just goes bungling along, acting in ways that build up resentments and distort the image of Americans.

One of the things that makes this so difficult is that a foreigner may live in a country for years and never learn that there are things in his conduct which are despicable in the eyes of the local people. Even the nationals who associate with him most closely may be too polite to tell him of his offenses, and when they give him the signals that they normally use to indicate to each other an overstepping of proprieties, he doesn't recognize them. If he were overstepping in similar relationships at home someone would be quick to let him know and he would be likely to get the signal.

That American is wise who walks humbly, speaks quietly, and listens for guidance in a foreign country. Even if he remains ignorant about many of the local manners he will not err seriously if he makes a sincere effort to live up to the best that he knows.

It is a compliment to us that so many times the people of other countries judge Americans who live among them not by their ethical code but by our own. I remember hearing a Buddhist criticize an American very harshly because the American had not displayed certain of the Judeo-Christian virtues. He even quoted our scriptures which I knew required at certain points a kind of conduct not demanded in the precepts of his own faith. This means that those Americans who may have drifted along being moderately honest or only conveniently unselfseeking on Main Street, U. S. A., must mend their ways or stand condemned in the market places of a foreign land.

We have all heard how the rigors of the wagon train migrations into our western territories separated the men from the boys. It can as surely be said that the mature Americans who move into foreign countries are easily identified and have the edge on those who didn't ever get around to growing up.

Motivation Is Basic

An American's reason for going to a foreign country has a great deal to do with how well he makes the adjustment to living there. If individuals or families leave their homeland because of a genuine concern to be useful in another place then there is a good chance that this goal will pull them through difficulties which might seem insurmountable to less well motivated people. This is particularly true if their concept of usefulness is not limited by a preconceived idea about what the foreign country needs. The altruist who has the blueprint for utopia all worked out may be sorely handicapped by his own impatience, and hopelessly frustrated by the fact that those who have had no part in creating his dream are far from being ready to help him make it come true.

Many who are working overseas with government or other technical assistance programs are so convinced that the jobs they are doing are important to the development of the countries in which they work that they are able to meet personal inconveniences and adjustments with equilibrium and are ready to make the extra effort required to make positive cross-cultural contributions beyond the call of duty.

Many missionaries fall in the category of well motivated overseas Americans. I could name dozens we have known whose outstanding contributions in education, medicine, agriculture and industry, and particularly in church leadership are matched only by remarkable abilities to understand, to improvise, and to endure. It doesn't follow, though, that because a man or a woman is a missionary he or she is sure to be endowed with an abundance of spiritual graces including a creditable motivation.

A missionary teacher, as well as an embassy secretary or any other American working abroad, might have gone ten thousand miles away from home in an effort to run away from something. These would-be escapees are the ones who are most likely to fall at the personal adjustment hurdle because the fears, prejudices, or failures from which they are running will surely pursue them and tempt them once again to despise themselves, to look down upon other people, to indulge in pretentious boasting or to reach too many times for a drink.

The challenge of a new job and the stimuli of a new environment and new associates do, sometimes, give a man a fresh chance to find himself. I have seen it happen to an expatriate. But the odds are so much against him, and the consequences of his potential downfall are so unfortunate, for him and particularly for his fellow countrymen, that I would hope a person who is in need of therapy would seek it before he leaves his own shores.

There are motives other than a service motive which send people abroad with a good chance of success at the personal level. A business man may want to advance in his career, so he will make efforts to keep his social behavior, and that of the members of his family, at an acceptable standard so that his company is not, because of him, discredited in the eyes of the local people.

The wife of an American engineer may be concerned about the American reputation and she will make a special effort to be considerate of local customs and will try to encourage other American women to join her in cultural studies and community projects. An exchange professor and his wife may be filled with curiosity and a sense of adventure and they will let themselves be interested in, instead of shocked by, the new things they see.

A foreign service officer may be motivated by a deep interest in international relations and his wife may be in sympathy with his desire to make a positive contribution to the processes of arbitration and negotiation in the realm of world affairs. They will be willing to make the extra efforts to keep their personal relations with the nationals of a country on an even keel.

There is no longer a place on the frontiers of our world for the ruthless adventurer who goes into someone else's country for the purposes of exploitation or domination. If he is trying to sell a worthless medicine there is likely to be one of his own countrymen who, for self protection as well as honor, will expose him as a fraud. If by treachery or swindle he is trying to gain control of valuable natural resources there is likely to be, even in a so-called backward country, a presiding judge acting on the authority of a modern constitution who will declare both his purposes and his procedures illegal.

There isn't even a place for the Americans who go to a foreign country with indifference. The absence of bad motives will not save them when the complexities of life in a foreign culture enmesh them, and when the demands of being responsible Americans at a time when the floodlights of history are focused critically upon our country bear down upon them as individuals. If an American does not have a good reason for going to another country it is better that he leave his traveling bags in the attic and keep himself and his family at home.

The Role of a Wife

The role of the wife of an American employee overseas is a unique one. In addition to being important to her husband in the same ways she was back home—as marriage partner, as the mother of his children, and as the mistress of his household—she is also, in a larger way than she may have been before, important to him in his daily work. Some of us in America live so far away from our husband's offices and know so little about the specialized work they do, that we are at times hard pressed to tell the children what to write on the school form which says *father's occupation.* All this is changed in most overseas situations.

In many of the jobs Americans do overseas the after-hours gatherings are essential. A man must go to these affairs and he needs his wife to go with him. He must entertain and he needs his wife to be his hostess. She meets his associates and his national counterparts. She must learn to listen with interest and to participate in conversation with discretion.

Many times a wife overseas is expected to work right along beside her husband. Missionary husbands and wives are both listed as employees. They may complement each other in their skills, but they are both at work in the same mission, and generally their home is the place where records are kept and where co-workers meet.

The foreign service officer is the one who goes to the embassy or consulate each day and the one to whom salary checks are paid. But when he is designated as a representative at an official ceremony, his wife is generally expected to accompany him. When he is on duty as the ambassador's aid at a reception, his wife is expected to be on hand to assist the ambassador's wife.

Not that the ambassador's lady just stands around being assisted. In even the smallest diplomatic post the chief of mission's wife has what amounts to a full time job with overwhelming responsibilities. She must juggle the hours of every day so that she may receive callers, attend public functions, write and acknowledge invitations, greet or bid farewell to dignitaries. She must find time to meet with, and to guide, the wives of junior officers of her husband's staff. She must manage to discuss meals and guest room arrangements with her servants. She must supervise the furnishings and upkeep of the embassy residence and gardens. She must preside at official dinners and stand through formal receptions.

In countries where the American ambassador is not married then the wives of senior officers must step in and do many of the things which the ambassador's wife would be expected to do to make sure that our country is properly represented in a foreign capital.

When a paleontologist goes overseas to search for the remains of some prehistoric civilization, who but his wife is the one who can be trusted to walk by his side with the padded basket ready to receive the fragment of an imprint of what might once have been a bit of a bone?

To the wife who has left her homeland wearied from being family chauffeur and telephone operator and errand girl this new sense of relationship with her husband's work may be exhilarating. Her days may hold new ranges of meaning and she may have a new sense of usefulness in the world. This is true, of course, only if she plays her role willingly. If she resents the demands that her husband's job makes on her leisure time, if she followed her husband abroad with dragging feet, if she thinks it is nobody's business how she dresses in any man's country or what opinions she expresses whenever she feels like it, then she is not going to like her new role and she is not likely to give her husband the kind of support he needs.

Even the wife who feels happy about the new dimensions of her life may find it hard going sometimes. Here are some observations I have made about wives who seem to have balanced the personal equation of an overseas assignment with a minimum of difficulty.

Flexibility Is Essential

The American wife who succeeds in being all that she needs to be in an overseas situation is a woman who knows how to give under strain, to bend with change, and yet to keep intact the core of her own personality. She knows when to pull and when to let go; when to hurry and when to wait.

Ellen is this kind of a woman. Her husband's job puts him in close touch with government officials in the country where they live. At one time a local political struggle for power caught him in a vise. He shouldn't take sides and he couldn't remain on the sidelines. He could only sweat out several months of tension and frustration. Ellen listened. She is probably the only person in the world who has heard completely his story of what it was like to be in the eye of that hurricane. But day after day she kept moving as usual in the community circles—always poised, always fresh and unusually pretty, never letting herself get pulled into a conversation about the political upheaval. Concerned as she must have been by her husband's dilemma she managed as only a firmly rooted but flexible woman could to remain close to, but detached from, what was necessarily her husband's problem.

Celia is by nature shy and retiring. She loves her husband and her children and finds her greatest joy in looking after them. Homemaking is both art and science to her and she has always pursued it with pride and diligence, leaving the work of the world to other people. When her husband was put on overseas assignment she looked wistfully back at the house where so much of her heart had labored, but she didn't cling to the house nor the neighbors nor the memories—precious as all of them were to her. She went with her husband because he needed her and her friends wondered how mousy little Celia would feel in a glamorous land of palm trees and garden parties.

Before long I began to hear reports about Celia. I heard that she was being a warm and gracious hostess; that she was taking a helpful part in the work with refugee rehabilitation. I heard about the courage she demonstrated when mobs stormed the section where Americans were living. How, I asked myself, could a shy woman have changed so quickly. When they came back on leave I saw her, and then I knew that Celia hadn't changed. She had only moved with change and in the process had opened up and blossomed.

Bev is a gal who is sure about things. One thing she has always been sure about is that she can go wherever her husband can go, and that where he stays, she and the kids will stay, too. A crisis occurred in a Middle-East country where they were living. American families were alerted. Most families were transferred to other places. But not her family. Her family couldn't leave together because her husband needed to stay with the small staff which would carry on a skeleton operation until the political situation was stabilized. Bev said that she would stay too.

The consular officer said it would be an embarrassment to the American government if women and children were in danger. Her husband said it would be a worry to him to feel uncertain about their safety. Bev faced the situation squarely and then without a quiver she bowed to the inevitable. She kept herself occupied and her children well and happy for four months in a hotel in Rome until her husband was able to join them and help them move to his new post in another country.

LIFE SAVING LAUGHTER

If a woman forgets to pack her sense of humor when she starts out on an overseas assignment she is running a serious risk that one time or another she will feel that she is out of her depth and can't make it.

In the same day a housewife might find the cook propping the refrigerator door open so that he and his friends could visit comfortably in the pantry, she might hurry to draw her bath before an important engagement and find that the water pipes were empty. Just after she had exhorted her cook to economy and had told him to buy only one chicken at the market her husband might call to say that he would need to bring six of the United Nations Area Conference delegates home for dinner. When all this and more happened on the day the children's nurse had to be away at a relative's funeral, if she couldn't open up and laugh, she would probably greet her husband and his guests with a face which said, "I've reached the end—the very end."

It is funny, isn't it, that a cook should decide to put to his own good use the boss lady's big machine which is designed to make hot air cold? And I know, because I have more than once gotten just enough water to be all-over soapy, how funny it is to live in a house that has four bathrooms all year 'round and running water only every now and again. When the dry season came in Burma our well pump couldn't reach the water; when the rains came, someone didn't get the motor lifted up soon enough and it was flooded so that when the electricity was turned on the whole thing was burned out.

I suppose I might have been annoyed when a "visiting fireman" enjoying our hospitality once said that he thought a committee back home ought to look into the business of putting a government official in a big house with four bathrooms. Instead, I was amused, because our big house was at that moment supplied with dirty water hauled from a nearby lake. Each of the bathtubs was tightly plugged to hold a barrel of the hard-to-come-by water. When we wanted to wash (in the tropics that urge occurs several times a day) we dipped a bit of water up with a basin and did the best we could to get clean. It was the basin also that supplied never quite enough water to operate the flush.

As for our house, it was a huge building all right but it could hardly be classed as an elaborate dwelling. The high ceilings had exposed beams. There were cement floors. Dark shutters had to be closed whenever a gentle rain suddenly turned into a downpour. The electric wires were exposed and the fuse board was spread out on the most conspicuous part of the living room wall. The hall closet had only a dirt floor and crawly creatures had a way of emerging. So it was funny that he should so quickly appraise our quarters and think we were in a mansion. (As a matter of fact, it was a delightful house in many ways and we all loved it and took pride in making it as attractive and comfortable as possible. Besides it was the only place available when we arrived in Rangoon soon after the war and we were very lucky to have it even though we ourselves would have preferred to be in a smaller and in that sense less ostentatious place.)

The application of a sense of humor isn't always related to amusing incidents. Fundamentally, I guess, humor and perspective are on the same plane. The people who find it hard to accept living quarters, or some other aspect of their life abroad, with a saving sense of humor are the ones who forget that things back home are not always perfect either. Granted we didn't have an efficient water system in Burma, but we did have barrels and men who could fill them for us and besides, when the heavy rains were falling and the nights were black but warm, what was to keep us from stepping outside a bathroom door with a bar of soap for a completely refreshing shower? When electrical power fails in suburban Washington we have no heat, no water, no lights, no refrigeration and no cooking facilities; and sometimes it takes the snow plow two days to get around to opening our road.

One day sometimes gets more than its share of calamities for anyone in the good old U. S. A. just as it does for an American housewife in a foreign country. Her humor quotient is slipping if she lets herself blame her adopted country instead of whatever universal law it is that lets things stack up too high now and then.

Amusing things do occur, though, for people living in a foreign country, and it is good to let them come along as comic relief.

A friend told me how anxious she was to have something especially nice for a company dinner in a place where food offerings had to be pretty much the same. She asked the cook to make a chicken pie. It was a new dish for him and he looked surprised. "It is very simple," she explained, "You just make creamed chicken as you know how to do. Put it in a casserole. Put biscuits on top, and bake it." She forgot that he had previously worked for English people for whom biscuits are little sweet cookies or cakes. The cook probably reasoned that for company the most elegant biscuits were in order. So when the casserole appeared the hostess saw that cookies with pastry tube icing sat grandly on chopped-up chicken and sauce.

The Leading Lady

A discussion of the personal performance of Americans, and particularly of their wives, overseas cannot be made without a specific reference to the place of the wife of an official, a business man, an armed forces officer, a clergyman, an engineer, a professor or whoever is in a foreign country in an administrative position in which other Americans work under him. If he has a wife, and if those men who report to him have wives then his wife has, in large measure or in small, a responsibility for other wives. The way she handles herself has an importance for her and for the other women which must not be underestimated. I wonder if enough thought is given to the guidance of the women who are going to be placed in positions of leadership with other wives.

The more complex and trying a foreign situation is the more a wife needs help as she moves into it, and surely the wife of the man who leads the operation to which she and her husband are related is the one who should be helpful. But the attitude of the senior woman towards the junior wives and her method of pursuing even the most worthy goals are of such fundamental importance that it can be said without exaggeration that the success of any overseas enterprise, whether it be the production of one small documentary movie or the running of one of the largest embassies in the world, can be deeply affected by the generosity of spirit, the wisdom, and the human relations skill of the wife of the man in charge.

My own experiences as a wife living overseas under the influence of women whose husbands have been senior in one way or another to my husband have in every case been so satisfactory that I find it hard to believe that a junior-senior relationship would ever pose a problem. The wife of the missionary who met us at a Chinese railway station in 1932 became not only the one who introduced me to the university community where we were to live and work, who shared with me her own insights regarding the local people, warning me at certain points and consulting me at others. She also became a good friend and my respect and love for her have survived long years of separation and even her recent death.

When we arrived in Burma my husband's chief sent us a note before time for our first meal: "My wife will be sorry she had to be away from Rangoon at the time of your arrival. But won't you please bring the children and come for lunch with me." On the day his wife returned to the city she turned up at our front door and shouted over the chatter of children, "Hello there Winfields, welcome to Rangoon." There followed days and months of what could only be called collaboration, and today, though our husbands no longer work in the same organization, my husband and I count those two people among our special friends. There have been other senior women with whom I have had congenial associations.

Yet in spite of my own good fortune I am constantly reminded by reports that filter back from many parts of the world that getting along with the wife of the boss may be the most difficult problem that some American women overseas ever have to face.

In some cases it is just a matter of age and mutual immaturity. A young woman may be so close to the time when she felt the need to cut the cord of dependence from the older generation that she arrives at a new post with a fear that someone may be waiting to tell her how she must do her homework. If the older woman who greets her has a wholesome life of her own and a respectful approach to people regardless of age or race or clan, there isn't any problem at all. The young woman will relax and behave like the grown-up the older woman assumes her to be. But if the older woman has a tendency to take over as a mother, or if she feels herself inadequate as a women whose husbands have been senior in one way or another to my then the chances for a good working relationship between the two are poor.

There is a chance of trouble also if the older woman has let herself come to feel that age itself is an assurance of special wisdom or gives one the right to make arbitrary decisions about another person's behavior. I have seen a young woman straight out of college who went overseas with her husband eager to go on learning, anxious to do her bit towards the nurture of the brave new world, and full of ideas as to what a better world would be like, come home from an overseas experience deeply disillusioned and lacking in self confidence because she had been so consistently criticized and browbeaten by the wife of her husband's superior officer who thought that all junior staff people were too young to have opinions of their own and that this young woman in particular had too many foolish ideas.

On the other hand, I know another woman who came home "fed up," as she said, with life in a charming foreign community because she was so tired of having the wife of her husband's boss take such a smothering interest in all her personal affairs. "She is a dear really and not a selfish bone in her body, but she just hovers too close and too much."

In a few cases a problem seems to exist because a woman whose husband is at some top rung of a ladder has harbored resentments and jealousies throughout his slow climb. For years she has hated the waiting and standing back, the docile knuckling under to someone else's needs or plans. Now that her husband sits in the front office, instead of remembering what it was like to be bossed around and coming up with a more understanding and creative plan for working with the women who look to her for leadership, she only re-enacts with a vengeance the old authoritarian pattern.

There is such a woman overseas today. If a junior woman comes to her with a complaint she berates her. If she comes with a problem instead of making an effort to help solve it or to show a troubled woman where she might go for help, she only says, "You girls today don't know what it used to be like," and she proceeds to enumerate all the things which she at one time or another has had to endure.

Junior wives, in whatever organization, should go overseas with the understanding that the situation will be likely to require more of them than is required of the wives of employees at home; they should expect to do their part when a special need arises, and they should do it in a good spirit. But it is too bad that they are so often set on edge by the proprietary way in which a senior woman calls upon them for help. Sometimes it is a colonel's wife. Sometimes it is the wife of a senior missionary, or the wife of a division chief, or the wife of a director who demands casseroles, servants, or assistant hostesses as if she were a lord.

Let me make it very clear that I would be the last person in the world to object to the idea of women helping one another. American women from the earliest colonial days have had a tradition of being helpful. In the pioneer days of our country women brought food for the settlers who gathered to build a log cabin and for the harvest hands who cut the wheat. But this tradition has always been on a mutual assistance basis, and deep in her heart any self respecting American woman resents a call for personal assistance that is couched as a command.

The wives who are in leading positions overseas surely have both the need and the right to solicit the help of other women related to their organizations. There is not a doubt about that. When great numbers of people are to be entertained more than one American hostess needs to be on hand. When refreshments are needed for a large function more kitchens than one are needed to prepare the food. When a state-side dignitary and his wife come visiting, arrangements must be made for their entertainment and for escorts to show them around. It is only fair that the junior as well as the senior members of the host group should help to share the load. The thing that isn't fair is that one woman should speak or act as if she thought the other women around her were pawns to push about.

"Just who does she think she is?" an irate American woman complained when she got a note saying, "You will send three dozen cookies" and again when a note said, "You will pour coffee promptly at three." She knew, of course, that the woman who wrote or dictated the note was the wife of her husband's boss, that she carried heavy responsibilities and that the help she was conscripting was not for herself but for the organization to which they both belonged. But she asked a valid question because the woman whose notes she resented had surely forgotten just who she was.

No matter how busy she is nor how important her cause a woman must remember that first of all she is herself a person and that each woman "under" her is an individual of worth. She dare not let herself get carried away with any of the perogatives of her own or her husband's position to the extent that she addresses other women as if they were just cogs in some big and impersonal machine. The woman who says, "You will" instead of "Will you?" has forgotten that she is an American and that only a woman who is willing to pay any price for her husband's promotion or who hasn't the confidence to think for herself is going to respond without inner rebellion to a call which is addressed not as to a respected co-worker but as to a servant.

Most of the wives overseas who carry leadership loads know well how important it is that they never let themselves be pressured into operational short cuts which violate courteous behavior and are too arbitrary to call forth full-hearted response from other women.

There are creative ways of enlisting assistance which not only succeed more effectively in getting particular jobs done, but which in the long run produce an atmosphere in which basic purposes can be shared and cooperation achieved. The director's wife who sent around word to a dozen ladies that they would send this or that dish to be served at a dinner for a visiting official would have been so much wiser if she had sent a note to the wives of all the division chiefs and told them that the visitor was coming and would they please come around on Thursday to help her make entertainment plans. Not a one of them would have objected to contributing food or loaning a servant or whatever was needed if they had been consulted as members of a team, and all of them would have profited from the sense of participation and the excitement of expecting the man and his wife from the home office.

Some of them might have come up with some new ideas for ways in which the visitors could be most helpfully put in touch with local people and might most profitably see the things of real importance in the community. As it was they had no part at all in the planning and many of them went to the dinner disgruntled about the dictatorial way they had been told to help. Their husbands were all uneasy lest they wear their feelings on their sleeves.

One of the most sensitive areas in which a wife who has responsibility for other Americans ever moves is in the realm of cross-cultural behavior. No American woman wants another woman to tell her how she should or should not dress, for instance. Yet, if she is dressing in a manner that is causing offense to the people of the country a warning may be in order. The manner in which it is given and the nature of the existing relationships between the two women make a great difference. If a senior woman hasn't bothered to be otherwise concerned about the offending individual then she hasn't earned the right to give her advice.

If an ambassador's wife lets it be known that she wants the women of the embassy to wear hose and hats and gloves when they appear at official functions in a warm and informal country, it might seem to the younger women that she is being unnecessarily fussy. And she might be. On the other hand, her instructions could be based on her understanding of the people of the particular place where they are living and her knowledge that the local women know how Americans dress for a formal occasion in their homeland and might consider less formal attire an indication of lack of respect for them. If this is the situation she is calling the signals on much firmer ground even though a question could always be raised as to which group of local people one is going to please, the conservatives who like Americans to be proper in a Victorian sort of way or the modernists who may like Americans because they are casual and informal. In any case, however right or reasonable the responsible woman's decision may be, unless she manages to communicate the reasons for it to the women around her, they cannot be expected to comply with understanding and without a feeling of annoyance.

A senior missionary wife in Africa knew that the Christians in their area were misunderstanding the free and easy friendliness which a young unmarried teacher displayed toward all the married men in the mission. One day as her husband was starting to drive alone to the market town the matron heard the young woman ask him if she could go along to get some things she needed. She had to decide quickly whether she should run the risk of letting a pretty young thing think that she, with her gray hair, was jealous or run the other risk of having the reputation of the girl, of the man, and also the mission damaged by groundless gossip. Giving the young woman credit for being mature and sensible enough to understand the situation when it was explained to her she called to her and stopped the innocent expedition. She made her move with enough good humor so that the young woman herself was able to laugh about it when, on furlough, she spoke to the members of her church back home.

In recent years all American organizations overseas have been increasingly concerned about the need for Americans to have wider and closer social contacts with the people of the countries where they are stationed. Official missions in particular have been making efforts to discourage their people from following the line of least resistance and spending their time socializing just with one another.

In one country where it seemed that the American women were letting themselves be too absorbed in their own affairs and were not making enough efforts to know and to associate with the local women, the ambassador whose wife was at that time out of the country asked the wife of the counselor of the embassy to see what she could do to improve the situation.

She called the other women together and began, "Friends, we have a problem—."

It wasn't any time until, under her open and inspiring leadership and with all the women participating in the discussions about their social relationships and how to improve them, the wives had not only mended their own ways but had initiated so many interesting kinds of cultural interchange that other Americans—men as well as women—and scores of nationals had been pulled into a framework of genuine fellowship and mutual respect.

Unfortunately, in a few places a similar problem has been handled in such an undemocratic way by the women who have undertaken to improve inter-cultural relations that they have actually retarded the very cause they were trying to promote.

In one case, a wife of the chief of a diplomatic mission tried to increase by edict the contacts between Americans and the people of the country. She sent out a terse message to the other women telling them that they might do no entertaining of any kind which did not include people of the country. Their associations with other Americans would, she told them, be limited to casual contacts at the commissary and at the swimming club. One woman was told that she could not even invite a newly arrived American family in for pot-luck supper unless a local person was present.

Her goal—the broadening of contacts between Americans and nationals—is such a commendable one and is so urgently needed that it seems tragic to me that even in one country it should have been distorted by a procedure which disregarded essential values in interpersonal relationships. Even those who already had many local friends and normally spent a great deal of time with them were unhappy that a rule should have been imposed upon them which stipulated just who they might or might not entertain.

Nevertheless, in spite of their personal reactions few wanted to defy the ruling of their chief's wife, and in that capital city a major head-hunting operation got underway. Americans scurried around in every direction hunting for any local person who might be persuaded to come for luncheon or dinner or tea.

When the top woman decided to hold a reception to honor national ladies, she sent a memo to her group of women which read something like this: "There will be a reception at the Residence on .... You are expected to be present by .... p.m. Any other engagements you have for that time will be cancelled, forthwith. You should not expect to shake hands with me when you arrive. I am not in this country to shake hands with Americans. You are expected to spend your time with the (national) ladies. Those of you who stand in groups where there are only American women will be embarrassed by having a monitor reprimand you on the floor."

Only a few local ladies appeared at the reception. When one arrived she was immediately surrounded by a dozen American women. If she managed to get out of the clutches of one group, another bevy encircled her while her previous attendants hurried to find another victim. Since the women of that country are smaller than Americans it made their hostesses look the more overwhelming when the head of one lone woman could just barely be seen in the center of each group.

The one aspect of this story which would be amusing if it were not so sad is that the grapevine telegraph operates most effectively in that country. I can imagine what fun the local people had laughing at the crusading Americans and joking about themselves knowing what a heavy price was hanging on each head.

This is an extreme, and, I am glad to say, a rare instance of leading lady ineptitude, but it does illustrate the importance of leadership being exercised with sensitivity and with due regard for our democratic ways.

Personal Enrichment

The people who measure up most consistently overseas are those who not only have resources within themselves for creative living, but do what is needful to keep their minds nourished and their spirits renewed. The ambassador's wife, the business man's wife, the general's wife, the missionary wife—and their husbands as well—must each manage enough time for personal enrichment otherwise they will get to the place where the work they do with other people has a false and weary sound. Any American abroad is in the limelight and this is a cause for strain. New conditions inevitably demand new answers. Those who live overseas must keep alert.

The wives who do not have clearly defined jobs as their husbands and professional women have and who must generally carry the brunt of the life adjustment load not only for themselves but for all the members of a family are particularly vulnerable if they let their reservoirs of spiritual energy get too low. Each woman must find for herself the particular kind of renewing activity that is most helpful but no woman can neglect to give some special time to her own growth and refreshment.

The pursuit of a hobby does this for some women. I have known many who felt that a most rewarding part of an overseas assignment was that, freed from some of the housekeeping and community busy work they had in America, they could at long last spend some time each week painting, composing music, making jewelry or any one of many kinds of creative activities.

One woman made beautiful wall hangings while she was in Burma by using an appliqué technique and the local landscape as her inspiration. A woman who knows and enjoys music reports that she takes a tape recorder with her on trips into the villages of Cambodia in order to capture the beauty of some of the folk music. A woman who enjoys gardening has joined a flower arrangement class in Japan. Another woman attends Chinese cooking classes at a YWCA in Malaya. More than one woman has started the "great American novel" in some far away place. Whether the novel ever gets a publisher isn't as important as the lift that comes to the writer as she works.

Activities which require physical exertion are especially valuable to the woman who has a lot of nervous tension to discharge. Swimming, boating, tennis, riding, golf, all meet a very real need for many women overseas. Some American women in New Delhi have had a most rewarding time studying Indian dance.

Card playing is a stimulating pastime for a great many people, but I have noticed that the American women overseas who get together day after day for cards are sometimes the ones who are most disgruntled with their surroundings. It is possible that it was a mutual inclination to be homesick which brought them together in the first place. But it is also possible that if any one of them had gotten involved in a more creative form of activity or had moved out into a wider circle of people, she might have avoided the rut of boredom which even a serious minded bridge player can slip into if she does little else.

Reading is a source of stimulation for a great many people. Some women report with triumph that while a magazine article now and then is the most they could manage during child-care days in America, they read book after book overseas. The United States Information Service libraries not only render an outstanding service to local people who read the American books, they also keep many American families intellectually awake. In some communities, families exchange books with one another and so extend their reading resources.

During our years in China twelve couples on our university campus formed a book club which meant a great deal to us in a place where up-to-date reading material was scarce and where living on small salaries we had to limit our book purchases. We all urged homeside friends to send us book reviews and after careful consideration of these, twelve books (some fiction and some non-fiction including poetry and plays as well as trends-in-science and state-of-the-world books) were selected and ordered. The cost was divided twelve ways. When all the books arrived a slip was attached to each indicating the route it was to take among the members. A member kept a book for one month. Then he checked his name and sent it along. During the time any one family had a book it was read not only by husband and wife but by other university colleagues not members of the club.

In Burma my husband and I belonged to a discussion group composed of about ten couples representing several countries and cultures. We read books and talked about them, or we selected a subject and one member would present his ideas as a kick-off for discussion. I found this especially worthwhile because as is so often the case of a woman overseas, I was doing lots of things just with women and we were doing a good many things with larger groups where a significant exchange of thought was not possible.

Many wives as well as other Americans overseas feel the need of finding a congenial worship center and of participating in a form of worship familiar to them. This is generally possible even in countries where the religions are quite different from the main stream of religious practices in our own country. It might be hard to find an exact counterpart of some one American religious sect, whether of the orthodox or liberal variety.

Even so, I have yet to know an American overseas who wanted contact with a religious institution or who wanted spiritual fellowship with a group of like-minded people who hasn't found something to meet his needs.

Roman Catholics may not always find an English speaking priest, but they can usually find a cathedral or a chapel where the form of service would be familiar. Wherever American service personnel are located there is likely to be a Catholic chaplain.

Catholic families who would like information about the location of overseas churches, material for religious education of children and adults, and orientation guidance for Catholics going abroad may write to:

National Council of Catholic Women
1312 Massachusetts Ave. N.W.
Washington 5, D.C.

The Council will act as a referral center sending inquires to the appropriate Catholic agency.

Jewish families who are of the reformed fold may sometimes find themselves in an unfamiliar form of service when they discover in a foreign city a very old synagogue, and a very orthodox congregation. But one mother said, "just to know that this group is here gives us a feeling that we are not cut off from our religious roots, particularly at the time of some special observance." In order to know where Jewish congregations are located American Jews might find it helpful to secure an up-to-date copy of the *Jewish Chronicle Travel Guide,* published by:

London Jewish Chronicle
32 Furnival Street
London E. C. 4, England

Christians may encounter a few countries where there is a state religion and the establishment of a Christian Church has not been permitted. In one such place American families had no trouble getting permission to hold Christian services and Church school classes in one of their homes. American Episcopalians frequently find themselves attending an Anglican Chapel with a largely British congregation. Pronunciation aside, the prayers in the prayer book are the same as those used in St. Mary's Church back home.

By and large Protestant Christians can find some kind of a congenial church association wherever they are. Those who want to make a particular inquiry about Protestant church opportunities overseas are advised to write to the:

Committee on American Laymen Overseas
National Council of Churches
475 Riverside Drive
New York 27, New York

Where there are Americans in the community there is usually an English language service even though the Christian congregation may be largely indigenous. Some find it interesting to attend a local language church service and feel that it is inspiring for them and perhaps helpful to a local church if they attend and support it rather than an isolated American congregation. Others feel that they need spiritual nourishment in a language they can understand and so seek out the English service. A few associate themselves with both a local language church and an English congregation. These English language services are frequently attended by English speaking nationals who may feel more at home with the American Christians than they do with the uneducated Christians of their own country who may compose the membership of the local language church.

In eighty-seven communities overseas there are union Protestant churches which have been developed on an interdenominational level by American and other English speaking families to meet their religious needs and interests. Forty-five of the union churches have full time ministers. The union congregations provide programs of worship and education similar to those in which Americans participate in their churches at home. They also provide opportunities for fellowship and for social service in the local community.

Many of the union churches have a long history. The church in Paris was established in 1814, the one in Beirut in 1823, Istanbul in 1849, and the ones in Bogota and Mexico City were started in 1868. With the present increase of Americans living abroad the union churches are growing both in size and numbers. The union churches are strong parts of the indigenous Christian movement abroad and, according to Dr. J. Quinter Miller who is assistant general secretary of the National Council of the Churches of Christ in the U.S.A., they frequently are supporting bulwarks of the missionary enterprise.

The move towards organic church union which is making headway in the United States today has fortunately been underway in other countries for some years. Many feel that this has strengthened individual congregations as well as the Christian movement in a country;

certainly it has helped to decrease confusion resulting from the differences in denominational names. Americans may soon find themselves affiliating with a Christian Church of India rather than with something like the Dutch Reformed Church of North America in South India.

The United Church of South India is one of the oldest of the united church bodies overseas. Plans are in process for a union of churches in North India; this will undoubtedly lead to a united church for the whole country. There is a United Church of Japan and a United Church in the Philippines. A movement towards union is underway in a number of other countries.

Sometimes one meets an American who (not just to observe as a tourist or even as a serious student of culture) attends a temple or a shrine of a religion other than the one which is by cultural inheritance his own. He goes as a suppliant and leaves refreshed.

For many Americans, those who are church related and those who are not religious minded at all in any formal sense of that word, the new vistas and the new demands of living abroad do call out a new wondering about the meaning of life and a wistful longing to concentrate, while there is yet some time, on that which seems most truly to have value. It is good if this soul-searching happens to Americans overseas and puts them on their mettle because though they may be on leave from a job back home, and though it may sometimes seem to them that they are living in another world, the fact remains that the years an American spends in a foreign country are still of the years of his life just as all the others have been and will be, and in these years, as in the others, personal failure is to be avoided at all costs.

Chapter VII

"ME AND MY WIFE AND MY SON JOHN"

When the five Finleys stepped off the plane in the dead of night at an Asian airport the buoyancy that makes them separately and collectively such delightful people was very much alive. Each of the three boys had his haversack on his back in the same nonchalant but responsible way a Boy Scout lugs his gear for a week-end camping trip. Their father, on loan from the staff of a distinguished university, was gay and casual, and their mother was relaxed and laughing even as she kept them all in line.

"It isn't hard. Our names are alphabetical," explained brother John as I was trying to introduce them to our own young people who were on hand to welcome the new colleague and his family.

Suddenly the whole picture of Americans following jobs to far off places became clear to me. It was natural, as natural as packing what you needed and going wherever the place was, just like for any other sort of trip. It was fun, like any family expedition. And when you take it as it comes it is simple—just like John coming after David and before Stevie.

A widely traveled friend has suggested that I might have put this section of the book first. He expressed the wish that we might start any discussion about living overseas not with passports and packing and complications and problems but with vignettes on typical American families living happily here and there. His point is well taken.

Whether a family be just a husband and wife or whether it includes from one to ten children, moving overseas and living in new surroundings can be just a normal part of doing one's work in the world, and it can be fun. Because my husband is related to an overseas staff of nearly a hundred people, we generally receive at Christmas time copies of a good many letters written from Americans overseas to friends and relatives back home. It is a highlight of the holiday season when we sit down and read these letters and the letters from many other friends overseas. They invariably reflect something of the local color and a feeling of what life is like where the writers are living. They may include significant first person accounts of a tense moment in history (a coup, an assassination, a throng cheering the President of the United

States). Without meaning to be particularly profound they sometimes contain a penetrating analysis of a complicated international situation. Yet, written as they are in the mood of the family-focused holiday season, they are always more than anything else letters about families and family members. It is in this that they reveal their greatest charm.

The Collins had a new baby last year. There being no doctor nor hospital he was delivered at home with the aid of a public health nurse. Three year old brother thought the newcomer was kinda nice but he was much more excited about the little wooden horse a visitor who had come to see the baby brought him as a consolation prize. Big sister Ann had lost her first tooth.

The Holmans report that both of the twins are thriving and that thirteen-year-old Paula helped her mother with the pageant at the church.

The Clarks report that Penny has cut her pig tails. One problem on their horizon: eight-year-old Clarence was elected Best South African Citizen in his school class. What if some super-patriots back home decide to make something of that? (Don't bother to report them—the name isn't really Clark!)

Bob and Thelma haven't any children but you should have read the description of how he dressed up like Santa Claus and went around to the homes of all their friends with a pack on his back.

A Family Closes Ranks

Two things are always made clear to me as we read the informal and newsy reports from Americans living overseas. The first is that families go on being families wherever they are. The babies come. The baby teeth go. People do things they like to do. Dreams take form and obstacles are dealt with one by one. Another thing which frequently is revealed is that in a new and strange situation family members are pulled closer together and there is a closing of the ranks.

This acceleration of a family's esprit de corps sometimes begins when the plans for departure are in the making. Sometimes it happens when the journey itself starts and the adults have time to stop being so busy with things. It may not happen until a family reaches its destination and the world around them sounds and looks and feels a little strange. Bonds of belonging which in the past may at times have seemed like fetters now become connections in a circuit through which the currents of mutuality and reassurance flow.

Another facet of the family angle of an overseas assignment is that there comes to many a respite from the rush of life. In few countries is the pace of living as intense as it is in the United States. In few countries do people get as involved as even the little Cub Scout can be in city or country or especially in a sprawled out suburban community anywhere in the U. S. A.

American mothers frequently keep a master schedule which puts the Grand Central timetable to shame. Family members sometimes see one another only in passing, and even when they are at home the television or the telephone may invade the living room, the dining room, and the master bedroom. Lots of people aren't happy about the situation but the encroachments have a way of moving in faster than controls can be devised. I have seen an American mother reply to a query about how she likes it in a place that is supposed to be less developed. She replied by smiling and taking a long unhurried breath.

Families who are not rushing around in so many different directions may find themselves more frequently together for meals and more regularly lingering after a meal is over to talk, to listen to records, or to sit down together to read. Not having a favorite program on the television to lure him, even our pre-school child joined the circle whenever his father took up a book to read aloud when we last lived abroad.

Adventure Without Wheels

Walking is a pleasure which we can only occasionally find time for in this country but one which we were able to enjoy regularly during the various times when we have lived overseas. Our now grown children tell us they remember with pleasure and fascination the times when we walked from the Cheeloo University campus in the suburbs of a North China city to *Ma An Shan* (Horse Saddle Mountain) about a mile away. The one who was the littlest then says she can still feel the delightful sensation of dancing along a narrow path where the waving heads of wheat were taller than her head. All of us recall that after we went through that wheat field we walked with awe along a road so old, and worn so deep, that even grown up heads could barely see the cultivated fields on either side. We usually walked four abreast, but sometimes we would meet travelers, and then it was a moment of great importance when we fell into a single file with the head of our family in the forward position to bow politely and perchance to engage the traveler in brief conversation.

When little feet began to tire I would take one child on my hip and the other one would be lifted high to her father's shoulders. Slowly, slowly we would ascend the humpbacked hillock until we reached the big flat rock where we sat down for a drink from the water flask and a long look at the valley stretched around us for miles and miles.

Farm plots in Shantung Province were unbelievably small and wheat grown by hand like a garden crop waved in immaculately neat patches with just the breath of a dividing line between. The only interruptions were the grave mounds here and there, new ones thrust high and twenty feet across, but the older ones grown smaller and smaller as through the years more and more of each mound was plowed back into the land. Occasional clusters of cedars hovered close around wayside shrines. As we walked home we might meet an old man or a young boy with a basket and a special fork picking up donkey droppings where travelers had been. This reminded us of the careful way the peasant salvaged every possible source of fertilizer and returned it to the soil which from ancient times had been so intensively used and yet was still supplying a yield per acre greater than most American farms.

Many years later we walked with younger children in the suburbs of Rangoon. Sunday after Sunday it was our habit to go out our back gate, down a palm-shaded lane, through a small cluster of thatch huts and across fields to the site where the World Peace Pagoda was being erected. We were fascinated to see that the huge lake, planned as a place of repose where worshippers might pause for meditation, was being excavated bit by bit as clay was dug to make the bricks which would become a part of the walls of the pagoda. In a land of monsoon rains the sprawling cavity would be filled in just one season.

The brick making process was always a wonder to us. It seemed incredible that so close to a modern city could be found an operation employing the materials and methods which had been used in ancient times. We saw the mud being mixed and molded, dried and fired in hand-built and hand-stoked ovens.

One day many months after we discovered the site, we were fortunate to be among the guests present when those bricks were all in place in what could only be described as a magnificent structure towering to the height of a ten story building. Astrologers had carefully divined the auspicious day and hour when the pagoda's *ti* was lifted up to the top of the dome. It is the umbrella like *ti* which indicates that a Buddhist place of worship is not just a shrine but is a pagoda which houses sacred relics.

This particular pagoda had been the dream child of U Nu the devout Prime Minister and had caught the imagination and support of the whole nation. On more than one occasion when we were walking we met U Nu, in casual dress strolling with his children or with a friend. We would exchange greetings and sometimes he would pause to show us some completed section or to explain the significance of certain things on the grounds or in the structure.

Visits And Vacations

Many people who have lived overseas have found, as we did, that opportunities for families to get together as families are greater than they are in most American communities. Those who live in Europe, or in certain foreign capitals where the European influence is felt, may find that in upper class circles, at least, children are for the most part segregated. But in most of the overseas places where Americans work and live, communities are very much family centered. One of the reasons why Americans so often find it easy to feel at home in a foreign community and why local people sometimes receive them more readily than they do Europeans is that we also are family oriented.

During the years overseas when we had teen-agers in our home, the various members of the family often went in different directions, and quite often my husband and I went to official functions where the children were not invited. Even so, it was natural and pleasant for us to plan to have other families come to our house or to go on outings with us, and we were frequently invited by other families to "come and bring the children." Parents visited while young people played badminton, tennis, or croquet. Adults and other children frequently sat together in the shade of mango trees in our Rangoon garden drinking cold lime juice, exchanging experiences, and explaining different national customs while little tots wandered here and there as little folks like to do.

We shall explore more fully in a later section the inter-cultural importance of family encounters, and look into some of the possibilities and problems. It is sufficient at this point to let ourselves be reminded that this is another one of the rewarding aspects of life overseas.

For overseas residents the possibilities for interesting and unusual vacations are endless. In most cases where an American is employed abroad he has regular and sometimes generous periods of leave time, and he is often urged to take it away from the place where he is working. It is felt that even though Americans are working without undue strain and though they are living happily in a foreign place, they are nevertheless under certain pressures because they are foreigners, and a change of scenery and sometimes of climate may be needed more urgently than a vacation might be needed at home. The eager beavers need a little prodding to get them loose from a job, but most people welcome the holidays because there are so many special things they want to do and so many special places they want to see in a new part of the world.

It isn't necessary to leave a country in order to have a change of pace. Many times one can find in the country where he is living pleasant spots which will provide the needed change of climate and opportunities for recreation. In many of the countries there will be historically renowned places which few would want to miss.

Those who plan to travel by car away from the big cities, or away from the villages where they are known, need to check with the local authorities so that they may know if the area through which they expect to drive is considered safe for motorists in general and for Americans in particular. Occasionally they are advised that travel is safe only during the daytime hours. In some cases the officials will want to notify the villagers along the route to expect them so that a friendly reception will be assured.

Whether in the country or in cities great caution is required while driving in foreign countries. In some places the traffic may be congested with modern vehicles trying to hurry along streets or roads where pedestrians are heedless of regulations, where cattle may be wandering at will, and where the men pushing wheelbarrows and those riding bicycles steadfastly refuse to relinquish a middle of the road position. Attitudes and regulations toward liabilities for injury caused by motor vehicles differ widely from country to country. All who drive should know exactly what the situation is in the areas where they expect to travel and should seek official instruction as to what they should do in case they are involved in an accident.

Americans often find it interesting to travel on local trains when they are moving around in a foreign country. Youngsters for whom trains are fast becoming a novelty generally love the experience of going by rail to the seaside, to the mountains, or to wherever the family is going. Adults as well as children have a good chance to see the countryside during the journey. A train makes it possible to go to places where motor roads may not be safe or dependable.

In many countries trains operate on a first, second, and third class system. In the heydays of colonialism, Westerners generally rode alone in the first class compartments. Today most Americans prefer to travel more simply and inconspicuously, often moving in with the crowds on third class benches. People with young children, and all who may want and need cleaner and more restful accommodations, find themselves in good company and not uncomfortable quarters if they choose to travel second class.

Since wayside motels are not prevalent in other countries as they are in the United States, it is necessary to make certain about a place to stay when overnight trips or extended vacations are undertaken. Almost any foreign country will have a tourist bureau in its larger cities where information about accommodations can be obtained. Sometimes it is possible to learn through personal channels about both nationals and Americans living in resort areas who will take in paying guests.

Reports come to us of families who exchange homes for a holiday—a business family from the city having a delightful change of scenery in a missionary compound in a village while the missionary family has a stimulating holiday in the city. Sometimes a foreign service officer from the capital city will trade his home (including beds and linen and servants) with a foreign service family related to a consulate in another city of the same country or in an adjacent one.

It is often possible to have relatively inexpensive holidays in other nearby countries. This increases, by yet another dimension, the cosmopolitan assets of an overseas job. We had a particularly rewarding holiday one year when we went for a three week round trip ride on a costal steamer which plied from Rangoon Burma down to Malaya and back. A Burmese friend went along as a member of our family party and her presence made our stops at the Burmese ports more interesting because in each of them we were met and escorted around the community by one of her friends or relatives. We had meals at their homes and saw things which they thought were worth seeing.

At all the stopping places we had at least eight hours and sometimes most of two days to be ashore, but our staterooms were always waiting for us when we wanted to sleep or rest. We were the only Americans on the craft which was operated primarily for the transport of cargo. There were about twenty cabin class passengers, representing several nationalities and we enjoyed living on an informal basis with them.

Our young son was quick to make friends with members of the crew and it was a high moment in his life when the first officer called him early one morning to let him set in motion the mechanism which lifted the anchor. We all were interested in watching the loading of cargo, and since much of it was tin ore we were intrigued when we were able one evening during a stopover to go on a launch upriver to see tin-dredging operations. Another day we visited a rubber plantation.

It was a fortunate thing for us that certain mechanical repairs were required when the *S. S. Metang* reached Penang. We moved to a bungalow type hotel on the coast of that paradise island and for three days we enjoyed a beautiful beach and rides through a picture-book jungle before we returned to our floating quarters for the slow trip back home.

During the time we were in Burma one of our daughters had a memorable holiday with school friends in Kashmir India. During a summer vacation period some young people with two of their Woodstock School teachers went by train from Dehra Dun in North India, where their boarding school was located, to Jammu, stopping at Amritar to see the golden temple. They completed the journey to Srinagar by bus. Their Kashmir hostel was a houseboat anchored out in a lake. A small cook boat on which their meals were prepared was tied to the side of the houseboat.

Whenever they wanted to make an excursion to some other point they hailed passing gondola-like boats that were cruising around. They sometimes went for a whole day's outing on the beautiful lakes or they just rode far enough to overtake a houseboat bazaar where they liked especially to buy the delicious cherries which were grown in the nearby areas.

One day they left the lake and hired ponies to take them up mountain trails to the snow line. It was a moment of great excitement for them when the fog lifted and they were able to look into a valley where little houses were snuggled among the tall trees and small children picked sweet wild strawberries while their parents wove the sheer wool cloth or carved the exquisite walnut pieces which are such a delight to tourists.

Special Days

Many Americans overseas find that the special days on their family calendar become more important to them than ever before. Birthdays somehow assume a new importance, especially for children. This may be because even a child who is happy in a foreign environment needs reassurance from time to time that he is who he is, and a birthday is certainly a good time for a child to be reminded that he is someone special.

I think that children often remember their birthday celebrations overseas because parents, not being able to buy the usual things so easily, have given more thought to making things and to planning unusual entertainment. So many homeside birthdays are celebrated with hot dogs, a cake-mix cake, and a child's best friends taken with him to one of the least offensive movies currently showing in neighborhood movie houses. Overseas the counterparts of these commonplace celebrations are hard to find so families come up with much more interesting and exciting things to do.

The other day I read a letter which described some of the difficulties a young family in Taipei was encountering on a certain day. The mother who was writing described several of their problems and then at the close of the letter she added a postscript which seemed to put every other consideration in the background: "Today is Teddy Bear's birthday and we are all getting presents." I knew when I read those words that whenever it is heavy weather in that household someone is going to give just any day a reason for being special and so provide a cause for good cheer.

Christmas is sometimes a happier occasion overseas than it is in the U. S. A. because there are still places where the "so many more shopping days" notices do not bombard you and where "Silent Night" isn't blaring out over loud speakers in every shop in town. For the most part the religious observances of Christmas are still left in the Christian homes and Christian churches where they belong, and gift giving is the personal expression of good will as it ought to be. Most people take a few Christmas tree decorations from home and, in the tropics where the familiar evergreens are missing, they often improvise with palm sprays or with branches of the cassarina tree.

The national holidays of our country, which at home are now sometimes known best for the big warehouse sales, are frequently observed with full flavor by families overseas. One family in Africa has written that all the Americans in a fifty mile radius gathered together to celebrate the Fourth of July with a picnic and a baseball game ("Our Daddy made a screaming home run" was the underscored line.)

American embassies in most countries have had to abandon the former practice of holding a reception for all American residents as well as the leading officials and many well-known local citizens in a capital city area. The membership of all these groups has increased so much in recent years that space can seldom be found where so many might be entertained and the cost of holding such a large party has become excessive. The official observances of our Independence Day are in most places now held by the embassy staff only for the diplomatic corps and for national officials.

Other overseas Americans may and do arrange their own celebrations and in so doing they are strengthening their ties with their own country. This is a good thing because one of the dangers related to overseas living, especially for those who take assignment after assignment, is that a sense of rootlessness overtakes an individual or a family. This isn't likely to happen to the families who cut out paper hatchets on

February twenty-second, who read the Gettysburg Address on February fourteenth, who pledge allegiance to the flag of the United States of America on the fourth of July and who gather together quietly with their countrymen on the fourth Thursday in November to offer prayers of gratitude for life's blessings.

The Second Honeymoon

I know from my own experience, and I have observed that it is true for many other American couples, that a move to a new part of the world can be the signal for a new quickening of the bonds between a husband and wife. I suppose in some cases it is just the stimulus of a new environment, a change of scenery and perchance a change in climate which reawakens the excitement of living life together. Sometimes it is the challenge of new responsibilities and the realization that new opportunities are opening for the pursuit of some long cherished goal which pulls them closer together. The experience of being foreigners in a far country may remind them of their good fortune in belonging, each to the other. In any case, there comes to many a heightened sense of meaning and fulfillment in a marriage which is already good.

For marriages that have slipped into a rut, not because foundations are weak or damaged but just because monotony or carelessness or preoccupation with the daily rounds has overtaken one or both partners, the new situation often provides a chance for a new start.

A wife who has domestic help after a long and exhausting period of caring for small children is able to take a new look at herself as a woman. She may see that she is much in arrears in reading and other forms of personal enrichment, and as she begins to do something about it her husband may find that she has more to offer in conversation and understanding. She may see that she has let herself become careless in dress and posture. With a little thought and some determined exercising she may soon give her husband new cause to find her attractive.

Using less time commuting to work and with fewer community demands made upon him, a husband may spend more time with his wife and they may have more time to participate together in sports or creative diversions. Romance long dormant may rise again under the same old stars now hanging in a somewhat different heaven.

I wouldn't suggest that a poor marriage will be better in a new country than it was in the old. To the contrary, a marriage which might have rocked along indefinitely in a familiar and supporting community may fall apart more quickly under the different conditions of overseas living. When this happens the other Americans can only stand aside while the unfortunate pair work out some kind of a solution or go their separate ways.

All of us who have lived overseas for any length of time have had the happy experience of seeing fellow countrymen starting, not on a second honeymoon, but on the first. It was fun on the mission field when a Presbyterian bride was "bought" for a Methodist bachelor. The Methodist ladies had all been playing cupid, of course, trying to pair off the only single man around with first one and then another of the Methodist spinsters, but to no avail. Then one fall a new young nurse arrived at the hospital which was supported by several denominations, including the Presbyterians. Our shy young man wasn't shy any more and before long rumors of a June wedding were in the air.

The couple didn't deny the rumors but the groom confessed that the date could not be fixed until negotiations were completed concerning the payments for the bride. It wasn't that her father in New Jersey was holding out for a good price, but the facts of life were that she was in the first year of service as a missionary from the Board of Foreign Missions of the Presbyterian Church. When she became the wife of a Methodist missionary she would need to resign from the Presbyterian Board even though it was commonly accepted that she would go right on working as a nurse in the same hospital. When a mission board has sent someone out to the field there has been invested no small sum for travel and outfit allowance. If the person resigns before the first term is completed then certain reimbursements have to be made. Happily, and as usual under similar circumstances, the treasurer of the Methodist Mission Board came forward to give the needed amount to the Presbyterians, and the bride's name was shifted from one roll to another with no interruption of her important work. The chapel bells rang out before the month of June was finished and with a gay escort of doctors and teachers and students the newlyweds rode in ribbon bedecked rickshaws to the railway station where they left on the North China Express for an undisclosed honeymoon.

Twenty years later in Burma I remembered the China mission wedding as I helped to gather delicate monsoon lilies for the wedding the chief of a technical assistance mission was giving for his secretary. On the day before the wedding the proxy father and his wife moved out of their air conditioned bedroom in order that it could be used as a depository for the masses of garden flowers that were going to be used in the bouquets for bride and maids and in the rooms of the residence where the reception would be held. There were hundreds of gardenias cut from gardens of friends, fragrant lilies and tuberoses and dainty white jasmine which was knotted into the ribbons of the bride's bouquet. Even the roads to the church were dressed for a high occasion because the flame of the forest, the silk cotton tree, the jacaranda, and the frangipanni were heavy with bloom.

The church had palms and pots of white oleanders, and the deep windows were all open with luxurious tropical growth outside. The bride was truly lovely and her beaming boss was as proud and considerate as if she had been his own child. In pews on her side there were half a hundred of her American friends and their sun-tanned enchanted children for whom the occasion was like something out of a story book. The groom's side was crowded with smiling Danes. On both sides Burmese friends and co-workers appeared, the men in silk shirts and kerchiefed turbans and the women in dainty jewel-buttoned blouses and gaily flowered sarongs. The chief's wife was ushered up to the place reserved for the mother of the bride.

The service had to finish before sunset so that the marriage would be legal according to the English civil laws that operated for Christians in that Buddhist land. But the reception went on gayly for hours in the evening with silk parasol covered lights in the gardens and torches beside the lake. The servants of the household had added their own special touch by transforming a boat which was floating in the lake at the foot of the garden into a magnificent illuminated swan. There was champagne with toasts in two languages, and dinner on the lawn. The high point of the evening came when the Danish wedding waltz notes were sounded, and with his countrymen singing and Americans tapping out the melody the big blond bridegroom claimed his American wife for the bridal dance.

Our host, no doubt, went back to his study after the wedding festivities were finished to read urgent cables and to plan the answers which he would dictate to a new and less experienced secretary the next day. But for him as for the rest of us the interlude had been but another reminder that life overseas holds, as life anywhere may, experiences that are rooted in joy and hours that are made for fun.

Chapter VIII

UNDER EIGHTEEN

Families with children under college age sometimes hesitate to take an overseas assignment because they are afraid it will be too difficult with young children, or too disruptive for school children. The experience of countless families lends weight to the opposing point of view, that little folks may be healthy and happy in almost any spot where American employees go, and that older youngsters frequently come back to their classmates with no handicap because of the two or three years' absence. In many cases the child who has had travel and a new language added to his school curriculum may be in an advanced position in comparison with other children.

The British, traditionally, have handled the children's angle of overseas service by sending their youngsters home from the outposts by the time they were nine or ten. The children live with relatives or, most commonly, are placed in boarding schools. The mother commutes between offspring and husband. This began when living arrangements in the British colonies were much less desirable than they are overseas today even in the most remote areas. It was supported, no doubt, by the need for British children to get into good schools in order to prepare for examinations and scholarships for the universities. The practice of sending young children to boarding schools was not limited to overseas British families. It has been a common practice among families in the homeland as well.

Americans as a rule are not inclined to favor the separation of children from their families. Early missionaries and overseas business people took their children wherever they went. The children learned to adjust. Schools were organized wherever there was a handful of American children.

In recent years, as the number of Americans going overseas has increased tremendously, the policy of packing the family along has continued. It can be done without undue difficulty, and it may prove profitable for the children, satisfactory to the parents, and a real boon to inter-cultural relationships. It doesn't follow, however, that the children's part in an overseas assignment works out well just as a matter of course. Special efforts need to be made.

Initial Adjustments of Children

Children have their own kind of cultural shock and need help in handling it. Little children aren't likely to be bothered by some of the things that disturb their elders. Dirt and disease and poverty which exists outside their own home are going to be thought about only by young children whose parents have been emotional about these things. The same thing is true about different racial characteristics or habits of dress or ways of doing things. This can all be just a matter of interest. It may, however, be a shock to a child when he realizes that he is going to stay in the new place, that he isn't going back to his own house and that he can't play again, for a long time, with the friends or relatives who have been left behind.

A two-year-old boy started screaming when his father took him from an overseas church nursery with the comment "Come along, son, let's go back to our new house." Some children let a cry work up. This particular one had the capacity to start at full blast and, to the embarrassment of his parents on their first day at a new church, he held his cry at full volume for what must have seemed to them like a very long time. Finally, he quieted down enough for them to ask what was troubling him. "Not to our house, to Uncle Ted's house," he sobbed and the volume swelled again.

Every Sunday that he could remember he had gone to church with his parents and then they had gone together to his grandfather's house where the special attraction was his school boy uncle who played ball with him. His mother and father had to make special efforts to help him accept the fact that Sundays in the new place couldn't follow the same ritual but that the new place had special and regular features all its own.

Some children miss the things they have been used to having around them and may feel a little frightened when the lights are turned off in a strange bedroom or when, for the first time, a mosquito net is tucked around them and they see no place to escape. If there is a familiar picture to hang on a child's wall or a favorite stuffed animal to share the new bed, the first night is sometimes easier. It is worth all the time it takes to explore a new house with a little child especially in a foreign country. He can learn to enjoy being tucked in with the mosquitoes tucked out but it may take a while for him to get accustomed to the arrangement.

It is not easy for a small child to get used to being surrounded by an unfamiliar language. The new nurse may come running every time the child calls but when she gets there if he doesn't know what she is saying or if she speaks English with a very different accent he may feel distressed. Some mothers have sent their regrets to welcoming parties in order that they could stay with young children and help them move with more assurance into their new world.

The fact that their parents may be performing in new roles sometimes proves disconcerting for little folks. In cases where families have had a very informal social life in America with baby sitters taking over with the children only on rare occasions, a child who sees his parents leave the house in dinner clothes night after night may become perturbed.

On our last overseas assignment my husband and I had to be away more nights than we were home. I did two things which I think helped. First, I always told the younger children where we were going and if I knew that parents of any of their friends were going to be there I told them about that so that they would have some point of identification. Then the next day I would tell them more about people we saw and anything especially interesting about the place or the food. The other thing I did was to arrange our dinner hour so that we always had supper with the children when we weren't going away and if it could be managed we sat with them while they had their supper on our nights out. When we had guests, as we did frequently, the children joined us unless the dinner needed to be too late for them. In that case, they greeted the guests before dinner and so came to feel that our new kind of social life was not so strange.

A good many women expect to make formal calls soon after their arrival in a capital city. Foreign service wives must make them in the first days. This presents a real problem when there are small children. Sometimes it takes a while to find and hire a suitable nurse. Hotels often have maids or *amahs* for special assignment but a child may not take kindly at first to a strange face and a foreign tongue, and a mother can't be at ease making calls when she knows her child is screaming in a new house or a hotel room. Some mothers have solved this by having the child and new nurse ride along in the car. Child and nurse sit in the car at each stop or get out and wander on the grounds. If another mother has been on the welcoming committee she might have a suggestion about a temporary nurse or might take the new children to her house while their mother makes her calls.

Older children and teen-agers in some ways have an easier adjustment than little children. They understand so much more about the new situation and in many cases have come to a new country with great eagerness. But they, too, miss their friends and can feel very lonely if parents are away night after night. The little ones go to bed soon after or even before parents depart, but evenings can seem long to children who are too old to be sleepy right after supper. It is very important to have a maid or nurse who can be a good companion to older children as well as to have one who can take care of the little folks. It is important also to help older children find friends. Adults find friends through their work but children who are not always placed in a school immediately have no special groups into which they will move when they arrive.

A group is not important to the very young child who frequently plays alone even when other children are around. When other children are available there are no special social adjustment problems for him. Clothes, skin color, sex make little difference. He will as quickly give a warm embrace to (or snatch a toy from) any strange child as to his own brother. With no effort at all he soon picks up a new language.

But the older child may have reached a stage where having friends his own age is very important to him and yet, having become self conscious about himself in relation to a peer group, he may be miserably unable to make a first move towards a child or a group to whom he is a stranger. There are the exceptional extroverts, of course, but even they may have their confidence somewhat shaken if the only children around them are children of the country whose code and whose language they do not yet know. So their parents need to give them some special attention in order that the social transition may be more easily made.

I recently heard a mother who had lived in several South American countries report that she always made a point of taking time to play baseball with her children for the first few weeks in any new community. She did it partly because it kept the children from being so restless at that difficult time. But she said the main reason was that she generally managed to hit the ball so hard that it went at least once into a garden where she had spotted children and that after that her children could be on their own. We have always made a point of inviting other families with children to come to our house, both local families and American families and in this way our children have made friends.

Once we joined a swimming club in spite of the fact that it had some exclusive clauses in its membership requirements (clauses which we did not like and which I am happy to learn have now been lifted perhaps because we and others who felt as we did registered a protest from within). We joined because we knew it would give our children, especially the teen-agers, a place to meet and associate with American friends. We have always welcomed the opportunity for our children to make friends with children of other countries and have felt that this has been one of the most rewarding parts of overseas living. But it has never seemed to us that this value negated the value of making friends with other American children with whom they might have special interests.

An American friend may be especially important for a child who has just left his homeland and is needing encouragement as he makes his way in a new situation. An American friend may also be important for him when he is about ready to return to his own country and is getting cold feet about how he will fit in back there.

An Attendant For The Children

The selection of a children's attendant is one of the most urgent and most important things to be done after arrival in a foreign country. European countries have licensed nursemaids who can be hired by the day or the hour. But in most other parts of the world a family with children needs a full time woman in order to have someone available when the mother needs to be away. In some countries a maid will double as a "sitter" but in many places a nurse expects to be responsible just for children and for light laundry and mending and perhaps for bedroom care. I have said in an earlier discussion that in most foreign places I would want a woman assistant for children of any age and especially teen-aged girls.

Finding a woman helper is most difficult in those Muslim countries where women are still sheltered and do not work away from their homes. Missionaries can sometimes find a Christian convert who has left her family and is in need of work. Sometimes a refugee from another country is anxious to find a home and may have good qualifications. Before employing an outsider, however, it is important to consider how she will be accepted by any other servants in the household and by people in the neighborhood. As a rule if a family lets out word that they are looking for a woman servant, sooner or later a suitable candidate will turn up.

The qualifications mentioned earlier for servants in general would apply as well for a children's attendant but there are extra requirements for her. The chief one is that she should be pleasant and attractive. She is going to give the children in the family the most intimate glimpse of the people of the country that they will ever get, and it is important that the impression they get is good. It is important also that she have a quality of teachableness in her character so that a mother can pass on to her not only ways of doing things but attitudes as well. I have always been as much concerned that the woman who is my stand-in should have a wholesome attitude towards our children as I have been that she know how to keep them out of physical danger.

Even the most understanding and conscientious children's attendant should not be completely unsupervised. I would make it a point to find out how things go when I am away and I would sometimes turn children over to their nurse when I am at home in order that I could observe from a distance how the relationship is working out. Without prying a mother can learn by listening to the things her children say to her how they feel about the person who looks after them when she is away.

In many places the nurses like to take young children to a central meeting place so that they may visit with each other while the children play. Within limits I think this is all right. It gives the nurse a chance to see her friends and it provides playmates for the child. However, I have observed that the meeting places may not always be suitably clean and that little children left to their own devices while the nurses are absorbed in conversation may not be as happy or as well supervised as they might be. If I learned that a situation like this was developing I would suggest that our nurse invite her special friends to come one or two at a time with their charges to play and visit in our garden.

If I saw that a helper needed more guidance at some point I would work along with her for a day or two—sitting with her when the children played in the garden, strolling along with her when they went for walks.

Occasionally one finds a nurse who holds the reins with too tight a hand. Then it is important to interpret one's philosophy of self direction and to point out ways in which a less rigid discipline has operated effectively with this particular child. I not only said to one *nanny* that we never hit our children and would permit no one who took over for us to strike them, but I took time to explain to her how we managed to achieve good cooperation in more acceptable ways. Another time I explained to her why we said to a child that unacceptable conduct was not good but that we never said to him that he was bad or that he was not acceptable. It wasn't easy to put concepts like these across but it was worth trying because gradually as Nanny listened to my explanations and observed our family in operation she was able to fit into it and to help us work towards the goals we held for our children.

More frequently than holding the reins too tight a nurse is likely to indulge the children too much. "But he wanted it," I have heard a kind hearted *amah* say when a child had eaten something he should not have had or had destroyed something he shouldn't have been given. Then I have had to explain to her the importance of a simple but firm "No." Sometimes a nurse will do things for children who ought to be doing these things for themselves. If I found a nurse dressing or bathing a child quite old enough to be independent in such matters I would encourage the child to take pride in being responsibly independent and I would admonish the nurse to let him help himself.

In addition to giving adequate supervision to the children's attendant I would always continue to keep an eye on the children themselves. It was important for our children when they were younger to know that even though there was someone who substituted for us a good deal of the time overseas their father and I were still responsible for them and still the ones to whom they were responsible. I have seen cases where parents lost control of their children after a nurse was brought in, and I think that this is not good.

Neither is it good for a child to lose touch with his parents because being freed from his care in good measure they neglect to give him as much of their time and attention as he needs. Actually an overseas situation generally offers more time for parents to have a give and take with their children, but I have seen a few cases where a serious break in a parent-child relationship occurred because parents, either too busy with society or too intent on good works, let their end of the communication cable slip.

Another reason for keeping an eye on the child's behavior in a situation where he is looked after by a nurse is that it can be easy for a red-blooded, vitamin-packed American youngster to take advantage of a servile minded national who wants to keep her job. I have on occasion seen an American child kicking or defying a nurse who seemed helpless in his hands. I have always wanted to be sure that our youngsters understood that in our absence a nurse, or any other servant who may have been left in charge, was to be accepted as the responsible authority and was to be treated with respect.

Sometimes a self reliant American child doesn't want to have a nurse. "But I'm not sick," a four-year-old protested when the *nanny* arrived, "Why should I have a nurse?" His mother was patient, explaining that there were no high school girls to call as sitters and that he couldn't spend week-ends with his grandparents as he used to do at home when his parents went out of town. She told him his nurse wasn't the kind who just took care of sick people but that her work was to keep boys and girls safe and well and to play with them and take them places where they couldn't go alone. He said, "O.K." and took the new attendant to see his ducks.

Older children sometimes feel that the presence of a nurse is a reflection upon their maturity. It may be necessary to explain to them that in the new community it is the custom to have another adult responsible for the welfare of a family when the parents aren't at home. This can be done without painting such an alarming picture that a child will become fearful of his new environment. But to keep the older child from feeling embarrassed at the idea of having to be looked after it may be important to instruct the nurse to keep in the background until the child accepts her as a companion.

It is more the rule than the exception that American children do rather quickly accept both the care and the companionship which a kindly woman gives them, and a mutually happy relationship develops. The nurse especially enjoys being included in family vacations and escorting the junior members to entertainments or parties. A birthday party gives a *nanny* a chance to wear her jewelry and her nicest clothes. In countries where attendants are likely to appear, a hostess generally sees to it that chairs are available for them to sit and visit with each other and that refreshments and sometimes favors are planned for them, too. They in turn take great pride in seeing that the children they are responsible for are properly dressed and that they conduct themselves with decorum. The hostess sometimes has to lure the *nannies* into a happy huddle so that the children can dash around and have some fun!

The most difficult thing about having an attendant for one's child on an overseas assignment is that the day finally comes when the Americans leave for their homeland and the nurse must find a new charge. Both of them are generally brokenhearted.

Educational Choices

Pleasant as it often is to live in a foreign country and educational though the experience in itself may be for children, parents who settle down to live abroad for any length of time should make inquiries about schools before they go or look into the school situation soon after arrival.

I have never been concerned overseas about schooling for a child under five or even six. I've always been a bit skeptical about the wisdom of mobilizing the moppets in any society, and I would want to be especially careful not to push a little child off to school too soon in a totally new environment. I would want to know that he felt enough at home to be ready to go away each day and that the program in the nursery school or pre-school class was suitable for him. It isn't in every country that one can find the supervised free play periods or the creative activities programs which generally characterize a nursery school in our country. In some countries three year olds might be set to fine muscle copy work or to rote memory exercises. Some American three year olds may be ready for this, but I suspect that most of us would want to let formal instruction come at a later time.

The question of whether or not a three- or four-year-old should be put into a school would depend on the child himself, on his readiness for a group experience, upon his need for companionship, and upon the particular school or class available. When our youngest child was four and five we lived overseas about twelve miles from the city where nursery and kindergarten classes would be open to him. He would have needed to be transported through the slow-moving traffic at the most congested time of day, and would have had to hurry through an early breakfast and arrive home for a very late lunch. These factors alone would have discouraged me even if I had thought he needed the social experience or had felt that the group to which he would have gone was outstanding. Fortunately, being a member of a large family his social experience had not been limited and since he was having numerous opportunities to play with other children the question of his being sent to school wasn't ever raised.

He had a competent and good spirited attendant, our garden had wonderful play places, and best of all, our sweeper's son was near his age and since the sweeper lived on our compound, those two boys could always find each other for happy hours in the bamboo grove or up in the mango trees. By the time we left he was beginning to learn from his friend how to shinny up the trunk of a coconut palm.

On rainy days we had handwork materials for him in the house and some older member of the family was always ready to read him a story. When we arrived back in the United States just in time to enroll him in the first grade I left a blank where it asked for a report on previous schooling. I felt, however, that he was not unprepared for the formal classroom and his easy adjustment and steady progress showed that I was right.

When our older children were pre-schoolers in China I once helped to organize an informal cooperative play group in our back yard, and it provided a happy experience for them and, I think, for their playmates. We were living on a college campus as were all the other faculty families so it required nothing but a safe and easy walk for the little folks to assemble. We had a large fenced-in backyard, and I saw no reason why it should not be put to good use especially since the North China winter days were cold but dry and almost always sunny.

Betty, a next door American neighbor, and I had no older children and therefore no regular teaching responsibilities so we took turns being on duty in the play yard. Chinese mothers who could be away from their homes also helped with supervision. Our husbands made simple but sturdy climbing equipment. Whenever a family went on home leave we were recipients of old tricycles or wagons, so with a few big balls and a huge pile of blocks on the porch we had everything we needed for the two hours the children spent together. It was the first time the Chinese, European and American faculty children had been brought together, and this provided community morale benefits in addition to the benefits the children had. Each mother spoke in her own language. Betty and I knew a certain amount of Chinese and some of the mothers knew English, but it seemed desirable for the children to hear each mother speak in her native language. Most of the youngsters became bi-lingual.

The pre-school years are a favorable time for culturally mixed groups or classes. Children at that age learn a new language readily and at that stage the curricular content of a program need not be related to later academic studies. Parents in various countries have placed their five-year-old children in local kindergartens and in some cases have put younger children in local language nursery classes. I have heard of several other places where an international or a bicultural group similar to the one we had in China has been started for young children.

Questions related to the education of American children overseas become more urgent when parents have children who are six years old or older. "What are we going to do about Johnny?" is a question of serious concern to many.

There is a great variety of opinions as to what is the most desirable kind of school arrangement. Some feel strongly that the only thing to do is to put children into whatever local language school is available and so let them have the full benefit of living in a foreign country and let the local people know that they do not hold themselves aloof. If parents hold this position as crusaders they are unlikely to be critically concerned about either the curriculum or the practices of the local school, or to be analytical about their own children's special needs.

At the opposite extreme, some parents feel just as strongly that while they are overseas their children must have as nearly as possible the exact counterpart of the educational program they would be having at home. Some even take textbooks purchased from their home town school board and ask the home school principal to write out a two-year curriculum. All parents in this later camp would at least want an American school or a correspondence course based on a more or less standard American curriculum. These parents also are more likely to focus their attention on the idea of a thoroughly American education rather than upon the experience or special needs of the individual child.

The vast majority of overseas parents do not hold absolute convictions, and are likely to make decisions which consider the needs of individual children within the framework of a broad range of values as they seem to be best met in an individual place. There is a variety of choices.

There are in all countries some local language schools which are attended by children of the country. There are some international schools. There are in many places English language (but not necessarily American) private schools. There are church-related schools. There are United States armed forces dependents' schools. There are company schools conducted by American or bi-national business firms. There is the possibility of being related by a correspondence course to a school in the United States. There are a rapidly increasing number of community or parent sponsored American or bi-national schools. In addition there are some well-known boarding schools.

There are ways in which any American family overseas can see that its children have good schooling. I have heard of one family in a far away place which discovered that there were four quite different kinds of school situations available in their community, and they decided that a different school arrangement was right for each of their four children.

No statistics are available as to the exact number of American children who are enrolled in local language schools throughout the world, but reports indicate that there are children in various places who attend the schools which children of the country attend. Many parents who are not in the small crusading group of those who insist categorically that a local school is the only correct choice for world minded people, have enrolled their children in national schools (or in parochial or other private schools attended by local children and using the local language) because they have decided that these are good schools, that the experience will be interesting and helpful for their individual children, that the children will be able to handle the foreign language, and that the presence of American children in the local school does represent a measure of international good will.

This enrollment of American children in a national school is more likely to be done in a place where the language of the school is among the more commonly used European languages such as French, German,

Spanish, Italian, Portuguese. But we hear also of a few American children in the lower elementary grades who are studying in schools where they use Japanese, Hindustani, or another of the languages which we Americans are inclined to think of as being more difficult. I know of some cases where American children study for a half day in a local school in order to learn the language and to associate with the local children and then do lessons in English at home for a couple of hours in the afternoon.

Some American children who are attending school where they study and converse in a language other than English may be enrolled in a school foreign to the country where they are living. One family, now living in Turkey, has two of their children attending a small German Embassy school there. Their children had previously lived in Germany and had some introduction to that language. American children are also enrolled in French schools in various countries including especially Vietnam. It could be added that American parents living in America frequently choose to send their children to French or German schools in the cities when there are such schools.

While the word "international" is sometimes used in the name of an American or bi-national school overseas there is a small group of schools abroad which are, in fact, international. That is, they are planned, supported, and administered by a multi-national group, enrolling children of various nations and employing a curriculum which is adapted to the multicultural needs of the students. The oldest, and perhaps the best known of this group is the International School of Geneva which was organized in 1924. The Geneva school has 1,246 students, representing fifty-six nationalities, including 525 Americans.

The International School of the Hague has 530 students, thirty-four nationalities with 217 American children. SHAPE International School, near Paris, has 1,100 children with ten nationalities including 130 Americans. It is of interest to report in this connection that the United Nations School in New York City which was founded in 1949 now enrolls a total of 330 students representing forty-seven nationalities and including 159 American boys and girls. A few of the American students are dependents of the American delegation or American staff of the U. N. but most of them are Americans from outside the United Nations who are attending the school because their parents appreciate the values of an international program and student body.

Some Americans send children to an English language school which is not American either in staff or in curriculum. There are now a good many private English elementary schools scattered throughout the parts of the world where there are large numbers of British people.

The reports indicate that these schools differ according to their leadership and according to whether they are patterned after old English programs and practices or are more like the modern English schools. A few Americans who like a no-frills curriculum and a no-nonsense discipline are satisfied with the old English set-up. Most want something less rugged and will consider an English school only if they know that it follows an up-to-date curriculum and deals with children according to a present day understanding of how they learn and how they may most helpfully be handled.

There are church mission schools, where classes designed for local children are taught in English, which are attended by some American children. In some cases attendance at the mission schools proves to be a profitable experience especially for a period of only one or two years. The danger is that the curriculum planned for children whose background is much less sophisticated than that of the American children and paced for children who know English only as a second language will not prove to be sufficiently stimulating for an American child. However, if the school is a small one and the teacher is understanding and resourceful the American child may be given additional material which will round out his studies and keep him from being bored.

Occasionally one finds a mission school which caters not to the underprivileged children of the community but to the children of locally prominent families of both the Christian and non Christian faiths. The non-Christian families permit their children to attend the devotionals and in some cases to take Bible study because they are glad for them to be in an English language school which enjoys a good reputation. Even in countries where the English language is, by law, no longer the language of instruction in the government schools (because for various reasons, including national pride, the country wants to strengthen the prestige of its own language) the private English language schools may be attended by the children of government officials.

In some cases a mission school like this provides a good education and brings the American children who attend into rewarding friendships with local children whose cultural background is broad. But I have heard of one case where children were taken out of such a school because it hadn't been able to resist the pressure to take more and more children and the student body had expanded much more rapidly than the curriculum had been revised or the teachers trained in modern practices. Parents decided that recognized cultural values of having their children meet local children were far outweighed by the limited educational values.

There are some outstanding schools overseas which were established originally for the children of North American Protestant missionaries and have continued to keep their emphasis on an American-type education with high standards. The schools for missionary children were the first American schools abroad (Woodstock School in India was founded in 1854).

We shall refer to the mission-related boarding schools in the later section dealing with schools for older children, but it should be pointed out here that some of the boarding schools have facilities and school programs for elementary children as well as high school people.

The missionary schools, both day schools and boarding schools, receive financial assistance from church agencies and are directed by mission board representatives so in cases where enrollment is limited, the children of missionaries must be received first. When space permits, other Americans as well as children of the host country and of other countries are generally received on a tuition basis.

The Schutz School for Missionary Children (called, also, The American School) in Alexandria Egypt is an example of a missionary school with boarding facilities (limited to sixty) for children as young as third graders. It was founded in 1922 to provide American education for children of United Presbyterian Missionaries in Egypt, Sudan, and Ethiopia. It is still operated for Presbyterian children but its student body now includes children from other missionary groups, and also from U. S. government families, from the World Health Organization and from the Sahara Petroleum Company. The Schutz School program extends through the twelfth grade with boarding arrangements for both boys and girls beginning with the third grade. English is the language of instruction but French and Arabic are taught as foreign languages.

A complete and up-to-date directory of schools available overseas for the children of North American missionaries may be secured for $1.50 from:

Missionary Research Library
3041 Broadway
New York 27, New York

This directory includes detailed information about many schools other than missionary schools which American children are attending. Designed particularly for the parents of some ten thousand North American Protestant missionary children (that number includes infants and up to college age), it is useful as well for other Americans who must find schools abroad.

In addition to the Protestant schools abroad there are also highly regarded Roman Catholic parochial schools available for Americans in major cities of the world including Bangkok, Djakarta, Havana, Lima, Paris, Manila, Mexico City, Rome, Santiago, and Tokyo.

There are a great number of American parents who have no need to assume full responsibility for their children's education overseas because they will find an authentic American school, sometimes complete with a yellow school bus, waiting for them when they arrive at the new place. The largest group for whom schools are provided are the children of military or civilian employees of the Department of Defense of the United States government. The regulations of the Defense Department provide that wherever there are as many as twenty children of elementary school age and as many as forty high school aged people in an overseas area, an American school may be organized and staffed by either the Army, the Navy, or the Air Force. Professionally trained civilian staff are recruited in the United States to conduct a school program which matches in detail a typical school in the United States. (In the case of a high school, it has to conform to the standards of the North Central Association by whom it is accredited. Inspectors of the association make bi-annual visits to all Defense Department high schools to make sure that standards are being maintained.)

The three branches of armed services do not maintain separate schools in places where more than one branch has dependents in residence. In many cases the first branch to have a sizeable group of children in need of schooling organizes the school and if that has been the Army, for instance, Navy and Air Force dependents are included as they arrive. In some cases it has just been an administrative decision which made one or another branch responsible for the organization and maintenance of a school for all service children. In a number of places where there are more than the minimum number of armed forces children, no school has been organized because a good American school is otherwise available, in which case the Defense Department assumes the tuition fees for Defense children and they attend the American school in the community. Taipei and Athens are examples of this. In both cases American parents have founded and are running good schools and the Defense Department has designated these as schools to which the children of their employees may go with fees paid for them.

There are cases where a small parent-operated school which may have lost its leadership or may never have had sufficient financial backing has been taken over by one of the branches of the Defense Department. Then the tables are turned and it is the children who are not related to the Defense Department for whom tuition is paid. Any school operated for the children of American employees of the Defense Department is open to other American children on the payment of tuition and on a priority basis as space permits. The priority is first for the children of other federal employees, then for those whose parents are not employed by the government but whose work is in some way related to the work of the Defense Department. After that, space permitting, other American citizens in a community could have their children admitted or placed on a waiting list.

There are a few cases where the child of a foreign national has been admitted by special arrangement to a school operated by the Defense Department. This would occur only if the child's parents were working in some close relationship with the U. S. Army, Air Force, or Navy. If such a child were accepted he would have to have competency in the English language, and he would pay the usual tuition for outsiders.

While regulations provide that a school for Defense employees' dependents may be started for as few as twenty there are not at the time of this writing any schools that small. Most schools have about 500 pupils. There are two Defense Department elementary schools in Germany which have over 1700 students each.

In Germany, France, and Italy the language of the country, taught by a national is included in the curriculum of the Defense Department schools beginning at the elementary level. In other countries efforts are made to include cultural studies related to the host country. In Japan, for instance, the Japanese language is not taught to the children in the armed forces school but the program has been enriched by the study of such things as Japanese art and dancing. In many places there are mutually helpful relationships between the American school staff and the professional personnel in the local schools.

The situation arises occasionally where a Defense Department employee prefers to send his child to some other American school in the area or perchance to a national or other private school in the country. He is free to do so but in that case he would have to pay his own tuition. The same restriction applies to a government employee not related to defense. A State Department employee for whom an education allowance is available may not receive the allowance to use at a private school if there is in the area a school operated by some branch of the United States Government and if space is available for his child.

The rationale back of this seems to be that educational allowances are provided for government employees because those employees would be able to send their children to free public schools if they were living in the United States. If a Defense Department school is available then it is assumed to be the counterpart of an American public school and parents who choose not to use it may pay for private schooling just as they would in the United States. But if a Defense Department school is not available for children other than those whose parents are related to the armed forces, then parents in other branches of the government may use their educational allowances at schools of their choice. I have heard parents express the wish that the regulations would be changed so that an educational allowance might be applied at a school other than an armed forces school if the parent felt that the other school had special advantages for his child.

A number of North American firms operate schools for their own employees overseas, particularly in areas where other American schooling is not available and the number of children involved is not small. There are about ten company schools in Asia and the Middle East, two or three in Africa, and about fifty in South America. Some of the company schools are small; a few are large. Most of them are for the children of employees only. Some accept other North American or national children.

The Arabian American Oil Company, to cite one example, has three schools in Saudi Arabia which are attended by 1,203 students. Aramco schools are open only to children of the company's senior staff employees, this includes the children of the Saudi Arabian senior staff members as well as children of other nationalities whose fathers are employed in senior positions. The language of instruction is English and the overwhelming majority of the students are American. The schools are tuition free.

The largest of the Aramco schools, with a student body of 627 is in the headquarters community of Dhahran. The others are at Res Tanura, the refining community on the Persian Gulf, and at Abqaiq, the oil producing center. There are sixty qualified American teachers in the three schools. No teacher is sent to Saudi Arabia who has less than three years' teaching experience in the United States; preference is given to those who have a Masters Degree and have had five years' experience. The schools operate on a trimester schedule with vacations for the months of December, April, and August. During the vacation months teachers are available for tutoring classes in order that those children who have been away from the country for the bi-annual home leave may be able to make up the lost time.

In all three communities the Aramco schools have classes from kindergarten through the ninth grade. The school programs are enriched with art, libraries, visual aids, musical groups, and sports activities just as they would be in good schools in suburban areas back home. After school classes in Arabic are available for those who want to make a serious study of the language of the country in which they live.

The story is told that one American child who was born in Saudi Arabia and had been attending the kindergarten at one of the Aramco schools visited his aunt in Des Moines, Iowa and asked her why the traffic signs were only in English. She explained that everyone there spoke only English. "Well, in my home town," he told her, "everyone talks two languages."

After the ninth grade the bi-lingual children must leave the community schools and complete their education at boarding schools in the United States, in Europe, or if they want to stay closer to their families, they may go to a boarding high school in Lebanon or India. The company pays an allowance towards the secondary education of the children of its employees and provides transportation for them to visit their parents during summer vacations.

In many foreign countries and especially in remote areas where no American type school exists and it is impractical to organize one, children study at home with materials supplied by an American school which operates a correspondence service. The best known home instruction course for elementary school children is that of the Calvert School in Baltimore, Maryland. Since 1906 American parents going on overseas assignments have been taking along with them the textbooks, the work books, the spelling papers, even the pencils supplied by the Calvert School. In addition to the supplies for the children the course includes also a day-by-day guide for the parent or other adult who will be doing the tutoring. For those who want it, there is also supplied a criticism service which relates a child to a particular classroom teacher in the Baltimore school. Once a month the child's tests and essays are sent to his teacher. She grades the work and sends back grades to the child and a report to the teacher-parent. Certificates of promotion are given when a year's work has been completed. The standards are high and children who have completed a grade of Calvert work can expect to move into the next grade's work wherever they may go. There are now 5,000 pupils enrolled for Calvert Home Instruction. The vast majority of them are American children living in foreign countries. The directors of the school report that Calvert students are to be found in virtually every country in the world where Americans are living.

During a period when I used the fifth and sixth grade Calvert materials with one of our children I found that it worked out very well for me to spend only about two hours with her each morning. She spent another hour working alone. During the afternoons she had a variety of interesting experiences with other children. At one time she attended an informal art class taught by the wife of a Fulbright exchange student who was both trained and gifted in art education. For a while she was a member of a drama group, made up of children of several nations. Throughout one season we arranged for a local dance teacher to come to our house for classes to which other children were invited. For one very happy month she attended instruction in the art of Indian embroidering conducted for young friends by the wife of a United Nations social welfare specialist. She regularly participated in childrens' activities at the United States Information Library, entering at one time a United Nations doll-making contest which the library sponsored. Upon our return to this country she entered the seventh grade without difficulty.

I enjoyed the Calvert experience as much as Nancy did because it gave me such a good opportunity to spend some special time with her. However, some mothers find that it doesn't work out well for them to teach their own children. I have known of a few cases where mothers exchanged children during school hours. Occasionally a family will employ a tutor who works with the Calvert materials.

Some parents have felt that the home tutoring program was not the best answer for them because neither parent was free or felt competent to direct it. Others have felt that their children needed the stimulus of a classroom experience which an individual instruction course could not give.

In a good many places small groups of parents, who have wanted for their children a classroom experience which individual instruction couldn't provide and a curriculum more closely related to the American system than a national school curriculum might be, have gotten together to start a school of their own. The results have been satisfactory in many cases. Some of the large and now well established overseas American schools began this way.

In Curitiba, Brazil, there is a parent-operated school in the first stages of its organization. Some Americans were teaching their children separately at home, some were sending them to a crowded local language school operated by a church. Neither group was quite satisfied. So, they decided to pool their children, their financial resources, their teaching skills and their ideas about education.

There is now in operation a small school which is preparing the children for the higher levels of schooling which they expect to have, and it is providing for the community a good example of modern educational practices. The school which is non-sectarian and operates on a non-profit basis is open to all children in the community whose parents want them to participate in a school experience where emphasis on fundamental knowledge and skills is combined with a creative use of cultural resources. The only requirement is that an applicant have a competent use of the English language and that he is prepared to do the work at a given level.

The exception to the language requirement is in the case of those entering the kindergarten operated for three- to five-year-olds. A bilingual teacher is in charge of the kindergarten children. Thus children who are not competent in English can make a beginning and go on from there.

The school is directed by an American residing in the community who has both training and experience in elementary education. Some teachers are parents, some are other Americans in the community who have training and are interested in the purposes of the school. Several members of the staff are Brazilian. All students in the school study Portuguese, the language of the country. They are all exposed to the arts and the history of Brazil.

Because there are some Brazilian teachers on the faculty there is an indirect feedback to teachers in the national schools who frequently come to visit the school and who have on occasion invited one of the American teachers to visit a local school to demonstrate a project such as creative dramatics. Children from Brazilian schools as well as children of other national groups living in the community have been invited to come to the American school to share their dances or folk tales. American children who have lived in other Latin American countries are encouraged to report on their experiences.

Instead of setting themselves aloof, the Americans in Curitiba who have organized a separate school are now not only demonstrating their appreciation of the local people and their culture; they are also in a position where they may make an effective and a creative contribution to the local schools. When the children were in a national school their parents, being foreigners, felt that it was inappropriate for them to make any criticism of the school or suggestions for its improvement. They did not even feel free, unless they were asked, to offer their special skills. Now the kind of situation exists where there is an exchange of information between teachers in the community, including the Americans who proved when they employed local teachers that they did not feel superior or self sufficient. Some local children whose background is such that they can profitably study in English are having the benefits of the American school and are in turn providing a valuable link to the community for the American children.

While the American children are all studying the local language and learning a great deal about the local culture, they are continuing to do their basic learning in their own language and are covering the subject matter which they will need to have covered when they return to a school in the United States.

The cooperative school of Curitiba has received helpful advice from the Inter-American School Service (IASS) as have scores of other bi-national schools in Latin America. This Service, an agency of the American Council on Education, has been operating since 1943. It is available as a clearing house of financial assistance and educational advice for approximately 340 schools in Latin America of which fifty three are community sponsored bi-national schools with about 6,480 North American children in attendance.

The Inter-American School Service works with schools which have been established by North American private citizens, companies, or religious groups "for the purpose of supplementing the activities of national school systems at the elementary and secondary levels." It helps the schools "to improve their educational program; assists in recruiting administrators and teachers; advises on procedures to secure acceptability of their graduates by colleges and universities in the United States; provides information on a wide range of educational and professional problems; and determines grants in aid to non sectarian, community-owned, non profit schools which admit a substantial number of Latin American pupils. Through these activities, the Inter-American School Service seeks to promote mutual understanding, confidence, and respect among the peoples of the Americas."

Some of the particular services of the IASS relate to the accreditation of secondary schools, to assistance in connection with plans for new buildings, to the counseling of students and families who are expecting to reside in any of the Latin American countries and are seeking information about schools. Encouragement is given to the holding of regional and general conferences for school administrators and teachers. Three such conferences have been held in recent years. Encouragement is given also to the organization of regional associations of American schools through which in-service training courses and other benefits for teachers may be provided. A professional *Newsletter* is published from time to time giving current information and news about the schools, as well as developments affecting the IASS program.

Readers who would like to inquire about the school possibilities in a specific place in Latin America or those already in Latin America who are interested in knowing how they might go about organizing a community type school for their children may direct an inquiry to:

Inter-American School Service
American Council on Education
1785 Massachusetts Avenue
Washington 6, D. C.

Parents who want information about schools or school services in Asia, Africa, the Middle East and Europe may write to:

International Schools Foundation
147 East 50th Street
New York 22, New York

or

International Schools Foundation
2000 Massachusetts Avenue, N. W.
Washington 6, D. C.

In 1955 the International Schools Foundation (ISF) was organized to provide a coordinating base and to be a strengthening agency for the international and American sponsored schools in Europe, Asia, the Middle East, and Africa. Offices were established first in Washington and then in New York. An extensive field study was made to determine the kinds of educational needs of the schools in those areas.

The directors of the foundation see it as their function, not to organize schools for Americans abroad, but to help existing schools or those which are in the planning stage, to the end that the education they provide may be of good quality despite the difficulties under which they usually must operate. Services of the ISF are available for all categories of American or bi-national schools in the areas of the world for which the foundation is organized; but the foundation is particularly concerned to be of assistance to the established community schools and to the small parent-operated schools which are appearing in many foreign communities where groups of Americans now reside. This later group of schools represents a dedicated and hard working group of parents, but in most cases they are in desperate need of guidance as they undertake the complicated responsibilities of establishing and maintaining a good school.

The cooperative schools use locally available teachers wherever possible. (It is reported that in New Delhi a committee from the

American School is at the airport to meet every newly arriving American and swoops down upon any likely teacher before she has a chance to get herself involved in other commitments.) All of them, however, hope to have an administrator and a few experienced teachers recruited from the United States. It is very difficult for a school isolated in some far away country to find and employ qualified personnel from America. It is difficult for such a school board to review the publishers' offerings in text and library books. They need help in developing their curriculum and in checking the progress of their students. At all these points the International Schools Foundation is prepared to be of assistance.

In addition, by keeping in touch with the scattered American schools and letting them know about one another the foundation is helping to meet a very real psychological problem: a sense of professional loneliness. It has held regional school conferences in Baguio, in Bangkok, in New Delhi, and is currently arranging for conferences in Europe, Asia, and Africa, to give the school people a chance to communicate with one another, as well as to learn at first hand what kinds of assistance are available for them and how they can qualify for it.

The foundation recognizes that the important ingredients in the parent-operated schools are the creativeness and devotion of the parents, and it is the basis of its philosophy to help American parents abroad to help themselves to operate schools which are not only adequate but are outstanding examples of the very best in American education.

There are now ninety-two community or parent-sponsored schools in Europe, Asia, Africa, and the Middle East. Approximately 12,000 American children attend these schools.

At present there are several sources of governmental financial assistance for American schools overseas. These funds are derived from the sale of agricultural surpluses (Food for Peace program) and from the State Department's cultural and foreign aid programs. Eligibility for assistance is related primarily to the usefulness of the schools as demonstrations of American education and secondarily as a means of assisting in the education of the children of government personnel assigned overseas.

An example of a parent-operated school which has grown from a small and informal arrangement to a system serving some 1700 students is to be found at Taipei in Taiwan. About twelve years ago a handful of American parents related to the Economic Cooperation Program put their eight children together for classes in one of the homes. Before long other parents joined them and the American School Association was born. Parents automatically became voting members of the association when their children entered school. Land was acquired; buildings were erected. Today the association, through its elected board of directors, operates a program which takes a child from kindergarten to high school graduation. There are two elementary schools, one of them recently built is as modern as any new school at home. There is a combined junior-senior high school plant. The high school is accredited by an association of private schools in the United States and graduates have been accepted by the leading universities in America. A recent graduate was accepted at all three of the outstanding engineering schools to which he applied.

The Taipei American School system has a professionally trained director, recruited in the United States. The rest of the staff is from the large group of Americans living in Taipei or from American trained Chinese nationals. Americans assisting the school are generally transferred out of Taipei after a few years of service but others keep coming in who have specialized skills and a willingness to teach or to work in some administrative capacity with the school.

A testing and guidance service is provided in the Taipei system, and those approaching graduation are assisted with college applications. The oriental studies program has been strengthened through the years, and students in the school have a variety of associations with the students in the national schools. The athletic program provides one area of contact because the high school teams (basketball and soccer are both locally popular) regularly play against Chinese school teams.

There are no racial or religious or national entrance restrictions. It is required only that an applicant have a competent use of the English language and that he be able to pay the tuition fees of about $300 per year. Of the seventeen hundred students in the three schools, about two hundred are Chinese and between fifty and seventy five are foreigners other than Americans.

A problem exists for Chinese students who attend the high school because, following as it does an American curriculum, the school cannot offer all the courses that are required in the national schools. A graduate of the American high school may find that he cannot be accepted by a Chinese university because he is deficient in certain required subjects. This necessarily keeps the percentage of the Chinese students low. Most Chinese graduates of the school hope to do college work in the United States.

Both because of the English language requirement and the relatively high tuition fee, the local children attending the Taipei American schools come largely from wealthy and well-educated families. While

American parents do not feel that it is fair to urge large numbers of Chinese to attend the American schools considering the handicap it might put upon them if they want to pursue higher studies in their own community, they appreciate the presence of even a small group of Chinese students and feel that they make a contribution out of proportion to their numbers.

Most American schools abroad would be happy to have local children in attendance, but it is not always possible to include them because some governments look with disfavor upon the attendance of their nationals at foreign schools, while others have laws which strictly forbid the foreign schools to accept children of the country.

In a country where large groups of foreign immigrants are residing a government may be apprehensive lest foreign schools encourage the continuation of foreign loyalties and delay the nationalization of a community. So they have laws to prohibit the organization of any foreign school. In such a place Americans who maintain a school for their children may need to do it informally and perhaps call it a children's center instead of a school. There is no instance where American parents who care to do it have not been able to work out a suitable arrangement for the education of their children.

Even in countries where the government has raised no objection to the establishment of American schools and to the enrollment of local children at them, the local parents may not permit their children to attend. Sometimes they fear that in the foreign environment the children will be educated away from their own families and their own community. They may be reluctant to have their children exposed to the social patterns related to American co-education. They may not be ready to accept the modern practices of American schools. For these reasons American schools cannot all be bi-cultural, even so, many American teachers are finding a way to bring the local culture into their schools and increasingly the local teachers are looking with interest to see how the American schools are operating.

The way in which small groups of American parents have organized and operated schools for their children in scores of foreign countries is a truly inspiring story. Sometimes they have had professionally trained educators in their ranks, but many times they have had to pull together a program and a curriculum in bits and pieces with whatever help they could find. In some cases they have been able to get substantial assistance from government or foundation sources. In others they have had to be completely self supporting. In every case where a cooperative school has succeeded in giving good education to its pupils, a group of zealous parents has given countless hours of constructive assistance in administration, in program planning, and in teaching. And they have done it willingly!

A few years ago in Teheran the Iranian foreign office gave permission for an American school to be established. The American Ambassador appointed a school board of representative Americans and they set to work to organize the educational talents of the Americans in the community. After a short while there was discussion as to whether or not the school should continue under parent direction or whether the Defense Department which has a large group of personnel in Teheran, should be asked to take over the school and operate it for all the Americans. A meeting of parents was called. The room was crowded. Parents who had no illusions about how much work and effort was required to run a good school voted nine to one to continue to operate as a parent-sponsored school.

The school now has 700 pupils in nine grades (older children attend a Presbyterian mission high school); it has a faculty of 39 people with three teachers employed from the United States. There is a budget of $35,000. There are 4,000 volumes in the library. Persian and French are taught as foreign languages, and U. S. standardized tests are given regularly. Iranian students are forbidden by their government to attend the school, but sports events bring the local students and the American students together, and the school serves as a demonstration center in a country where education is making rapid advances.

An American who has worked closely with the Teheran American School for a number of years says it has been fortunate to have broad community participation and many people have contributed their talents and have had a voice in school affairs who could not have been able to do so if the Army had been asked to come in and run the school for them.

Schools For Older Children

Some special factors enter the picture when parents are making educational choices for children above the elementary level. The college career of a ten year old may not be affected significantly by the fact that he has or doesn't have Virginia history at that level, whether he goes to an American or German or Japanese school or whether, in fact, he is actually in a formal school for a couple of years. But it will make a good deal of difference what he is doing academically when he is sixteen.

Parents are inclined to weigh their decision more carefully by the time a child is in the tenth grade. Many people overseas are now situated near a good American high school. The school may be accredited by one of the secondary school associations of our country and credits may be transferred to a high school in the United States or may be offered for entrance into a college. Some parents of teen agers find themselves near an outstanding English, French, or German secondary school and feel that these schools will prepare their children for college entrance examinations even though the children may not earn the standard number of American high school credits.

In some cases high school age people are having the benefits of living overseas with their parents in places where suitable schooling is not available and are managing to keep up their high school work by following correspondence courses. A number of American universities have extension services for students at the secondary level. Students enroll in a given number of courses and upon the satisfactory completion of work receive credits towards a high school certificate. In some cases a parent will supervise the work. Sometimes a tutor is employed. Occasionally a tutor is used only for highly specialized courses. It might be valuable, for instance, to have as a science tutor a college instructor who might be permitted to take the student into his laboratory. Language courses might profitably be supervised by a person found in the country for whom the language is a native one. Some well motivated students work independently and seek out help only when they feel the need of it. Information about high school extension courses might be secured from:

Dr. Gayle B. Childs
Class and Correspondence Instruction
Extension Division
University of Nebraska
Lincoln, Nebraska

or from:

Extension Division
University of California
Berkeley, California

I have known cases where a young person has used correspondence courses for the first or second year of high school and then has attended a boarding school in the area for the completion of his high school work. In many cases an American teen-ager goes to an overseas boarding school for his complete high school course.

A few overseas high schools with boarding facilities are listed below.

A number of them have been in operation for many years and have standards so well known in educational centers in the United States that their graduates have no trouble getting into the colleges of their choice. All of these schools have limited capacity and applicants sometimes find that they must go onto a waiting list until a vacancy occurs. Some of them must operate on a priority basis, giving preference to children of a specific group for whom the school may be endowed or by whom it may be directed.

Cameroun	American School (Evangelical Lutheran) Meiganga, via Douala, Cameroun, W. Africa Principal, Miss Olive Touson
Chile	Santiago College (Methodist, girls only) Casilla 130-D (Calle Lota 2465) Santiago, Chile Principal, Miss Elizabeth C. Mason
Colombia	Marymount School (Roman Catholic, girls only) Apartado, Aéreo, 1912 Barranquilla, Colombia Director, Rev. Mother Vianney Steuart
	Marymount School (Roman Catholic, girls only) Apartado, Aéreo, 6838 Bogota, Colombia Director, Rev. Mother du Rosaire McNulty
Egypt	American School (United Presbyterian) 51 Rue Schutz, Alexandria, Egypt, U. A. R. Principal, George W. Meloy
India	Kodaikanal School (interdenominational) Madurai District, Kodaikanal, Madras State, India Principal, Mr. Herbert L. Krause
	Woodstock School (interdenominational) Landour, Mussoorie, U. P., India Principal, Mr. Samuel R. Burgoyne
Japan	Canadian Academy (Inter-Board Protestant Missions Committee) Nada-Ku, Kobe, Japan Principal, Mr. Douglas Bishop

Lebanon	American Community School Beiruit, Lebanon Principal, Mr. Dwight E. Knox
Malaya	American School (community school) 15 Rochalie Drive Singapore, 10 Principal, Mr. James S. Aven
Morocco	American School of Tangier (private, non-profit) 2 Rue de Belgique, Tangier, Morocco, North Africa Director, Mr. Robert Smith Shea (boarding facilities for limited number only)
Philippines	Brent School (Episcopal Church) P. O. Box 35, Baguio City, P. I. Principal, The Rev. A. L. Griffiths
Switzerland	International School of Geneva (international community school) 62 Route de Chene, Geneva Switzerland Co-Principals, Dr. Aleck H. Forbes and M. F. Roquette
Taiwan	Morrison Academy (Interdenominational) Taichung, Taiwan Principal, Thomas J. Means

I know, because I faced it, that an American parent, female gender, does not always find it easy to decide to send a sixteen year old to a boarding school in a foreign country or out of one foreign country and into a second one to attend a school no one in the family had ever seen or even heard about previously, especially if the school is in an isolated part of a high range of mountains. I have had many occasions to be grateful that my uncertainties were overridden both by a sixteen year old and by her father. I survived; and the experience of attending Woodstock School in North India was most rewarding for our eldest child and for a sister who followed her the next year.

Academically, they couldn't have had a firmer or more stimulating preparation for college work. For one hundred and seven years Woodstock has been getting young people ready to enter either American or British universities. There is a highly qualified faculty of about thirty-five full time members for a student enrollment of four-hundred-sixty.

There is a library of nine thousand volumes. Instruction is in English but Hindi, French, German, and Latin are taught as foreign languages.

Socially, they had an opportunity to associate happily with boys and girls of their own age who represented about thirty different racial, religious, or national groups. Physically they thrived on a diet of plain food and a daily climb of several hundred feet up and down the staircase trails that linked the girls dormitory with the school halls.

Students who want to take American College Entrance examinations are able to arrange to have them sent to an educational institution in their area, where they will be given. An inquiry might be addressed to:

College Entrance Examination Board
Educational Testing Service
Princeton, New Jersey

Children vis-a-vis Community

American parents who move into a foreign community frequently find that their children often break the ice and make it possible for a whole family to become acquainted with their new neighbors more quickly. Little children especially are usually natural and not afraid of making a culturally wrong move so they smile and say "hello," and even the most formal person is inclined to respond. Many times it is the curious or friendly American child who brings adults together for a conversation in a park or public building or on a railway train. Occasionally such a casual introduction may lead to a rewarding friendship, but even if it does not go beyond a brief encounter it may have provided a mutually interesting exchange of information and have been the source of a good impression of the national group which each party represents.

Families with children are likely to establish an informal give and take with local families more quickly than others who haven't the good excuse of children to move outside the formal patterns. I know that in foreign countries where we have lived we have sometimes had in our homes humble people of the country who might never have felt at ease to come to a formal gathering but who came comfortably on a family basis. We have also, because of our children, been able to entertain informally prominent people (both nationals and people of other countries) whom we might otherwise never have had the opportunity of knowing personally.

When our teen-aged children were enjoying conversation with some

English young people at a swimming pool one morning I said to their mother, "Would you bring your children over to our house one day. We have some American films they might enjoy."

"And could I bring my husband along, too?" was her reply. At the agreed upon hour an old car with a man in a comfortable sports shirt at the wheel drove up to our front door. The driver who had left his chauffeur, his limousine, and all the appurtenances of his office at home was the Ambassador of Great Britain to the country in which we were residing. We gave him and his delightful family fried chicken, hot biscuits, and cherry pie. After supper we all saw a color film of the Tanglewood Music Festival.

Children frequently are responsible for leading their parents into discoveries about the community itself which they might never have made except that they took the time to escort the children on a sight-seeing jaunt. Older children who can wander around on their own sometimes bring back reports and descriptions which may spark an interest in a closer identification with the community on the part of their elders who might be inclined just to do their work and take the community for granted. Sometimes gregarious American youngsters make friends on every corner and, in the good old American way, often keep open house for local children.

I know of one case where American parents, eager to demonstrate friendliness, had encouraged their children to make friends with local children and then were wondering how they could possibly cope with the ensuing problems. The first problem arose when the head servant of the household put his foot down. "These children," he said, "are children of the alleys. They do not know about honesty. I cannot be responsible for their being on Master's premises." Next, the master was dumbfounded when he learned that as many as thirty bottles of coca cola had been used to refresh the visitors on just one day. Then the young host was bewildered when, after every one's insistence that the hospitality operation be kept in reasonable limits, he attempted to meet his friends at the gate and to admit only those who were known to him by name. Soulful eyes pleaded as the boys spoke with a mixture of their own language and of English, "But this one must come. He is my other best friend and these are his little brothers" or "But my cousin wants also to play with the friendly American." The last I heard the parents still held on to their belief in international friendship but had eliminated refreshments and had limited visiting hours to a time when they themselves could give some direction and supervision to the play.

It is gratifying that so many American children are free from a snobbery which would lead them to shun the children of the streets or the children of servants. But congenial and important as the casual contacts are, it seems to many that it would be too bad if their children have no contacts in a foreign country with children who are in one way or another their cultural peers. Sometimes this can come about by association in a bi-national school, sometimes it happens as families become acquainted through professional or business contacts. It may happen at a swimming pool or a sailing club.

One of our children made friendships with young people of the country through associations at a youth group of a church. A number of teen age local children who attended an English language school, came also to a church where the English language was used. Under the friendly supervision of an adult sponsor the mixed group of young people went together on picnics and swimming parties and hikes.

In some places an association of nationals and Americans plan projects designed to bring older children together. Two of our teen-age daughters had a pleasant time with Burmese young people at a weekly square dance held on the paved tennis court of an American home. The dances had been arranged by the Burma-American Association.

In a few communities an integrated social program has been inaugurated only after American young people, unoccupied and unguided, have created a bad name for themselves in the community and the parents have stepped in to do something about it. Noisy and aimless "horsing around" is not understood in most foreign communities and in some cases it has gotten out of hand.

One report has come in from a foreign capital where a few American young people whose energies were not being channeled, drifted into local gangs and were involved in escapades more serious than the usual tearing about. American fathers got together and organized a teen canteen which not only helped to provide a wholesome outlet for the energies of their own children but was gradually accepted by sophisticated local families as a proper place for their children to join the Americans for fun.

Parents are neglectful if they do not manage to convey to their children an understanding of their responsibilities as guests in a foreign country. This guidance in good manners must begin with little children and continue all the way to those of high school years, otherwise our children may, in ignorance or carelessness, conduct themselves in ways which will reflect unfavorably upon the reputation of their parents and of all the Americans in the community. Sometimes it need be only a reminder that local people are not to be excluded from the usual courtesies which the children have been taught to observe.

Other times it may be necessary to help them learn some of the mores of the country so that they can make the moves or give the kind of responses which the local people understand.

I remember one American who was overseas for the special causes of democracy. He was hard working and seemed sincere. His wife shared his interests, and the two of them were away from home most of the time. They were out making friends for democracy but young Billy left to his own devices and to servants who had no control over him, terrorized his neighborhood, teaching neither friendliness nor democracy. He learned the local swear words and hurled them with rocks at every passing car. He managed to lift the lid off of a neighbor's well and tossed in rotten fruits and trash. He was so rude to servants at other homes that American mothers felt compelled to take Billy to his home and tell him to stay there if they needed to leave when he had come to play. What a difference it would have made if his mother had given more attention and more guidance to her lonely and neglected child!

In European communities American children sometimes need to learn to behave a bit more formally in relation to grown ups than most of our children do these days. Without imposing a Victorian set of manners or without spoiling the spontaneity which is frequently the charming hallmark of an American child, parents can explain to them that they are living in a community where behavior patterns are more standardized and more formal than they are in America and that their good will may more easily be understood if they go through the accepted motions whenever the family is visiting or entertaining guests of the country.

Some of these gestures of courtesy which American children learn to make will be left in the country where they are appropriately used. Others of them will stay with our children for a while, or for a lifetime, as gracious and effective expressions of a kindly feeling towards people—a feeling which has been strengthened and enriched during their months and years abroad.

Chapter IX

THE WORLD AROUND US

The Shwe Dagon Pagoda in Rangoon is one of the most strikingly beautiful and culturally significant shrines in the world, yet a well-educated and socially prominent Westerner, who had lived within sight of its magnificent, gold-encrusted dome for nearly twenty years, told me that she had never once taken off her shoes (as one must respectfully do) and gone into it. Another western woman, also a long-time resident of Burma and one who has a special interest in religion, told me that she had never attended a Buddhist wedding, but wished she might.

In the first instance, the colonial-minded lady thought the shoe business was undignified and wouldn't bother. In the latter case, a missionary family busy with Christian friends had never become sufficiently close to a Buddhist family to be invited to an event as common in an overwhelmingly Buddhist community as a Buddhist wedding. Neither of these women is a typical Westerner in Burma today, where with colonialism a closed chapter, there are many evidences of a friendly give and take.

When my husband and I went to a university campus in China in 1932, we lived for a while in a missionary residence which, years before, had been designed so that Chinese guests who came on business or to make formal calls could enter a reception room detached from the rest of the house and furnished according to the Chinese fashion. One explanation was that in the early days of the missionary enterprise this arrangement was devised because the Chinese in that northern section wore padded garments in the winter, never heating their houses, and that they would be uncomfortable in the living quarters which the missionaries kept at least a little warm. Others said that the low and cushioned chairs of the Americans would not seem dignified to the more formal Chinese. Another report was that the missionaries, often so far removed from medical doctors, and without the modern drugs, couldn't risk the exposure of their children to visitors who might be carrying small pox or some other disease. In any case, I am glad that by the time we reached the Cheeloo campus rooms like that were being used for game rooms or for storage, and Chinese and Westerners were working and playing together with mutual respect and appreciation.

Americans who go overseas and keep themselves separated from the people and places around them, not only deprive themselves of rare opportunities for adventure and enrichment, but they also give to the local people an impression of aloofness which is unfortunate.

The Market Place

Even transient visitors in a foreign country should find their way to the local markets, not necessarily because they want to buy things, but because a market is such a fascinating place. One can see the common products of the country and the common people off their guard. A North American recently returned from Mexico city tells of his great disappointment that the pressures of a conference prevented him from seeing more of the places of special interest, but he said "I did walk through one of the food markets, and I want you to know it is one of the most fabulous places in the world."

The Mexico City market he visited is a modern one, with fruits and vegetables displayed in a spacious hall and kept under sanitary conditions. In some places a market may be a group of stalls under a mat shed or rows of neatly spaced wares spread out on the bare ground. In parts of North Burma the market moves from place to place on a regular rotation so that it may be market day in Kalaw on Tuesday and the market is somewhere else on the following day. The markets there operate on a five day cycle. When sunset comes at the end of a given market day the baskets and bundles of commodities are put on public buses and the market moves away. The occasion of a market day is of such central importance in the life of a community that all other plans revolve around it including the designation of the day to be observed as Sabbath.

The floating bazaar was another interesting phenomena in northern Burma. Way out in the center of Inle Lake the people who live in stilt houses and cultivate farms on floating islands buy necessities and small luxuries from traders who carry their wares around in boats. We are still using straw hats which we bought by bargaining across the heads of occupants of several intervening boats.

Many families lured by the fascination of a market will get up early on a first morning in a foreign city intent on exploring a local bazaar only to find that a small market has come to them. On the sidewalk outside the hotel doors they will find that peddlars may have their wares spread out just to serve the hotel guests. I remember seeing shaggy-haired Tibetans with charming bits of copper ware and jewelry displayed on an old worn cloth in front of a fashionable hotel in New Delhi.

The temptation to start buying things immediately is one which few can resist. More than one returnee from a foreign assignment has said to me "Tell people not to spend all of their money the first week." The newcomer who makes a look-see exploration with his pocket book at home is generally better able to resist things which may catch his eyes at first but might not seem so attractive after he had been in the country longer. This is especially true in a part of the world where the art forms, the color combinations, or the materials are quite different from the ones people have known at home.

I have inherited a large grass-linen dinner cloth which I bought for my mother-in-law soon after we arrived in Peiping. A good many times I have rejected it when I have looked in the linen chest for a table cloth for a special occasion. The linen is still beautiful, the cross-stitch work still exquisite, but the colors and design are so showy that I generally look on for something more simple. I learned after I had bought it that the shop where I found it catered primarily to tourists and that for the same amount of money I could have bought a cloth of even better quality with graceful chrysanthemums embroidered all in white or with water lilies in pale yellow or with sprays of drooping wisteria in a very pale blue.

Newcomers need a little time not only to acquire a taste for local merchandise but to learn to judge the values of things and to gain experience in learning how to agree on a price in those places where bargaining is the practice. In many places one may see a sign on a shop window reading ONE PRICE STORE. In most cases this is a bona-fide notice and may be depended upon. In fact, shopkeepers who are maintaining a fixed price store and look upon it as a progressive step indicative of their status in the modern business world may be offended if a foreigner, who has been warned about bargaining, tries to talk a price down.

Next door to the one price store may be a shopkeeper who expects to talk price. In some countries only the open stall bazaars now follow the old bargaining procedures, but in a few countries the law requires that even the itinerate peddlar display a wholesale cost price and a fixed sale price. There is little chance for bargaining except in cases where the merchant is pressed for money or the product is ripening too fast and he is willing to take a loss in the accepted margin of gain.

In many places quantity buying may reduce the price per unit, but when the products are handmade the price may go up instead of down for people who want more than one of some item. I remember once in an Asian market after I had agreed on a price for a small basket I said to the shopkeeper "Very well, then I shall take fifteen." He made noises of dismay telling me that my extravagant buying would leave his shelves embarrassingly empty and nothing could alter his decision that one cent should be added to the cost of each extra basket.

When bargaining still exists, it can be a spirited exercise in both stubbornness and flexibility. The customer generally starts. The first move is crucial. If he makes it too high his opponent knows that he is inexperienced. If he makes it unreasonably low he may insult the dignity of the shopkeeper and so put him in a bad mood for debate. Sometimes a compromise is agreed upon quickly. Sometimes it takes a long while, and if the expenditure of any sizeable amount of money is at stake it may take place over cups of tea or coffee or wine. It is said of the Chinese merchants that when they buy from one another they sit at a table, each with a hand pressed on an arm inside the sleeve of the other, giving no facial signs of readiness to come to a bargain. The whole transaction is done through pressure on an arm by fingers so that no outsider ever knows what the final figure was.

If a customer in a market can't get the price he wants he may move to go or actually walk away. If the merchant has spoken his lowest price he will let the customer go with a shrug, but if he is still open to suggestion he may wait until the stubborn one has walked a few paces and then run after him pressing the item into his hands with an "All right, I give it away to you." There is a barrage of complaint if the customer says "Oh I didn't want it anyway" and tries to walk away from his own top price. Having stated it as a price he is honor bound to pay it if the shopkeeper agrees to accept it.

There is no fixed rule about how buying and selling is done in any area. It differs from country to country, from city to village within a country, and unless there are state laws it may differ from shop to shop.

The everyday things to be bought in another country may be of great importance to the Americans who are anxious to live as much as possible on the products of a country. The luxury items and especially the old art pieces and the remnants of an earlier civilization can be interesting and valuable acquisitions if they are bought with care and for a good reason.

Unfortunately, a certain number of Americans in every country fall victims of the buying fever. They start at first buying souvenirs or buying in relation to a hobby and then, being lonely or bored, they buy as if they were addicted to buying and just couldn't stop. An American in a Mid-East city told a visitor recently that she had bought so much she ran out of space to put things and now had rented a room in a warehouse to keep the things she goes on buying day after day after day. Another compulsive shopper said that once she acquired a few pieces of fine jewelry she lost all interest in everything else in the country. Nothing excites or lures her now but the chance to see and preferably to buy another valuable ring or bracelet or uncut stone. Instead of letting the market places of foreign cities open to them new tastes, new contacts, and new opportunities for cosmopolitan living, these people have let themselves be drugged into a total absorption with things.

The Countryside

Any country offers its foreign guests a chance to observe at leisure the terrain of its countryside, the architecture of its cities and its villages, and the landmarks of its history and of its changing culture. Some places have more spectacular or more satisfying scenery than other places have. Some may be described as exotic, a few might fairly be called forbidding, but there isn't any place of which it can be said "There is nothing, simply nothing to see here."

The seeing of the new place frequently becomes both a pastime and serious project for Americans living overseas. They hear about the special places and go to them—the temples of Kyoto, the ruins of Ankorwat, the wailing wall of Jerusalem, the ancient capital at Pagan, the Acropolis, the pyramids, the Black Forest, St. Peter's, the Louvre, the Tower of London, the murals on the walls of the University of Mexico, Macchu Picchu, the inimitable Taj Mahal. No list could include all of the outstanding places those living in different parts of the world are generally careful not to miss. But an American abroad should also keep his eyes open for glimpses of the ordinary places. His experience in a foreign country will be the poorer if he ever gets to the place where he rides or walks along and doesn't remember to look.

One time or another I have read a good many books about China but none is more vivid in my memory than one called *Chinese Characteristics* which I read some thirty years ago. It was written by a Dr. Arthur Henderson Smith who lived and worked in China until he was a very old man. The book which became somewhat of a classic was written not at the end of his distinguished career but near the beginning. He had been there only a few months when he began to write down the descriptions of the people around him. In later years when people would ask him where and how he learned so much, it is said that he would smile, wet the tip of one finger and hold it out in front of his eye. He was dramatizing the fact that in such a manner he had noiselessly pushed peep holes in many paper covered windows and so had been able to put his eye where he could observe the common people in their daily rounds.

A newcomer's focus is generally sharper in the first few months than it ever will be later on so it is well for him to find as many kinds of peep holes as he can. Chances are if he acquires the habit of watching and looking, the habit will stay with him and he will continue to see things of interest and of importance until the day he leaves. Many feel that they can see only with a camera in their hands. The camera certainly has its place on an overseas tour, especially for those who want to be able to share the experience with relatives and friends at home. But those who want the shape of things in their adopted country to be printed clearly in their memories need only to start out with their eyes open and to look long and deeply even at the things which become most familiar, until objects and actions take on meaning as well as form.

Like the ordinary places, the ordinary people are always worth seeing. In countries where there has been little racial mixing people may at first seem to be all alike. But gradually as one begins to see more of them, and especially if he is able to use the language and converse with a great variety of people he begins to learn that they differ as individuals even though they may all share common characteristics and common traditions. Some are more lazy or more energetic, some are more dependable or more fickle. Some are sturdy. Some are frail. Once an American begins to see these human differences he stops saying "all the Thais" or "all the Greeks" and sees them as individuals. This discovery is a fundamental one and each foreigner must make it in a new country for himself.

He generally discovers also that even in a country where the people seem homogenous they have emerged from different tribal or regional groups and so to a greater or lesser degree carry certain differing characteristics or customs or loyalties. It is good to know about these background factors because it may explain what might otherwise seem like baffling actions or attitudes. One family serves hot curry; another makes it mild. Mr. M teams up well with Mr. P and Mr. O but collaboration is at a standstill when Mr. N is brought in. The students from the North are phlegmatic; the ones from the South are eager for a strike.

Sometimes the observant American learns to spot the tribal or regional background by certain physical characteristics or mannerisms. When he has progressed this far then he is able to identify with a person of the country even more completely. He sees him as a national, as of some special part of the nation, as well as an individual with human fears and feelings. By this time he can say "just like me" because he knows that he too has the human kind of strengths and weaknesses, that he belongs with pride to a country, but that he also is a boastful Texan or a stubborn Missourian or a fighting Irishman from New York.

There is a further stage in person-to-person understanding. It comes to those who, even though they are able to think of people of another country as individuals, can go beyond the "just like me" stage and can look for and see that difference itself—as it shows up both between and within cultures—is a factor to be recognized and respected. It is essential to get to the place where we are able to see that people who are in some ways unlike us are human just as we are and that they have group characteristics and loyalties just as we have. It is the mark of real maturity, however, when a man or woman can admit that there are cultural differences—sometimes very profound ones—and can be free enough not to let the fact of difference be the determining factor in the way he judges or values people. For the one who attains this kind of freedom from cultural egocentricity, every common man he meets on the streets of a foreign country will be uncommonly interesting, and the men and women he is fortunate enough to know personally will not be held at a distance by any kind of an artificial barrier.

Jerry and I were fortunate when in 1932 we left the shores of our homeland for the first time and were seated in the dining room on a trans-Pacific steamship with an elderly woman who had lived in China for many years. Day after day she told us about the people with whom we would be working. We could not help but sense the high regard she had for the Chinese as a race of people, the warm and deeply personal concern she had for various individuals whom she and her late husband had known through the years. But the thing we remember about her most vividly and for which we shall always be grateful is that as she talked with us she made no effort to pretend that there were no cultural differences between Chinese and Americans. She pointed out many of these differences to us, telling us how interesting some of them were, showing us in what ways it seemed to her that the differences effected the attitudes and conduct of the people we would be living among. Never once did she express a judgment about the people which was based on a point of difference from herself or her own race. At times when we have been tempted to conclude that some different kind of person was good or bad, worthy or unworthy just because of some racial, cultural, or personal difference we have remembered Mrs. Brewster and been glad that we made our first crossing from one cultural community to another with her.

The Open Door Policy

Carefully observing people of another country is a helpful way of understanding what they are like, but it is at best only a detached kind of knowledge which one gains in this way. I am sure that while Dr. Smith was making detailed observations of strangers he was also availing himself of every opportunity to know Chinese people as friends. It is only when we are able to leave the sidelines and actually move into the arena of personal encounter that we can know what men of another country and culture are like.

The most fortunate Americans are those who manage before their tour of duty in a foreign country is ended to have a number of friends who not only accept their invitations but who also open their own doors. The achievement of family give and take may come slowly in any country. In European societies it may be necessary to wait for proper introductions before proposing social intercourse. In some cases the social status of the national will have something to do with his willingness to make friends with newcomers. But if an American is not too hasty and if he invites people of the country to the kind of gatherings where they are most likely to be comfortable (in some places this would be a formal dinner, in many places it would be a small tea party or a simple family meal) he generally finds that they come and that both hosts and guests enjoy the occasion.

In parts of the world where English is not widely used, women especially may be reluctant to come to an English speaking home unless the hosts speak their language. (This is one more reason why Americans, particularly women, should study the language of the people with whom they live. National men with whom Americans are associated overseas have frequently studied English but in many cases their wives haven't.) If one can at least say a few words of greeting in the national language, then a guest will feel happier. A hostess needs to make a special effort to communicate with a guest whose language she does not know. It is possible with gestures and smiles to indicate personal interest, but the best thing to do is to make sure that at least one woman guest is present who knows both the national language and English. The bi-lingual guest could be seated near the one who understands no English to keep her company and also to interpret conversation with the hostess and other English speaking guests. It is a mistake to assume that a guest who speaks no English does not understand our language. Sometimes they understand but are fearful of making a mistake so refuse to speak in the presence of English speaking people. Good manners would, in any case, restrain a host family from making personal or inappropriate remarks in the presence of any guest.

In some of the less modern countries women do not go out with their husbands because their husbands prefer that they stay at home. This may be related to cultural patterns, or in some cases where women are not sheltered a modern man may feel ashamed of his uneducated wife and is unwilling for her to appear with him in public. American women occasionally find that local women enjoy coming for an informal morning coffee when no men are present, and if the language barrier can be eased either by the hostess or by a guest interpreter, the women may have a delightful time observing an American household and conversing about subjects like food and children which they understand.

Americans often ask me what kind of food they should serve the people of the country where they are living. My own practice has always been to serve American food because I know that local people are generally curious about it just as I would be about theirs. Also, no matter how long I lived in another country I would never feel qualified to judge whether or not I (or my cook) was preparing a national dish so that it would seem good or proper to my guests.

At holidays I try to serve the traditional American dishes because they are interesting to local people. I have made heart-shaped cookies and told people about the valentine theme. I have served cherry pie on George Washington's birthday. We've made pumpkin pies and invited people to appear in costumes for Halloween. It has always been interesting to find the local fruits and vegetables to fill a cornucopia for a large Thanksgiving table to which both Americans and nationals have been invited. We have made dozens of Christmas cookies and bundled them up with red ribbons to distribute to national friends.

Our guests have been interested in knowing about things we serve which are regional favorites back home—New England clam chowder, Boston brown bread, southern fried chicken and hot biscuits, *chili con carne* from the southwest. When we have explained that a food prepared in a certain fashion is characteristic of one or another section of our country then national guests have told us how food preparation may differ in different parts of their country. In Asia, especially, the men seem to take a good deal of interest in food preparation, and I have frequently had a highly placed official tell me in great detail the way he thinks prawns are best fixed, or the kinds of foods that should be served together.

I have noticed that nationals are always interested in any dishes which we have prepared in our manner out of products common in their land. They like to go home and try new dishes just as we do. They feel discouraged if we always serve them foreign imports, but if a tasty food is made from supplies in their market then they are very pleased and often ask how it is done. I gave a recipe for coconut macaroons to scores of Burmese guests. They had plenty of coconuts and they had sweetened condensed milk in their shops but many of them did not know that they could so easily be combined into a delicious confection.

There are two things I always consider when I am planning for a meal which will include guests who are not American. The first thing is that I make every effort to learn in advance if the guests have any special food habits related to religious or cultural practices. If the group is to be small then I plan a meal which all guests can eat. For instance, we once entertained Brahmins who were vegetarians except for the fact that they would eat eggs. So we had creamed eggs with rice and plenty of vegetables. If a group is to be large with buffet service, I might have two main dishes so that guests could make a choice. If we were serving fried chicken which I knew some local guests would enjoy I would have a large platter of deep fried okra for vegetarian guests. I was particular to show this platter to guests I knew could not take meat. Even when I served two main dishes I would be careful that neither dish would be seriously offensive to any guest. I never served pork in any form, if I knew that we had a Muslim or Orthodox Jewish guest.

Most devout Buddhists and Muslims will not drink alcoholic beverages. We happen not to serve them, in any case, so our fruit drinks or tea or coffee have always been acceptable in situations where abstainers were present. But it has often occurred to me that Americans who regularly serve wines and liquors might well give some special thought to the drinks they offer to local people who do not take the alcoholic ones. I have felt sorry for a teetotaler who has had to consume some of the insipid substitutes offered them by Americans who serve only the finest brands of sherry, brandy, or Scotch. Sometimes they have their cooks concoct something that is mostly fruit coloring and sugar water; sometimes they buy locally bottled drinks that are made from artificially flavored water that has been charged a little bit.

Natural fruit juice is always the happiest choice to offer a non-drinker, lime juice with just enough sugar and the right amount of water, lemonade made from fresh lemons, or orange juice, grape juice, apple juice. American soft drinks are popular many places overseas. When Americans serve ginger ale or one of the "colas" they generally find their national guest pleased to drink them, though older guests may prefer the uncarbonated fruit juice.

I also think about whether or not the food I am planning to serve to local guests is likely to please their taste even though it may not be unacceptable from a religious or social point of view. In some cultures people like their food greasy or highly spiced. Others prefer food with little fat or very bland. Some people are accustomed to sweet foods, others find even a little sweet too much. If I know these things, at least the first time a national guest is coming I try to choose the kind of American dishes most likely to suit his taste. Later on they may be more ready to try the things which are different from their own foods.

The entertainment of guests should also follow an understanding of the kind of activity they are most likely to enjoy. People who are fun loving might enjoy parlor games or they might like to learn an American square dance. If people are sophisticated they would be likely to enjoy being grouped for conversation and might like to listen to musical recordings after dinner. If children are included it is wise to see that suitable play equipment is ready for them. In many places it is possible for Americans to borrow films and sometimes records which may be used for home entertaining from the United States Information Service Library.

The one warning I would give to Americans who want to make friends with the people of the country where they live is to avoid the big-party pattern. The big party has its functions, but getting acquainted personally with people to whom one is a foreigner can not be accomplished when one has a room full of people circulating this way and that with hands holding glasses and eyes roving for familiar faces. It may take many more parties, but entertaining local people is certainly more rewarding if it is done with few enough people and in a sufficiently relaxed atmosphere for a genuine kind of rapport to take place.

Many Americans feel that they are making friends and that nationals seem to respond happily when they extend invitations, but they are disappointed that many times the nationals never extend an invitation to them. There are a number of reasons why this so often happens. One of the most common reasons, perhaps, is that any American home seems elegant to people in many other countries and they are reluctant to bring their American friends into dwellings which they feel are so humble in comparison. Most Americans would go happily and would not be in the least disturbed by the size of a house or the simplicity of its furnishings but the national sometimes has a hard time bringing himself to the place where he can let them come.

In some cases it is a matter of money. The national would be unwilling to entertain Americans unless he served the kind of feast food which he couldn't afford. Americans would probably be much more interested in the everyday kind of food than in the rich or expensive dishes encountered at official dinners or in public restaurants. In many places the host would not feel that he was doing his duty as a host if the food he served were not special so he doesn't invite until he can afford to buy the makings of a feast. Those who are invited to the homes of people whose economic resources are very limited are often torn between pleasure that the host was willing to ask them and pain that the cost to him would be so great.

Sometimes Americans who know a local family may stop by to see them without an invitation, making sure that it isn't meal time and feeling assured the family is not likely to be upset. They may go dressed informally just to leave some flowers or fruits from a tree in their garden. Sometimes a gesture like this is all the local family needs to convince them that the Americans would not be unwilling to take them as they are, and an invitation for a family meal may be forthcoming.

I heard recently of a couple in Italy who had several times entertained a local business associate and his wife. Finally, just before the Americans were ready to leave after a two-year stay, an invitation to dinner at the Italian home came. The host explained that they were sorry they couldn't have the honor earlier but it took time for them to have their rooms redecorated and it had taken time also for them to save money so that they could hire a maid for the evening. In this case it was better that the Americans had not presumed upon a friendship but had given a formal man time to express his friendship in a formal way.

Sometimes Americans can ask local friends to go with them to see places of historical interest in order that they can have the benefit of their explanations, having made the request they can then assume responsibility for transportation and if needed provide picnic food. If an interest is expressed local people will in turn frequently include them in the observances of special occasions in the community.

Festivals And Ceremonies

Every country has its special festivals and its colorful ceremonies, and Americans overseas find it worthwhile to find out about them and as far as possible to participate in them. Local friends are always ready to talk about their special days but are not likely to do so unless they know that you really care to hear. I have frequently said to a national with whom I might be seated at a dinner party "What is the next special day coming up?" There has never been any problem about conversation after that. He would respond eagerly to my questions about the holiday or festival, giving me the traditions related to it and sometimes telling me how the observances vary throughout the country.

One spring the American women's group invited a history professor from the University of Rangoon to meet with us and tell us about the water festival which marked the beginning of a new year on the Burmese calendar. She gave a fascinating lecture telling us several of the different mythological stories related to this festival which is so important to any Burman.

One story is that long years ago two princes in the heavens were fighting and one cut off the other one's head. This presented a problem. If the head were allowed to fall on the land, the shock to the earth would kill all the people. If it fell in the sea, the water would flood all the earth. So the head had to be held by seven princesses. For three days each year they are relieved of their burden and come down to the earth where the grateful people throw water to remove stains from their hands and to wash away their sorrows.

However far apart people may be in their interpretation of its origin everyone in Burma, including the Christians, gets wet together when water festival time comes around. The Burmese go about, not only to wish their close friends and relatives a happy year with all the sorrows and trials of the departing year washed away, but to pour the symbolic water on everyone they meet. In the old days people walked and sprinkled perfumed water from dainty silver bowls. Now trucks, jeeps, and buses have crowds of laughing people who may have barrels of water and big squirt guns ready for constant use. School classes, labor unions, literary societies, women's clubs—just any sort of group—will band together, rent a truck, decorate it as a float, and then plan some special entertainment, usually singing and dancing, to perform at special pavilions set up for the purpose all along the route. Some stands have judges who designate the winning teams and floats.

Wet as you expect to get, and that means really soaked, you wear your best clothes as is fitting on such a special occasion. No one minds being wet because the festival comes at the end of winter when everything is dry and thirsty for the rainy season which may be several weeks and many hot days away. Just as it isn't cricket to go out in a raincoat, so it isn't being a good sport to ride around with the car windows closed. We didn't relish the idea of getting the inside of our car soaked because the car we had in Burma didn't have water shedding seats; so we rented a jeep and joined the fun. Swimming caps are now acceptable because with fire hose attached here and there by overzealous well wishers, a hard stream of water can really damage the inner workings of an ear.

The celebrations go on for three days beginning at first with a dry day when people make formal calls to pay respects to elders and special friends. Our younger children remember that early on the morning of the first wet day they stood outside our gate with buckets and small water guns calling out and sprinkling whoever passed by. They shared water with or accepted water from little Burmese neighbors across the way.

In many parts of the world the New Year celebrations assume a special importance. Wherever Chinese people are living the debts get paid, new clothes are prepared, and special foods are made. There is a great stir as families go around to make New Year calls. In North China the steaming and delectable meat dumplings, *chiao tzus*, were always served. Little children were given coins. Dragons with the legs of men danced during parades. Pudgy little children with dragon shoes upon their feet bowed low bows to their elders chanting *"Hsin Hsi, Hsin Hsi, Hsin Hsi"* (New Year happiness).

Many countries have some variation of a harvest festival and likewise a spring festival which may relate both to planting time and religious symbolism. Several religions have a period similar to the Christian lent, preceded by a Mardi Gras type of merry making. Throughout South America where the Roman Catholic influence is strong, North Americans may join in Mardi Gras celebrations. Those who have lived in several Latin American places report different variations according to the pre-Christian practices that have come into celebrations at different places.

Each society has its special ceremonies for initiating the children into the religious or social practices of the elders. Sometimes ceremonies are related to the time of puberty and sometimes they are not. In Burma quite young girls may squeal their way through an ear boring ceremony (the squeals are expected and applauded as indicative of high spirit) after which they will wear gold or jeweled earrings in their ears. Every Buddhist boy in Burma goes through a ceremony of entering the Buddhist priesthood as a novice, generally when he is about twelve but sometimes much younger.

It was always interesting to us to see the colorful procession which was sometimes preceded by a band of musicians or by a car with recorded music. The lad would walk, ride a horse, or sit in an open topped decorated car. Others would proceed and follow him carrying gifts that had been sent by family friends for the boy to present to the monastery. The initiate would be dressed in jeweled headgear and ornate robes symbolizing the fact that Guatama Buddha was a wealthy prince before he renounced his princely position to seek enlightenment.

After the boy reaches the pogoda his head is shaved, he puts on the saffron robe of a priest, and vows to observe the ten precepts of Buddhism. Generally for one month—though in a few cases only for one night and in other exceptional cases for life—a boy submits to the discipline of the head abbot. He studies the scriptures, and each morning before he has eaten he walks along beside an adult priest carrying a begging bowl from house to house for several hours begging for food. This begging serves not only to get rice for the monastery, it also gives the donors a chance to earn merit for their act.

The marriage ceremony is a happy one in any country and it is always a pleasure for Americans overseas when they are included among the wedding guests. In Burma the Buddhist wedding is a family rather than a religious affair. A senior friend of the family takes charge and in addition to offering sage advise to the young couple leads them through a traditional ceremony in which water and the leaves of certain plants play a symbolic part.

Those who live in a national capital may find themselves celebrating the festivals and observing the ceremonies not just of their host country but also of many other countries represented in the city. The Festival of Lights was one observed by the Indians in Rangoon. It seemed especially delightful to us to ride about the streets and lanes at twilight and see the twinkling clay lamps with mustard oil fed wicks bordering the doorsteps and sometimes the walls and gardens of the Hindu families living in Rangoon.

History In The Making

"Happy Independence Day, Mother" our daughter, Nancy, shouted as she dashed in from school on a cold fourth of January after we had returned to the United States from our assignment in Burma. I was clearing away Christmas clutter and for a minute I couldn't fathom her excitement. Before she had finished her, "How could you forget?"

I remembered the date and I was back with her in warm and beautiful Burma celebrating again with that relatively new republic its freedom and progress. Our children's identification of themselves with the national celebration of another country and their first hand contact with world history as they saw a newly independent government hold its first general election are not-to-be forgotten parts of our family experience overseas.

Americans do not participate directly in the governmental affairs of another country, but wherever they are living they can watch the political scene and are sometimes able to feel the pulse of a growing and dynamic national body. It is generally unwise for them to speak out for one side or the other in a political struggle, but they can listen and ask questions and come to their own conclusions as to where the country is going and what forces are in the lead.

It is useful to read the local papers if one's grasp of the language is adequate. In many communities there are English language papers which carry the local news and editorials. I have often found that the "Letters to the editors" section of an overseas paper may provide the most interesting reading because it shows what subjects arouse popular interest. One must watch, just as he must at home, for the political slant of a newspaper, and if possible read more than one.

The fact that Americans must usually remain detached from national affairs in the foreign country where they live and work doesn't mean that they have no influence at all upon the trend of public affairs. They may of course respond, in a personal conversation, to a discussion of the national problems, and being in a somewhat detached position they are frequently able to make observations which may influence the thinking of a local friend. To observe without passing judgment or attempting to persuade is an act which more of us who live abroad should strive to cultivate.

Americans in a foreign country need to keep their heads when they read or hear rumors that Amercians are not wanted or that this or that group is doing a poor job. There could be times when a rumor like that represented a government supported policy or was an expression of popular opinion, but it might be only the indication that an internal debate is going on. If the party in power invited some group of American technicians or if the government had passed legislation permitting some American business to operate, the opposition party might be using criticism against the Americans as a way of criticising the party in power. I have known cases where a scathing "Go Home Yankees" editorial hadn't anything to do with Americans at all, but had a great deal to do with internal politics.

In addition to the political developments in a foreign country Americans can have front row seats to watch communities grow and change. It is truly a history making process when an agrarian society begins to shift to cities and industries, when a disease-ridden country begins to set up programs for public health, when village fathers agree to supply land and labor to build their portion of a cross country road.

I remember when the wife of an official visitor to Rangoon exploded at the end of the first day because she had been shown by her hostesses only the jewelry stores and curio shops where tourists so often want to go. She went to the man who was arranging her husbands program. "Look" she said to him "My husband is on travel expenses but I am paying my own way and it is costing me fifty eight dollars and thirty five cents every single day. I have no intention to pay that kind of money just to look at souvenirs. Please find someone who can show me what is happening in this country!"

The new hostess had to run to keep up with the energetic matron but she showed her a new cotton mill, a new public health center, a low cost housing project. She took her to see national women who work with welfare programs. They went to a day nursery and saw how the United Nations Childrens Fund was providing the powder used to prepare milk for the children's lunch. In two days she saw more than some Americans see during a two-years tour of duty. She knew that history was in the making in every foreign country they visited and she was determined not to miss seeing it in process.

Most Americans who live overseas do not have to pay their own transportation, and seldom have the occasion or the inclination to calculate their losses in dollars and cents if they do not manage to see what is going on in the foreign country where they are living. Even so, the example of a visitor who did take seriously the opportunity to learn at first hand about the problems and the progress of a country is surely a challenge to all who live abroad.

Opportunities For Service

Although Americans have neither the responsibilities nor the privileges of citizenship in the foreign countries where they may be working, they do find everywhere opportunities to be helpful to individual people and to communities.

We have mentioned already the possibilities of assisting servants and members of their families to have medical care and schooling. We have no way of knowing how many Americans have found individual people overseas whose personal needs they have investigated and are now assisting. A war victim in Korea is being fitted with artificial legs. An artist in Taipei is being supplied with much needed art materials in exchange for drawing lessons for the donor's daughter. A talented and ambitious Haitian orphan is now in an American college because her boss took time to write to a scholarship committee. The only son of an Indian laborer is alive today because an American contributed the railway fare for his father to take him to an Indian hospital where a complicated operation could be performed.

Americans generally give help like this quietly, and they often hope anonymously, because they are only wanting to help and not to gain any kind of publicity. A few people hesitate to help in places where they see a need and feel able and willing because they are fearful that it might become known. The idea of being a helpful sort of fellow has somehow been downgraded in our society and some who are actually generous spirited feel they must manage to escape the label.

It is as well that those who give personal assistance overseas do it without publicity because there are so many needy people in most foreign countries that any known benefactor would be engulfed with requests for assistance. Most Americans confine their financial assistance to people whose backgrounds are well-known to them and do not give to passing beggars even though it is never easy to let oneself ignore the outstretched hand of a suffering or needy creature. In most countries where beggars are still commonly seen the welfare workers are glad if foreign residents and tourists cooperate with them in their efforts to get beggars off the street and into productive activity. It has been discovered in many cases that the children of the so-called beggar kings are being victimized by having physical ailments neglected or deformities displayed in order that the rich foreigners would drop coins at their feet. A woman who feels anguished at the sight of a boil covered baby whose mother begs for pennies, might best contain her impulse to give the mother money and go instead to the nearest hospital or clinic or welfare agency and say "Is there any way at all in which I might be of help to you in your work?"

So many American women are giving their time and skills to community welfare projects overseas that it is said in many countries that the work of the volunteer American technicians compares favorably with the work of employed Americans in assisting local governments to meet the needs of their people. Some women merely roll bandages along side local ladies whose friends they become in the process. Some help with unskilled chores in a hospital. Women in a Middle East country have organized their teen-age daughters into a group of teen-aids who go regularly to a children's hospital to give bedside care;

feeding children, combing their hair, bathing and dressing babies. The girls are so responsible and so efficient that it has made a great deal of difference to an understaffed hospital to have them. It is also an encouragement to the few educated women of the city who would like to see the local girls freed from some of the restrictions that surround them so that they too might be trained for useful community service.

Many times the work that American volunteers do is of professional caliber. A graduate nurse with years of hospital experience is working with the teachers of student nurses. A trained social case worker is assisting the local director of a newly organized family welfare clinic. A teacher who is on leave from a university faculty while her husband is on an overseas assignment with an engineering firm is participating in a work shop at a local teacher's college. A wife experienced in religious education is helping local pastors train people of their parishes to teach church school classes or to direct youth groups.

In one country in Africa the wives of American technical service employees prepare educational kits for use in rural schools. They work without pay on assignment for the educational division of the local government which could not afford to employ such highly skilled help. The women feel that they are involved in a most creative task.

Americans frequently find their service jobs through personal contacts or personal inquiries. Many times they work through local organizations. Our government cooperates in many countries with the establishment of bi-national institutes where cultural exchange programs are sponsored. Such institutes are always needing teachers of English and teachers of the arts; music, dancing, painting, creative writing and such. Churches operate day nurseries and clinics and in times of disaster soup kitchens and hostels, and they are always needing extra hands. In many cities a YWCA will want to offer a course in American cooking (wives plead to be taught how to make apple pie for husbands who studied in the U. S. A.) or in modern child care and they welcome American teachers.

In many foreign cities the civic and service organizations welcome any who will help them with the running of their organizations. Frequently the educated men and women want to get themselves organized for useful service in the community but feel the need of the kind of leadership know-how which many Americans have. Men in Kiwanis or Rotary Clubs overseas not only contribute a note of good will by their attendance; they frequently help local men see how they might go about formulating a program and organizing committees to carry it out. In many countries American women have served on the board of directors of the Young Women's Christian Association, encouraging the local women to assume responsibilities and counselling them as they seek to meet the needs of women in rapidly industrilizing areas, as they establish suitable residences for professional women, as they organize recreation centers for children and adult education centers for their mothers.

In more than fifty countries there are now University Women's Clubs which are affiliated with the International Federation of University Women. Association with the educated national women who belong to the university clubs is a rewarding experience for an American who has belonged to a similar group at home. If she is skillful enough to contribute suggestions without letting herself take over and run the club she may make a significant contribution to the purposes as well as the structure of the group.

The democratic process of group planning and of broad membership responsibility in group projects is one of the most important concepts which American women have to share with women in other countries. It isn't the kind of thing which can be taught as one would teach another person to do the Virginia reel or to apply a first aid dressing. Techniques of creative leadership and of dynamic program building can be taught best by those who participate unobtrusively but contagiously, with less experienced people. The women who are helping local women to carry out their own goals for their own communities are rendering an important service.

A growing number of people feel that it is better for Americans abroad to let their talents be put to use by an indigenous group than to work independently or with an American club. I am one who believes that an American wives group may be very useful as a supporting group for new or lonely American women and also as a group able to organize lectures and tours for Americans who want to learn more about a country. But I question the wisdom of American women letting their own associations become so large that they overshadow the local organizations.

When American women get going in any organized way they can be so efficient that they sometimes discourage local ladies from assuming positions of leadership or doing what they might to strengthen their own organized efforts. I think we are generally not wise to organize independent charity projects but should more frequently assist local women in starting and supporting projects which they know are needed and for which they will continue to assume responsibility after individual Americans have gone.

I feel strongly that Americans who give assistance in communities overseas should do it freely, so that a heart as well as a hand is doing a good deed. It is unfortunate when the boss' wife assigns the women she considers are *under* her to do this or that charity chore. If she feels there is some good reason why her group should work on the same project, then the least she can do is consult the other women before she decides just what the project will be. Individual women should always be free to decide the amount of help they can or want to give. Certainly if a woman has a special skill and a special interest she should be permitted to let that guide her into some avenue of useful service and should not be regimented into some every Tuesday assignment that may make sense to everyone but her. To argue that some women might never exert themselves to be useful in a community if someone didn't tell them to, is to me a spurious argument. A volunteer isn't a volunteer if she is pressed into service. It is good for leaders to give other people a chance to be useful and it is important that the fact of a need be made known to those who might help to meet it. But overseas, as at home, each one of us must be the steward of her own leisure and talents, and in that regard no one has a right to set herself up as another woman's keeper—not even as time keeper and certainly not as judge.

I would not give the impression that women have a monopoly on community service overseas. Unemployed wives, especially those with servants, may have more time to give than their husbands or professional women have. But just as working women overseas frequently find ways to use their skills or hobbies helpfully after hours so do men make their contributions. American men are teaching swimming, tennis, sailing, skin diving, even ballroom dancing in clubs where nationals and Americans associate together. One man I knew spent an hour every morning before he went to his office at a home for orphan boys leading them in exercises and teaching them group sports. Men are leading scout troops where their sons may be the only American boys. They are singing in choirs where they have to tone down their volume lest their language deficiencies show up too much. Men are serving on boards and committees for bi-cultural schools.

The men, like the women are most likely to be rendering helpful service if they work because they see a genuine need, choosing freely to try to meet it; and if they are working within the framework of the local situation.

The report has come back to us of one American man who was walking near the water front of the Ganges River late one night. He found a man sick and dying. Instinctively he knelt to help him, but when he felt how slow his pulse was he knew that only expert medical assistance swiftly rendered could possibly save his life. He tried first to get a taxi. With his limited use of the local language he managed to get a driver over to the man's side but instead of helping to carry the old man, the driver only shook his head. The American himself lifted the frail body. When the taxi man saw this he got into his cab and drove away. He left the sick man where he found him, hailed another cab and managed to get himself taken to the nearest hospital where he explained the urgent need to an English speaking staff member. He too shook his head.

The compassionate American went from hospital to hospital. It was almost dawn when an American missionary doctor who had been for long years in the country said to him "In the first place we do not have the authority to bring this man to the hospital, and the doctors in the government hospitals no doubt feel that they have no right to deprive a pilgrim of his long cherished wish to die by the sacred river. Who can decide that those doctors are not right. Surely neither you nor I."

Compassion must sometimes bow to ancient customs, but communities everywhere have need of warm hearted Americans who can help to shoulder the stupendous load of needs that are recognized and pressing.

CHAPTER X

CULTURE TO CULTURE

There is a two-way impact whenever people from one part of the world move into a community in another part of the world. Each group is affected by the behavior of the other. Within each group individuals may react differently to the exposure to a foreign culture according to their individual capacities, the rigidity or flexibility of their upbringing, and according to their preconceptions regarding the other people. It is beyond the scope of this book and outside the competence of the writer to discuss the fascinating and important studies that have been made by anthropologists.

For many years students of human behavior have been reporting, not only upon the characteristics and conduct of the members of various tribes, races, and nations, but have also been studying the nature of the reactions that occur when people from different backgrounds have short or sustained associations with one another. Much of this research now has been put into books designed for the lay reader, and any American who expects to live abroad will find the experience more enriched if he reads at least two or three books dealing generally with the cultures of people and then reads more thoroughly about the particular culture into which he is going.

Three paper-back books which would be interesting and useful to anyone moving abroad are:

Patterns of Culture by Ruth Benedict

Human Types by Raymond Firth

Cultural Patterns and Technical Change edited by Margaret Mead.

These books are issued by the new American Library and are available at fifty cents a copy. *Customs and Cultures* by Eugene A. Nida (Harper $4.50) is also highly recommended. Edward T. Hall's book *The Silent Language* (Doubleday & Co. $3.95) is an intriguing account of the non-verbal factors in communications between peoples of different backgrounds. There are many other useful books for the overseas Americans who would be even casual students of social anthropology. I hope that the readers of this volume will find them.

Let us now, however, take a layman's look at some aspects of an overseas experience to see how the cultural impacts might be clarified and enriched.

Host To Guest

The American who goes into a foreign country behaving like a guest and feeling like a student is the one who is most likely to gain from the experience and to make a useful contribution as well.

He needs to learn just as quickly as he can what the polite practices are in the country to which he goes so that from the beginning it will be obvious that he wants to behave respectfully in relation to the people of the new country. Even one who has read a great deal about a given culture would still be wise to say to the American residents who seem most perceptive and to any local people with whom he has a reasonable degree of closeness, "Are there special things I ought to know?"

A woman who returned recently from a Muslin community said, "Why didn't someone tell me that it is rude to pass food or to offer gifts with the left hand?" She had been doing this for months before someone explained to her that the hand which is used to take care of personal body functions is never used, in the place where she was living, to offer things to other people. Other Americans had learned this but it had never occurred to anyone to tell her when she first arrived. The new arrival must take the initiative both in observing carefully and in inquiring.

We cannot assume that gestures, for instance, imply the same thing to people in foreign countries as they do at home. American men, whether they are Rotarians or not, frequently approach one another with a hearty slap on the back to indicate friendliness and informality. In places where the Chinese culture is dominant such an approach may have exactly the opposite effect. A turtle has a back. A turtle crawls on the ground as the lowliest of creatures. To call attention to a man's back is to imply that he is like an animal of the dust. To reflect upon a man is to reflect upon his ancestors. And to call a man's grandfather a turtle is the vilest form of swearing. "Why didn't somebody tell me?" a good hearted American said one day in Formosa when it had finally been brought to his attention that he was known as the "insulting American." It hadn't occurred to him to ask for help from those who could have given him some pointers about being an acceptable guest.

Knowledgeable nationals will know that a friendly foreigner who is courteous in his own way intends no disrespect when he violates the social rules of a culture with which he is not familiar, and they forgive him. The harm is done when a national unfamiliar with Americans interprets their conduct as he would interpret the conduct of his own people. He may then form an unfavorable impression of the newcomer and close his mind to the possibilities of his good intentions, or cut himself off emotionally from the chance of becoming better acquainted.

The national who may be well enough informed about American social practices but has deep rooted prejudices against Americans can be ruffled by even innocent social mistakes. But when an American says to such a one, "Teach me how to conduct myself with your people" then even a hardened anti-American will probably relent and assume with patience the role of a teacher. To put one's self in the posture of a student is the first responsibility of every American overseas whether he be eighteen or eighty and, however elevated his professional position may be.

Language Study

Because language is one of the most obvious barriers between peoples it stands to reason that an American living in another country should make great efforts to learn the language. Those who care to look into studies about languages and their importance in history and in modern life will find books on the subject in any good library. I would recommend another paper back (also fifty cents from the New American Library) called *Language A Modern Synthesis* by Joshua Whatmough who is professor of comparative philology in Harvard University.

It is easy enough for me to say, as many Americans are saying now, that those of our countrymen who live abroad should learn the language of the country to which they are going. This is sound advice, but we need to recognize that there are some problems Those who go to parts of the world where the European languages are used have little difficulty in finding good teachers and good study materials and may already have, from their school days, an elementary grounding in the language. Certainly anyone going to French, German, Italian, Spanish, or Portuguese language areas should be expected to become proficient in at least one of these languages.

Many other languages are so different from the European ones that Americans do not always learn them quickly, and employers who sometimes speak loudly about the importance of learning a language do not always give their employees time to acquire a language nor provide money for the teachers and language learning materials they may need.

When my husband and I went to China many years ago we were given a full school year for study at the Peking College of Chinese Studies where seven hours every day we studied under Chinese scholars who had great experience in teaching their language to Westerners. They used the direct method in a large classroom, in small groups, and then for two periods each day in personal tutorial sessions. We spent several hours a day studying on our own, and we used much of our free time mingling with the people of the city trying to use our expanding vocabularies and listening to the sound of the language. Even so, at the end of the first year we had a very limited command of the language. My husband was put on only a part time teaching schedule the next year in order that he might continue working with a tutor, and it was expected that each of us would spend several hours a day with a teacher throughout our first five-year term. How many employers today can afford to give a man that much time to learn a language, especially if his term of service in any one country may be only two years?

It is true that there have been many strides made in the techniques of learning a foreign language and Americans are now frequently getting a beginning grasp of a complicated language in three months of concentrated work. Such a course cannot be inexpensive and there is still the fact of an employee's need of a salary during the time of his study. There is a question, too, as to who will pick up the tab for his wife to take the same course, and a problem about care for small children while she is at a language study center in this country.

Our government went through one of its frequent economy attacks a couple of years ago and rulings were made that barred dependents from language courses provided for overseas employees. Ironically, this happened at the same time that government spokesmen were advocating more language study. Many wives who were eager to learn were not permitted to enter unfilled classrooms where a teacher was being paid to teach their husbands who were government employees. I am glad to report that policies have relaxed and more government men are being given language study opportunities and some of their wives are being permitted to join them in classes both in this country and after arrival on the field.

Another practical complication is that it isn't always easy to know just which language an American going abroad should learn. Nigeria has about fourteen languages. Only one or two of them are taught in this country and an employee whose work will require him to move about is hard put to know just which language he should study. Those going to Cambodia may be willing to study the language of the people there, but the facts of life are that much of the business of the country is still operated in French and all highly placed nationals use French. Should Americans going there study French which they will use a great deal or should they study Khmer which they will learn more slowly and use less frequently? Those who have a good ear for language might be encouraged both to improve their Franch and to begin a study of Khmer so that they can at least greet the men and women of the villages as friends and not continue to be vocal representatives of a former colonial power.

In spite of all the practical difficulties it is still extremely important that Americans living overseas work at learning languages. In many ways this can best be done when one is surrounded by people who are speaking the language. A good tutor is the most important language learning aid and can usually be employed at a modest cost. In addition phonograph records or tape recordings of suitable language materials make possible repeated hearing and speaking drill when a tutor is not at hand. Persistent practice with these mechanical aids can speed considerably the rate at which spoken command of a language is acquired. Listening to and conversing with children is another good way to get language practice.

People who learn a foreign language are wise to be sure of the circumstances in which they use it. Unless an American has a very good grasp of a foreign language and is reasonably good in pronouncing the words and inflecting the sentences, he should confine his public speeches to a few words of greeting in the local language and then speak in English with an interpreter who can give his remarks the dignity and respectability he wants them to have.

For any matter of official or business discussion an American needs to have an interpreter speak for him unless his use of the local language is flawless, because his limited knowledge of the language might cause him to say something he didn't mean or prevent him from understanding the full import of something a local person might say. He is fortunate, of course, if his practical understanding of the language enables him to follow a discussion as it goes along and to check the interpretation that is being given to his words.

Communicating through an interpreter requires special skill. A person who expects to use an interpreter should take time to get personally acquainted with him, and give him the chance to become acquainted with the subject matter and purpose of the communication. Here are four simple rules for the effective use of an interpreter:

1. Talk slowly and have each sentence or paragraph interpreted.

2. Use a simple vocabulary. Replace three and four syllable words with shorter more common ones.

3. Keep a simple, clear sentence structure.

4. Stay psychologically on the job while the interpreter is speaking. Don't cut yourself out of the communication circuit by showing lack of interest while the interpreter speaks.

Using an interpreter is always a tedious and in some ways a difficult job so one must be patient and persistent in order to use an interpreter effectively.

The use of a local language is most helpful in informal social contacts in the community. Americans should try to use a language, even if they use it badly, when they are with friends because in that way they demonstrate to their friends a willingness to identify with them, and by use they can improve their language ability. One of the real advantages of learning a language in the country where it is used is that the American who puts himself in the hands of a teacher and under the tutelage of local friends is demonstrating most sincerely his willingness to be a student.

There are times, however, when even a gifted student must use discretion in displaying his talent. A missionary nurse in Portuguese Angola who made a brilliant record as a language student in Portugual and lectured in flawless Portuguese to student nurses in the African hospital decided that she would also learn the language spoken by the Africans in their villages. She found a teacher and being a good student of languages she learned quickly and well. When she was in the market one day she saw one of her students, and thinking it would please him as well as give her some practice, she addressed him in his native speech. He froze. She later learned that she had greatly offended him by implying in the presence of bystanders that he, a student, could not understand Portuguese, the status language. After that she spoke the local language only with shop keepers and the uneducated hospital patients. She spoke the language of the ruling class when she talked with those who aspired to positions of importance.

History-Religion-Arts

An overseas American who takes seriously his role as a student must study a country's history. An understanding of history can come most readily, perhaps, from books. A few countries may have a limited amount of history recorded in English and in some cases very little in a language of their own. These would certainly be exceptional places. There is generally a considerable amount of historical material. Americans are wise to consult local historians as to which English writers they feel have best represented them, and then read books they suggest in addition to books they may have found on American lists.

In addition to reading which Americans can do individually or as families it is interesting and stimulating to join classes organized for those who want to learn about the historical background of their host country. Sometimes groups of families will get together and invite a university professor to speak to them and to guide them in their studies.

Visits to museums, shrines, and old ruins, with a well informed guide, are enlightening to any who are truly curious. Naturally, those who go to a place just to be going somewhere or who think only of comparing it with something back home will learn little and will not impress the local people that they are genuinely seeking to be informed. I shall never forget the day when a friend and I were given the responsibility of escorting a visiting American to the Shwe Dagon Pagoda (a 2,500 year old Buddhist shrine) in Rangoon. Because of the importance of her husband's position the visitor was met by one of the prominent patrons of the pagoda who was prepared to explain politely and in detail about the shrine and its history. She chattered incessantly exclaiming in superlatives about how fabulous everything was so that the host hardly had a chance to speak at all. She noticed a candle burning at one small shrine and forgetting what the man who was there to be her teacher had said about the age of the pagoda, she said, "Oh, isn't it touching. There is something you have taken from catholicism." The floors were solid marble but Elsie and I felt we would fall right through them in our shame!

Geography can be another interesting study for Americans overseas. A country's culture is frequently related to the harbors, the rivers, the fertile plains, and the mountains. To see what the lay of the land is in a given country and to learn how this relates to the things that have happened to the people is a study which will fascinate even young children who live abroad. Field trips are essential to this kind of study and there are books that will help, too. Again it is the school or university that can help one find the best books. Sometimes it is possible to borrow geography books used by school children and have them translated by local friends. Unfortunately, in some very interesting parts of the world children whose countries have been for years under a colonial power may not have many geography books written about and for their own country. But in many places local geographers are at work preparing such material and sometimes they are happy to let visitors look over their shoulders as they write and go along with them as they make their own explorations and prepare to draw their own maps.

No culture can be understood apart from its religious traditions. We frequently find that the religious heritage consists of not just one strand but of many threads, sometimes carefully interwoven, sometimes matted so that it is hard to tell which is which.

It is best whenever possible to learn about a religion from those who are its followers. We were fortunate in Burma because many of the world's active religious groups are represented in Rangoon. Some of us who attended a church there decided to start what we called a Religion in Life Forum. It met before the English language worship service while the children were in church school classes. We began with a study of Buddhism, which was the religion most prevalent in the country. We invited a Buddhist scholar to speak to us for an hour at a time for six or eight weeks. He gave illuminating lectures about the history of the Buddhist movement, its various branches and the precepts of the faith. He prepared mimeographed copies of his lectures, and was most generous in answering our questions.

In one discussion the speaker told us something of the animism which preceded Buddhism, explaining that *gnats* (evil spirits) were believed to inhabit stones, trees, and the earth. Since they were thought to have great power, it was considered important not to irritate them, especially by stamping a foot. Many Buddhists still fear the *gnats*, but he rejected such superstition by saying, "I stamp my foot at *gnats*."

After he had gone a well educated Burmese friend who was attending the group remarked, "I agree with him that a belief in *gnats* is superstitious, but you know," and she said this earnestly, "I think he really shouldn't have stamped his foot."

This reminded us that in any country even well educated people may still have in their emotions a reluctance to defy the superstitions which have survived in even the most sophisticated religions.

There followed weeks when we studied Islam. The first teacher was Dr. M. A. Rauf, who at the time was India's Ambassador to Burma. His lectures were rich in historical material and were warm and human, coming as they did from a man who was a dedicated adherent of a faith whose history and scriptures he knew so well. One or two other followers of the Prophet Mohammed spoke to us. For another series of weeks we studied the various facets of the Hindu faith, again inviting both scholars and laymen to guide us.

It was always a surprise to us to discover how other religions have, as Christianity has, dozens of splinter groups and a wide range of opinion as between an orthodox and a liberal point of view. It was helpful for us to hear followers of other religions say that there is sometimes quite a gap between the highest teachings of their faith and the common practices of the followers of that faith. Knowing how far short we come in applying the precepts of the faith we claim, we had a fellow feeling towards the speakers who pointed out that such failure is not exclusively confined to those who have a Judeo-Christian heritage.

The Hindu studies were followed by a study of the Parsee movement and the teachings of Zoroaster whose concepts of monotheism may have preceded and contributed to the Hebraic concept of one God. The studies led by a Parsee scholar, whose ancestors had fled from Persia to India many hundred years ago, caused us to realize how frequently people of one religion have wrong concepts about another religion. Most of us went to the first lecture expecting to hear about people who worship fire. The man who spoke to us insisted that his people had never worshipped fire but explained that the flame of the fire which is never permitted to burn out in any of their temples is to them a vivid symbol of abiding and universal realities.

It isn't in every country that so many religions can be studied at first hand, but in any country there are religious traditions to be explored. Those who work out a way of doing this find that they are better able to understand the social practices of the people, some of the events in their history and particularly the indigenous art.

In some countries Americans discover that local artists are busy being western artists who simply use local themes or landscapes for their subjects. This happens especially in countries where for several generations the people have been ruled by western powers and where the few artists who have had special training have studied in the west or under western teachers. However, with the upsurge of nationalism in many places there is a revival of interest in indigenous art forms, whether they be primitive or sophisticated. Sometimes when Americans express an interest in finding typically native art, local artists are encouraged to view their own cultural heritage in a new light. Some of them, inspired by the visiting Americans, are becoming more appreciative of their own heritage and through this are beginning to express themselves in a more creative way.

Many countries, of course, have never abandoned their own artistic traditions and in those countries one can find much to see and much to learn. In his zeal to see the old art in a country an American needs to be careful not to overlook the fact that in other countries as well as our own there are contemporary artists who are designing new patterns out of the old traditions. It is always worth asking who they are and good to give them a chance to say for themselves what they are trying to communicate.

Music and dance are art forms which can be appreciated everywhere. If the musical scale is different from ours, it may not sound very melodious at first, but gradually as we hear local music we may begin to have a feel for it. Some buy a local instrument and have great pleasure in learning to play it. Travelers into interior places often report happily that they heard the strains of folk music coming from the huts at twilight or echoing across a lake where men sang as they rowed their boats. Years later and miles away these sounds may still linger in their memories. Dances also may seem either too stylized or too wild at first, but as their movements become more familiar they speak as the movements of dancers anywhere speak to spectators about the mystery or the meaning of life.

The theatre, too, provides a fascinating study. In many countries one finds a revival of the old dramatic forms where mythology and folk lore are related to the stories of the beginnings of a people or a nation. It can be an enchanting experience to see such a play in Bangkok, for instance, especially if a Thai on either side of you is able to fill in the background information you need in order to get the full import of the drama. A theatre need not be a formal place or even a fixed place. Some of the most interesting kinds of dramatic activity may be seen in courtyards where performers have been hired to entertain wedding guests or at a village square where a wandering troop hopes to get coins from the market day shoppers. It is more interesting if one can understand the dialogue that may go on in the troubadour performances, but if he is only a lone bystander the experience of watching the players and watching the audience can be very entertaining.

Changing Patterns

Many thousands of Americans are scattered throughout the world precisely because change and a desire for change is underway in the places to which they go. Yet some of these same technicians or their wives can be heard to say, "It's a pity they don't wear the beautiful hand-woven sarongs any more" or "I do hope nothing will ever change this sleepy peaceful village." Few generalizations can be safely made in a discussion about foreign countries, but I think I am on safe grounds when I observe that change is one of the most dependable facts about today's world, whether one is talking about Africa, Asia, Europe, or any part of the Americas.

It is hard to say just where change in a country begins; whether in education, in economic development, in government, in scientific progress, in religious and philosophical concepts. It's a cycle with change at one point both making possible and stimulating change at another. For whatever reasons and in whatever manner social changes are occurring in other parts of the world, it is to be expected that behavior patterns are changing as well. Intrigued as Americans may be with the old costumes and the old manners, they shouldn't be dismayed when they see evidence that these too are giving way to the demands of a new day.

The American who maintains the attitude of a student finds himself not only delving into ancient history to see where a society had its beginnings and reading more recent history to see how the present order came about, but also observing on-the-spot how people are reacting under the impact of such forces as nationalism, communism, industrialization, aviation, and maybe even television. The impressions he gets are not always clear (does a person in a state of transition ever know himself just how or where he is going?). Sometimes the results are amusing (a clear plastic raincoat on a bare little boy). Frequently they are distressing (modern machinery put into use before safety devices have been ordered or understood). Occasionally they are heart rending (an old man, the patriarch of a family, being ridiculed by a well educated but brash grandson).

Those who stand in the midst of change as guests and students are fortunately not required to draw up a list of appraisals or conclusions. The situation in almost any place is still too dynamic for that.

There is an excellent pamphlet *When Americans Live Abroad* prepared at the Foreign Service Institute by Glen H. Fisher as a supplement to an orientation seminar in Working With Foreign Peoples. In a thought provoking way it combines theoretical principles and practical suggestions. It includes eight pages of titles and brief descriptions of suggested readings as samples of the literature which may be useful for further reading. *When Americans Live Abroad* is small enough to be carried with a passport and I would recommend that anyone who is even contemplating an overseas assignment should get it and study it. It may be obtained from the Superintendent of Documents, U. S. Government Printing Office, Washington, D. C., for 25 cents.

In the same connection I would recommend that all who are employed in overseas positions as well as those who select and train Americans for employment abroad should read *The Overseas Americans* by Harlan Cleveland, Gerard J. Mangone, and John C. Adams (McGraw-Hill Book Company, $5.95). Based on two years of research at the Maxwell Graduate School of Citizenship and Public Affairs at Syracuse University and including interviews with hundreds of American and foreign nationals on five continents, the book describes the range of overseas assignments now handled by hundreds of thousands of Americans abroad, and analyzes their policies and performances. It discusses the elements needed for successful performance in overseas assignments and suggests an imaginative program of action for the recruitment, selection, and training of personnel in various categories of work who, whether they know it or not, are all carrying important responsibilities for United States foreign policy.

Guest to Host

When I urge Americans to go into other countries with a "Tell me about you" approach to the people I am assuming that at the same time they go with a willingness to let themselves be known. This is the two-wayness of cultural exchange, and with rare exceptions it is greatly desired by people in other parts of the world. Few people have not heard of America or Americans, and many people are eager to meet an American in the flesh. Even those who may be jealous or critical of our country will press forward to see us. In the less developed places curiosity prompts even shy children to reach out and touch an American child.

"Why did he want to touch me, Mommy?" a child said one day when he had been startled to have a very black hand reach out to touch his white leg. "I guess it is because he wants to know if your body feels just like his does even though it is a different color outside," his mother told him.

Women missionaries who worked in Chinese villages some years ago used to report that a question frequently asked when they entered a Chinese home to visit with the women was, "Do you wear trousers or not?" A worded answer was not enough. The missionaries had to show what kind of garment was worn under the western skirt. All the women the villagers had ever seen had either worn pajama-like pants under or instead of a long jacket, and so this was a very natural question for them to ask.

In some places Americans are startled to be asked bluntly, "How much did your automobile cost?" "How old are you?" "Does your husband also have a younger wife?" These are generally not prying but just curious questions. Americans may evade the more personal ones if they prefer but they endear themselves to the questioners when they respond as many times as possible and satisfy their desire to know what life is like for the ones who have come from afar.

Aside from the childlike questions there are more profound things the people of other countries want to learn from us when we are living among them.

First of all, hundreds and thousands of them want to learn our language. They want to know how to read and write and speak English because they know that it is a language of modern technology. It is a language in which much history and great works of literature are written. They want to learn English so they can get to an American college. They want to learn English so they can get a better job at home. Most Americans overseas have not had special training in how to teach English to those who are foreign to our language, but many are doing good jobs with English classes even so.

In many overseas cities there is now a bi-national (American and national) institute in which a staff member is likely to be trained in linguistics and is able to teach a willing American how to teach the eager nationals.

Those who are called upon to teach English in places where there is no one to guide them in knowing how to do it or in deciding what kind of materials to use are advised to consult:

Center for Applied Linguistics
1346 Connecticut Avenue, N. W.
Washington 6, D. C.

Whenever I think of teaching English to other people I remember the missionary who taught some Chinese students English because they wanted to learn English and she wanted to teach them the New Testament. One day she gave each of them an invitation to have dinner in her home. One reply read, "My dear Teacher, verily, verily, I say unto you, I shall be glad to come."

Even though an American may teach English simply because a local person is wanting to learn it and with no special purposes of her own in mind, the process does, nevertheless, set up for two people or for one teacher and a group of students a channel through which information of a great many kinds may be passed. A student increases his vocabulary by asking his teacher questions, and naturally he asks about her family, her country, and her way of life. He increases his vocabulary sometimes just because he wants to get to the place where he can ask questions about special things he wants to know about democracy, about the rights of women, about his child who never learned to talk.

In addition to teaching English in formal classes or through informal contacts, Americans also render a useful service when they take time to talk with people who have studied English in a classroom and want to become more able to speak and understand it. Young nationals who have returned to their homelands after years of study in the United States are sometimes very lonely for America which became a second home, and they are delighted when an American speaks to them and includes them in parties or discussions with other Americans.

There is often a good deal of curiosity about American geography. People in small countries where a tropical climate keeps temperatures pretty much the same throughout the country and throughout the year sometimes find it hard to understand how Niagara Falls can freeze and how it can also be hot in the United States. A collection of road maps and a big stack of Chamber of Commerce information-for-tourist folders would be good things for Americans to take when they go overseas. Copies of magazines like *Holiday* and *The National Geographic* which have such good pictures of our country would be useful to have, too. It is possible in many foreign cities to direct an interested national to a United States Information Service Library where he may find many books about America. Films and slides are generally available there so he can see things about America with a hand viewer or in a hall where scheduled films are shown. Americans can sometimes arrange to borrow USIA films to show to groups of nationals at their homes.

Our history is also of great interest to people overseas. Everyone who goes abroad might well take along a good high school level history of the United States because he will surely have occasions to loan it to interested people abroad. Sometimes inquiries come about special persons or special periods in American history, Abraham Lincoln especially, and the story of our western expansion. Local high schools or colleges sometimes invite an American to give a lecture about some aspect of our history, and when that invitation comes he is glad if back there in his own high school he did some homework! I knew one wife who was invited to go once a week to a local language high school to conduct a class in a discussion of American current events. She didn't know the language of the country well enough to use it with students, but she prepared her reports and gave them in English and the teacher who knew English translated and then moderated the discussion which always followed.

Questions And Answers

We can't expect to get by overseas just by telling people about the settling of our great wild west or by quoting wise words of Abraham Lincoln. Everywhere the people are pushing us to bring them up to date, and they want straight answers. The questions Americans are asked overseas range from inquiries about the status of the American Negro to the patterns of dating, the care of the aged, the winning baseball teams, the relative powers of the House and the Senate, on and on, and back again to the status of the Negro.

Public Affairs Press (419 New Jersey Avenue, S.E., Washington 3, D.C.) has issued a very useful reference volume called *The Facts of American Life* ($5). This book edited by M. B. Schnapper lists many of the questions commonly asked by people throughout the world about the United States. The answers are based primarily upon information from various agencies of the Federal government. Major emphasis is placed on people, government, business, labor, agriculture, science, education, culture, and world affairs. Within these categories those going overseas will find much information which will enable them to answer many questions more accurately and more thoroughly than they otherwise might do.

Questions about America differ according to the country and the prevailing concerns of the people. There are few places where sooner or later a question isn't posed about the place of the Negro in the life of our country. I remember one night about ten years ago when a noisy square dance was underway in our house in Rangoon. A change of partners was called and as a young dark skinned Asian diplomat stepped up to my side, he said, "Mrs. Winfield, how is it that you still have slaves in America?"

I saw that his eagerness to talk was greater than his interest in the next figure so I beckoned for a couple of people to take our places and we found chairs where we could converse.

I decided that there were two things he needed to know. First, it was important for him to know that I knew that there was a problem and that I was concerned about solutions. He himself knew a good deal more about the actual situation in our country than his question had implied. Next, and this was actually his most urgent need; he felt he must find out if I personally had prejudice against people of color so that he could decide if I might have reservations about him.

The non-white peoples throughout the world are asking Americans what they think about race problems and they are genuinely interested in our answers; but they are most of all concerned to watch us and see how we feel about racial differences. When our guest learned that all members of our family truly respect men for what they are and that our belief in social equality has no qualifications at all, then his own defenses dropped and during the months that followed we became good friends and were able to communicate freely at many levels.

Americans who consciously or unconsciously harbor feelings of racial superiority or who have a creed of brotherhood which has restrictive clauses written into it, had better stay at home and find some smug little isolated corner in which to hide. There is certainly no place for them out on the crossroads of the last half of the twentieth century.

We have found whenever we have reached the place where we can have serious conversations with nationals that they want us to tell them how we feel about our country and what we think its purposes are, or ought to be.

We always remind them that we speak as individuals. We try to give them some picture of the heterogeneous make up of our people and a concept of the broad spread of opinion which could be found on almost any subject. Then, having explained the nature of our individuality, we have as individuals given our opinions on any subjects that have been presented to us. We have always found that we need to keep reading and thinking about America in order that our own ideas may keep fresh and growing.

Max Lerner's *America as a Civilization* (Simon and Schuster) has proved to be stimulating for us and we think it is well worth the cost for those who want to think seriously and deeply about our country. A paperback edition of this work is available in two volumes at $1.95 each.

Memo for Overseas Americans by Stuart Gerry Brown (Syracuse University Press, $1) is a small enough paper-back to go in a flight bag and is condensed enough to be read en route to an overseas assignment. It is worth reading more than once. A few other titles out of a great many which would be helpful to Americans who are willing to try to interpret their country abroad are:

The Search for America edited by Huston Smith (Prentice Hall, $1.50).

Goals for Americans, the report of the President's Commission on National Goals (Prentice Hall, $1).

Characteristically American by Ralph Barton Perry (Alfred A. Knopf).

Art and Life in America by Oliver Larkin (Rinehart and Co.).

INTERPRETIVE ART

The best way for the music, drama, and art of a country to be interpreted by citizens abroad is for the people in other countries to see performances and to participate with Americans in productions or projects. The easiest way to accomplish this in the musical field is to have a good record player and a supply of records of the kind which you yourself most enjoy (no use trying to expose other people to things which bore you!) and then invite groups of local friends for musical evenings. It makes the experience more interesting for guests if they can be told something about a composer and, in the case of a musical show, something of the social framework in which the plot has its setting.

An even better way to give people an idea of American music is to have a live concert, either a one or two-man program in a living room or a performance in a hall with the musically talented Americans from the community assisting and large groups of local people invited. The best way of all, because it has such creative overtones, is for American music lovers and national musicians to get together regularly or for special occasions to play or sing for and with each other, using music of two countries and cultures.

From time to time the United States Government sends well-known individual Americans or musical groups on tour to other parts of the world. Their arrival in a community gives the Americans there an opportunity to invite local people to attend performances and frequently opens the way for other musical contacts.

When a visiting North American chorus was singing at an informal gathering in a Brazilian city some months ago a woman from the United States who had Brazilian guests with her asked the director if he would tell the audience something of the background of a folk song they had just heard. He did. Afterwards a Brazilian professional musician whom she had not previously met came up to her and thanked her for the explanation given and then told her about the background of some of their folk music.

During this conversation he learned that she played the cello, that she had played with orchestras in her own country, and that she would enjoy playing with Brazilians. She felt she was out of practice and persuaded her new friend to become her teacher. Before long the pupil was recommended for membership in the highly respected symphony orchestra of the local university. It was the first time in that part of Brazil that a North American had been a member of such a group. Thanks to the graciousness and humility of a talented and unusually attractive American woman who was ready to push herself to study in order that she might give a creditable performance and who was able to convince a director that she wanted no special treatment but expected to be corrected (in Portuguese) for mistakes just as others were, the reputation of the United States was considerably enhanced in that place.

Even nationals who do not understand English enjoy attending theatrical productions put on by Americans. An amateur theatre group in a foreign city not only gives its members a good time; it can also give another picture of what America is like to the local people who attend performances. Whether a play which is presented is a take off on American politics such as *The Best Man,* a searching look for values like *Raisin in the Sun,* or just a corny bit of Americana like *Boy Meets Girl,* an overseas audience will see Americans looking at themselves, and this is good. Also they will enjoy attending the play with the Americans in the community, chatting with them during intermission and jostling with them when the inevitable traffic tie up occurs after the performance. This is good, too. The only thing that is better as far as American theatre overseas is concerned is to have local people working with Americans both before the footlights and back stage.

Those who draw or paint or mold clay or hold a camera with precision as well as those who only look with appreciation upon artistic expressions have opportunity overseas to speak about our country. Ordinary words get in our way so often. They mean such different things to different people. But a picture speaks for itself, a jug has its obvious shape, the lines in a photograph can be read by an illiterate and also by a scholar.

False modesty too often keeps overseas Americans from displaying their work abroad. There is no reason why a woman should not say to her national friends, "I enjoy working with clay, would you care to see some of the things I've been doing?"

If an exhibition of the work of amateur artists is announced at a local institute there is no reason why an American woman who follows another profession but paints for a hobby should not enter her paintings. In fact, there are many reasons why she should: she lets people know that she is willing to submit her efforts for public criticism even though she is a person in a prominent position who may be only moderately good as an artist; her willingness to join in will encourage local amateurs; attendance at the exhibition will indicate her desire to be friendly with the people of the country and may introduce her to some who will become congenial friends.

Those who don't do creative work themselves can find many ways in which they may be useful in the art field. They can assist with the arrangements for an exhibition. Sometimes they can be instrumental in arranging for a loan of paintings from a home town museum to be used with a collection of paintings done by artists in the country where they are living. They can help to set up after school art classes where American children study with local children and Americans who are trained in art teach alongside local artists.

One of the most creative people-to-people projects in recent years was the Asian Artists in Crystal exhibition which was made possible through the joint efforts of Asian artists of sixteen countries who submitted drawings, American designers of the Steuben Glass Company who designed the crystal forms onto which the drawings were engraved, American craftsmen who blew the glass and engraved it, and the United States government which sent the exhibition on a tour of the sixteen countries and then presented to an appropriate museum in each country the pieces which carried the drawings done by artists of that country. This enterprise represents many of the elements of collaboration which are so sorely needed in the world today.

It would be good if in all the countries where Americans are now living, those who have art skills would work out ways in which from time to time their efforts and the efforts of the local artists might be made to complement each other in some form of creative expression. The results might be modest in comparison with the magnificent and expensive Asian Artists in Crystal project. Yet, like those delicately beautiful pieces, even the most humble creation of a joint endeavor of artists of two countries would interpret something more than their two cultures; it would translate into visible forms the aspirations of sensitive individuals who are in the vanguard of an emerging world culture.

Problems In Communication

It is easy to see that there are many points at which people of two countries can have mutually helpful cultural contacts. But we find ourselves stymied sometimes because there is interference in the communication channels. We see this happen in the use of words. There is obviously a problem if two people from different countries try to work together with neither knowing the other's language. Sometimes the problems are no less acute when both speak English, for instance, but have a different understanding about the meaning of certain words.

Here is an example. When an American technical mission went to an Asian country a few years ago one of the first things the government there requested was that a group of pre-clinical teachers be supplied for the national medical school. They had good clinical instruction from trained doctors who practiced in the community, but they couldn't find qualified medical people who would give up medical practice to work full time on university salaries to teach anatomy or physiology.

The school's need was urgent. The medical officer of the technical mission knew that he could get just the kind of teachers they needed from an American medical school. It could have been easily arranged under our country's university contract plan. He suggested that an affiliation between the local medical school and a certain well-known American medical school be set up at once. He had no response at all from this suggestion. He mentioned it again both to the dean and to members of the faculty. No one made a move to start the affiliation process.

Months went by. Each time the medical officer mentioned the medical school affiliation he met evasion and delay. He simply could not understand why. Finally he had built a close enough personal relation with one man on the faculty who risked explaining the problem to him. It was that one word *affiliation*. The medical school men had all been trained in the English use of the English language; in that usage the word "affiliation" implies a relationship between a superior and an inferior. As they understood it this proposed affiliation would put their medical school under the control of the American one (as a colony is under a colonial power). With nationalism a burning issue in their country they would close their medical school before they would permit it to become affiliated with a foreign institution on those terms. When it was explained that the American plan referred to an association between equally independent and sovereign institutions with the one in America only supplying, on contract, certain faculty members who would work under and report to the dean of the local school the whole problem was cleared up but so much time had been lost that the project was never carried out.

Another problem also grows out of national pride but is related to status symbols rather than vocabulary. People in developing countries are anxious to have Americans help them know about some of the discoveries that our scientists have made and they want useful information put before their people but it must be done in such a way that it will not offend the sensitivities of the uneducated people.

Cartoons are often used effectively to teach new methods or skills, but an American has to check carefully with a local person before he produces a strip. In one case, an American technician designed a cartoon strip showing an elderly farmer going to an agricultural center to ask questions about improving his crops. The extension agent was shown displaying pictures and charts which gave the information the farmer needed. A national associate suggested a basic change. He showed the old man accompanied by his young grandson and the grandson asking the questions. In that community it would have been humiliating for an old man to be shown asking questions which showed that he was ignorant. It was perfectly all right for him to listen to the answers that were given to a young boy's questions.

Sometimes it is a feeling of pride in relation to the outside world which makes it difficult for nationals to accept the kind of aid they need. Americans helping with a census survey in a Middle East country found that the results indicated one hundred per cent employment for all the men in the country where it is common knowledge that many men are not gainfully employed. The local census takers were not willing to have the Americans see figures indicating that there were many beggars in the country. When a man replied to a question concerning his employment that he was a beggar, the enumerator would not write that down but pressed the man to give another occupation. If a man had ever done anything else the earlier occupation was listed. If he insisted that he was a beggar and the son of a beggar then he was pressed for his grandfather's occupation. The beggar might then be listed as a drummer or might be assigned to some random category, but no beggars were listed in the census that was designed in order that unemployment as well as other national problems might be more knowledgeably handled.

A failure to communicate can occur if those on one side do not understand the traditional attitudes of those on the other side. A good illustration of this is an incident that occurred in Japan a few years ago. An American educator was assigned to set up teachers' workshops for the study of democracy. She heard that a well-known American scholar was visiting Japan and she made arrangements for him to open the workshop with a lecture on the meaning of democracy. He was a man with such a well-known reputation that an outstanding Japanese scholar was assigned to him as interpreter. The lecturer arrived eager to give a convincing presentation. He wanted very much to show the teachers in his audience that he had the spirit of equality in his attitude as well as in his speech so to signal this he sat on the edge of the table and talked informally. He was thanked by the Japanese chairman and politely applauded by his audience, and then he left to keep another appointment.

Pandemonium broke loose. There had never been such a heated discussion at any of the workshops. The American who organized the workshops was thrilled that the lecture on democracy could arouse such interest. She turned to her interpreter and asked what was being said, but he only told her that they were talking about the American speaker.

"But what are they saying about him?" she kept asking.

"They are saying that he sat on the table," he answered evasively.

"What does that have to do with his speech?" she insisted.

He faced her hesitantly and then he told her boldly, "In Japan the top of table is sacred. The bottom of man is not!"

The very actions that the lecturer had intended should indicate equality and democracy were the ones that so outraged his audience that they heard none of his fine words about democracy.

There is still another problem related to the give and take between people of different cultures. It is that societies differ in the degree to which personal relationships are paramount. By and large Americans are accustomed to work in situations where a certain degree of objectivity exists in working relationships. Suggestions are made in relation to projects or goals. Disagreements are aired in relation to principle or values. We have laws and regulations. We interpret them, we defy them, and we change them, but still the rules are there and we operate in relation to them. All of us get personal now and then in our actions or reactions, but when we do there is generally someone to tell us to put personal feelings aside and stick to the issues.

People in other countries may not have the same pattern. Even in the places where the law of an outside colonial power has operated for many years, in the vital aspects of life the people have been ruled by men rather than laws, by the priest, the chief, the elders. Around these men intricate systems of personal relationships have evolved. Life has been tolerable for many of the people of the world only because their personal relationships have been kept in balance.

Americans are sometimes confused when they get into a place where even though there is now a constitutional government there is still a tendency to think first of the personal angles of a situation. A technician makes a suggestion to a group of community development people. They say "yes." He outlines next steps and they nod. But nothing happens. American wives are consulted about plans for a day nursery. They go into high gear and come up with a design for a building and a daily schedule for the children. Nothing happens. In both cases for one reason or another the original suggestion was not suitable to the local situation or sufficiently in line with local customs. But people accustomed to making or responding to suggestions indirectly and personally do not know how to speak out in committees and say "That won't work because—." Not knowing how to deal with the matter-of-fact Americans they only can say "yes" and let an important project die by default rather than risk what they think might involve a break in personal relations. Americans must learn to understand the pattern of social relationships in the communities where they live.

Here again, as in our earlier discussion of shock absorbers, we are reminded of the need for each American to find some local person who can be eyes and ears for him, thus helping him to push aside the barriers that can stop the flow of information, the cooperative activities, and the person-to-person understanding which are the most essential ingredients in all our undertakings overseas.

The interplay of culture with culture is so intricate and is of such great importance in all the enterprises of international cooperation that there is no end to its fascination nor to the need for Americans to seek to understand it. The possibility of acquiring skill and insight in this area is one of the special satisfactions of living overseas.

Chapter XI

DIPLOMATICALLY SPEAKING

In addition to all the adventure which is a part of any overseas assignment, and the fascination of living in a different country and becoming acquainted with the people and customs of that country, those who go abroad—especially those who live in a capital city—may find themselves related to a cosmopolitan group of people who compose the diplomatic community. There will be in that community representatives from every country with whom the host government has diplomatic relations. This chance to see at close range and in many cases to know on a friendly basis people from a great variety of cultures is for most of us an extra dividend of overseas work.

The social procedures in diplomatic circles differ from those which might operate in any one country. It is therefore necessary for those who expect to have any formal relationships with the officials of the country and with the diplomatic corps (the term used to refer collectively to the heads of foreign missions and their staffs at the capital of the country, including in popular usage the wives and children as well as the representatives themselves) to learn about the social practices of diplomacy and to act in accordance with them whenever the nature of a situation is such that diplomatic procedure is appropriate.

I would stress at the beginning of this discussion that even in those circumstances where the rules of protocol must be followed it should never be assumed that formal procedures preclude the possibility of friendly and sincere associations between the people involved. Whether an American overseas is a diplomat and must therefore be continually involved in official functions or whether he is a citizen working abroad in some non-official job and finds himself only on a few occasions participating in diplomatic society, he and his wife should, in either case, be able to find pleasure in knowing as many people as possible and in keeping their relationships with other people at all times comfortable and kindly regardless of the formalities that must sometimes be observed.

Respect to the Host Government

Most of us were taught as children to find the hostess and greet her as soon as we arrived at a party. Americans should remember this overseas. In most cases it is not practical or desirable for visitors to call upon the wife of the head of a state or at the home of the principal ministers. These ladies may not speak English. They may not care to have large numbers of foreign visitors. They certainly couldn't receive all of the American women in places where there are several hundred. Nevertheless it is unbecoming, I think, that so many times American women get in a great flutter about wearing just the right things to call upon the American ambassador's wife and dash here and there to leave cards at the embassies of other countries and frequently ignore completely the women of the country whose guests they are. Such people sometimes say at the end of a tour of duty, "No one in this country ever invited us anywhere."

We ought to make particular inquiries as soon as we arrive in a foreign capital as to ways in which we can respectfully and appropriately greet our hosts. In Burma there was a President's book kept at the gatehouse of the residence of the president of the country. It was a courtesy for foreign residents to sign the book once each year. This way they were able to indicate that they considered themselves guests in the country and wanted to pay respects to the head of the government and his wife. Those who signed received invitations to certain state functions.

Some Americans who hadn't bothered to sign wondered why they were not included when many Americans were invited to a state reception. Unless they were on a list of official Americans there was no way for those drawing up the guest list to know they were in the country. Naturally, those who had indicated special interest in being received would be most likely to be put on a guest list not only for a once-a-year reception but also for announcements about the opening of an exhibition, a national music festival, or other nationally sponsored affairs.

In some countries there are local ordinances which foreigners should learn about and follow, regarding deference to the head of the state. In Liberia, for instance, it is forbidden for anyone to walk in front of the executive mansion while carrying a parcel, or to drive any type of vehicle except a sedan past the front of the mansion. If a car is driving by the mansion when the Liberian flag is being raised or lowered, the car must stop. All cars must stop when the President's car passes by.

Outside of official circles, a newcomer might inquire of the local person with whom he works most closely to determine whether it would be convenient for him and his wife to make a courtesy call at the associate's home. For instance, an American employee in a bank in a foreign city might ask his local counterpart if he and his wife might call upon the national and his wife.

A Fulbright professor might ask the same question of the chairman of the university department with which he is associated. Americans would be surprised if they knew how many times local people hold back because they assume that the important and well-to-do foreigners wouldn't want to see them socially. In most places we must make the first move and within the framework of international etiquette it is proper that we should.

We sometimes unwittingly offend by seeming to be so much more interested in the nationals of some other country than in those of the place where we are living. This is a thing to watch especially in a newly independent country where the residents may be unduly self-conscious and sensitive.

An American and his wife in an African capital city are not being received as warmly as they would like to be and observers have reported that the local people feel wary of them because they have so much to say about Ceylon, the country in which they previously worked. Ceylon was their first foreign assignment. They made an all-out effort to get acquainted there and had many friends. They are just as anxious to make friends in the African city, but before they had made any local contacts they hurried to the Ceylonese Embassy and became involved in a whirl of social activities with friends of friends there. At gatherings where they meet local people they talk a great deal about Ceylon and recount experiences they had there.

I heard recently of an American executive who had to be transferred out of a certain Latin American country because he couldn't manage to detach himself psychologically from another South American country where he had last been assigned and where he had operated most successfully. Every conversation in the new country eventually included a reference to the way things had been done in the former place. Local people expect foreigners from the United States to talk about their home country and to mingle freely with their own countrymen. After all we are United States citizens, and nationals expect people to love their own country and admire them for it. But they find it hard to understand or respond to the good intentions of a visitor who seems to be enamored of a third country.

Even in affirming loyalty to his own country an American should be careful not to be over-zealous. Modesty calls on one who is living abroad to be discreet even in the way he speaks about his homeland. It is obviously important for us to be unusually careful about the way in which we speak about a host country, remembering always to speak as courteous guests.

Representatives of Other Countries

It is possible to know and to become acquainted with people of other countries living in the host country without neglecting or offending the local people in any way. Aside from the diplomatic representatives upon whom Americans may call or whom they may meet in other ways, there are frequently other groups of foreigners whom they may get to know.

The "old timers" in a cosmopolitan community overseas are frequently the ones best able to help the newcomers get acquainted with other foreign residents. They are likely to know a good many people and should assume some responsibility to help new arrivals make calls and should see that introductions are made when the new people are attending large gatherings. Then just as soon as they are beginning to make friends, the newcomers in turn should make efforts to help any newer Americans begin to find happy associations in the international circle.

The United Nations has technical services representatives in many places. They are drawn from a great variety of countries, generally speak English, and often welcome a chance to get acquainted with Americans. A cultural affairs officer at the American Embassy may be able to supply a list of U. N. representatives in the city with their home addresses. Two or three American women sometimes get together and make calls on wives of United Nations representatives. In one place the wife of a principal member of a United States technical mission holds an informal morning coffee every few months with the United Nations wives as honor guests, in order that she may introduce newly arrived American women to them. Happy and mutually profitable associations have often grown out of such gatherings. In some cases family friendships have developed and continued long after both families have moved on to other places.

The presence of British people in many countries offers a chance to get acquainted without the language barrier which so often handicaps the relationships between people of different countries. I'm not overlooking the fact that the Queen's English and the English of the Americans has its differences in pronunciation, in usage, and in vocabulary. Our trucks are *lorries,* our gasoline is *petrol,* our yards are *gardens,* our radio is *wireless,* and their *tiffin* (a word British people use overseas) is nothing more elegant that a noonday lunch. Nevertheless, the

Britons and the Americans have a great deal in common and in many places are enjoying one another very much.

There are some differences, which are more fundamental than vocabulary, and the cause of Anglo-American friendship would be better served if these differences were taken into account. Generalizations are as faulty in this case as in any other where a statement about the characteristics of a foreign people is made. But in general, British people are more reserved with strangers than Americans are. Because this is so, they sometimes conclude that Americans are forward and we conclude that they are cold. Unfortunately, these first impressions may keep two individuals from caring about becoming better acquainted and may even carry over as prejudice against all Americans or Britons. I heard a story which illustrates this point.

An American couple in Africa decided on their first Sunday after arrival to go to Church. Since they are Episcopalians they chose to attend an Anglican Chapel rather than the American Methodist mission church. They walked into the small building before time for the service to start and waited for an usher as they were accustomed to doing at home. There were no more than twenty others and they were regular attendants so the usher could not have been unaware that they were new to the church. Yet he gave not the slightest smile of greeting but said formally, "Will you sit here?"

After the service was over the Americans moved out to the church yard where the parishioners talked in small groups. No one noticed them at all. The words of the usher upon arrival were the only ones addressed to the couple during the whole time they were present. They missed the "right hand of fellowship" which would have been extended had they gone to an American church.

Imagine their surprise a few nights later when they were introduced to those same Englishmen at a reception and were greeted with, "How nice to meet you. Didn't we see you at church on Sunday?"

In the months that followed, warm friendships developed between the American couple and the English couples with whom they worshipped. It is fortunate that the reception came when it did otherwise they might have let themselves feel unwelcomed and never gone to that chapel again.

It isn't coldness or indifference which holds a British person back. On the one hand it may be the custom of waiting for a proper introduction before speaking to people, and on the other hand it may be the reflection of a kind of respect which doesn't too quickly presume that a stranger will want to be spoken to. Americans who tend to be extremely outgoing should not be hasty in judging others as unfriendly, and should restrain themselves, at least on first encounters, from being so garrulous or familiar that the British will decide they never want to see them again.

The Ambassador of the United States

Nominated by the President and confirmed by the Senate, an American Ambassador is our country's accredited representative in a foreign country. In most cases he is a man of exceptional ability who has come up through a career in foreign service or has been tapped from public life. In any case he is the deputy of the President of the United States and respect accorded to him is respect to the elected head of our nation. If Americans by intention or through carelessness show disrespect to an ambassador or to his wife it may be interpreted by those of another country as disloyalty or as lack of confidence. It should be remembered that it is the office and not necessarily the political person of the President which is the object of respect.

Whatever an American's feelings may be about an ambassador as a person and however much he may disagree with the policy of the party whose successful presidential candidate appointed him, it is important for Americans abroad to show respect to their ambassador just as they would stand for the national anthem or salute or otherwise give dignified attention to an American flag. If an ambassador is personally weak, then there is all the more reason for his fellow Americans to try to bolster him up and fill the gap.

There are a number of ways in which respects are paid. When an ambassador (or a minister in countries where we have a legation instead of an embassy) and his wife enter a room where there are as few as twenty people, all those present, both men and women, stand until the honored ones are seated. Thoughtful Americans extend this courtesy to the heads of diplomatic missions of other countries as well as their own. American guests at a party or reception wait until the American Ambassador has departed before they move to go At a small party, if an emergency required a premature departure, the guest would ask the ambassador's permission to leave.

Sometimes it is a difficult thing for a new ambassador (or for any other newly appointed official of high rank) to remember that it is his obligation to be the first to go home. Almost any foreign service officer could recount cases of junior people being kept frightfully late simply because their seniors were having a good time at a gathering and didn't think that others might be wanting to leave.

A proper form of address to any ambassador is "Mr. Ambassador" and this should be observed in public even by associates or personal friends. Introductions are made *to* an ambassador even in the case of women to whom men are generally presented. An American ambassador's wife is addressed simply as "Mrs. Smith" even though the wives of the ambassadors of other countries are most frequently addressed as "Madame ...." During an ambassador's absence from a country the one delegated to carry his responsibilities receives the courtesies normally accorded to the chief himself. If the ambassador's wife is away the wife of the next ranking officer assumes the duties of the first lady and is accorded the same courtesies which the ambassador's wife receives.

In addition to observing these various signs of respect in relation to the American Ambassador, citizens abroad should have a better understanding of his function and more appreciation for the work load of an ambassador and his wife. It is not uncommon to have an American returned from an overseas assignment, or particularly from a short tour, complain that the ambassador or the members of an embassy staff neglected them, meaning that they weren't invited to dinner at the embassy or may not have received an invitation for some reception given by the ambassador and his wife. Some who are going abroad are so anxious to receive attention from the American Embassy that they put pressure on a congressman who writes the ambassador insisting that red-carpet treatment be given when there may be no reason at all why the particular American in question should have special attention in the country where he is going.

An embassy assumes certain responsibilities for the safety and interests of its citizens, and Americans should register at an embassy or consulate, if they expect to reside for any length of time, in order that the officials may know of their presence. They should realize however that while it is part of the official function of an embassy to protect Americans against discrimination, an embassy must treat its citizens as fully subject to the laws, administrative practices and customs of the host country. Above all, an embassy cannot be a travel service or a social service and must not seek unfair advantage whether it be fixing a parking ticket or calling on the king.

The ambassador and his staff are in a country to represent the United States government and their time and attention must go first and for the most part in the direction of the local government to which they are accredited. Entertainment allowances given to an ambassador or his staff are by law limited to functions where a significant proportion of the guests are people of the country and others as needed specifically to promote the national interest. It is expected that Americans who attend such affairs are there either because their presence will contribute in a special way to the purpose of the occasion or because they are needed to assist in entertaining special guests. Those who are invited to an embassy affair should try to find out why and then work at being useful.

In a great many cases an ambassador and his wife find time to receive groups or individual Americans who are living in or passing through the country, but it is unreasonable that entertainment should be expected as a right.

It is also unreasonable and naive for Americans visiting a country to walk into their embassy and ask to see someone who will fix it up for them to have an interview with the prime minister of the country. Americans living in Thailand say that they have learned not to be surprised when a tourist shows up for dinner and blurts out, "The wife and I would like to meet the King while we are here. Do you suppose you could ask the ambassador to arrange it for sometime tomorrow?"

These are exceptional cases of course, but they are reminders to all of us that an ambassador and his staff have an important job to do, and that it ill becomes us to ask them to dissipate their energies in order to humor fellow citizens or to listen to absurd requests.

The Order of Precedence

Only a very small per cent of the Americans who live abroad will ever be involved with the full range of the intricacies of diplomatic protocol. Diplomatic representatives and those hostesses who remain close to the diplomatic corps are the ones who have occasion to follow the rules in detail. For those on the sidelines it is primarily a matter of interest to know how diplomatic society operates.

Protocol is defined in the handbook *Social Usage in the Foreign Service* as "that part of social procedure which is set out in definite rules prescribing the etiquette in ceremonies of state. It is the code prescribing deference to rank and adherence to due order of preference and to correct procedure in diplomatic exchange." It was at the Congress of Vienna in 1815 that diplomatic protocol as it has been observed in recent years was first codified.

In the spring of 1961 the plenipotentiaries of eighty countries convened at a new Congress of Vienna, this time under the auspices of the United Nations. They reviewed the old rules of diplomatic practice and after six weeks of deliberations were able through compromise and conciliation to arrive at certain changes, which were acceptable to all.

To the uninitiated the rules about who walks first and who sits where may seem a little silly as well as burdensome, but to those who work and live within official circles the rules provide a standard way of establishing and maintaining relationships with people of other countries no matter how diverse their own social rules might be.

Every embassy has a protocol officer whose responsibility it is to be acquainted with the rules regarding such matters as the seating of officials, the expression of condolences, or the acceptable form of addressing different diplomats. He keeps an up-to-date list of all diplomats in the country with the rank of each noted so that he could supply this information wherever it is needed.

In cases where two ambassadors are to be seated at a dinner or on a platform, the one who is senior in length of residence in that country would be given the position of honor. The ambassador who has been officially in a country longer than all the other ambassadors is referred to as the Dean of the Diplomatic Corps.

Great care has to be exercised by those who plan official gatherings to make sure that the rules are carefully followed because if they are not it might be considered that a lapse in protocol was a deliberate offense against the country whose representative was in some way slighted. If there were no fixed rules then our representatives and those of other countries would have no end of confusion to deal with, and would frequently be hard put to keep from making decisions that might give a wrong impression of our government's attitude at a given time. With protocol social situations are handled impersonally.

Invitations to official affairs are formally engraved, printed, or hand written. They are answered promptly, and the formal answers are hand written unless, as is becoming increasingly acceptable, a reply to a given telephone number is requested. Official parties generally have a reception line, and it is frequently the case that a butler or a staff assistant will be the first to greet the incoming guests in order that he may announce the name of each visitor to the host. Husbands and wives should enter together and are generally announced as a couple. Unless one has been assured that promptness is not expected (as may be the case at a continuing reception) good manners require that a guest arrive within a few minutes of the hour stated and that he leave on time if a departure time is given on the invitation. At a dinner party other guests leave only after the ranking guests have gone.

It comes as a surprise to many that it is the newcomer rather than the established resident who makes the first call in a diplomatic community. The American who gets her new house all ready for visitors and then waits to be called upon is going to wait indefinitely unless she is an ambassador's wife or some other highly placed person upon whom initial calls would be made. Otherwise, she takes her cards and goes around and presents herself saying in effect, "I have arrived. I want to pay my respects to you." By this token she indicates in a changing community that she is in residence and that she is ready to have social intercourse. If she herself is the wife of a diplomat she will make her calls upon the senior woman in her own embassy soon after arrival—usually within two days. Calls upon appropriate persons in other embassies and in the local government would be made within the first weeks.

Foreign service officers and their wives are always briefed concerning their responsibilities in these regards. The information included here is primarily for those outside the diplomatic service who may need or want to participate in diplomatic society. It is not required of any Americans outside of the foreign service and not related to principal positions in other government missions that they enter the social arena in a capital city. All those whose husbands have positions of prominence in their organizations generally do participate, and others who care to present themselves through the accepted procedures and as a result enjoy occasional or frequent contacts with the members of the diplomatic group.

It is necessary to inquire upon arrival in a new capital city as to the custom regarding calls. If an American has no one in his own organization to guide him at this point he or his wife could speak to someone on the staff of the protocol officer of the American Embassy. From that office he would not only learn the hours when calls are generally made, but also could find out if it is customary to go unannounced or by appointment. A new arrival should ask in particular if the wife of the American Ambassador or the wives of other senior American diplomats expect to receive American callers and the circumstances under which they prefer to do it.

The protocol officer is sometimes able to furnish a list of the members of the diplomatic corps to those who expect to call at other embassies as well as our own. (In many countries an up-to-date diplomatic corps list may be purchased at local book stores.) He might be able to tell the newcomer about the use of English among the wives of foreign diplomats. If a wife does not speak English and the American does not speak her language then it might be kinder to leave cards at the door rather than actually entering for a call. The two people might later meet at parties where a third person could help bridge the language gap.

Those who expect to participate in diplomatic society should have calling cards which are in much greater use abroad than at home, even though within the diplomatic corps the custom of dropping cards is fast being reduced and is thought by some to be a formality which in time may fade away.

Cards used by foreign service officers have traditionally been engraved, but this is not a requirement for other Americans and some use less expensive cards of good quality. The important thing is that cards should be dignified and formally worded. A woman, for instance, would never use a *Mary Brown* card, but would have a card reading *Miss Mary Brown* if she is unmarried and *Mrs. John Henry Brown* if she is married. In some cases women who are overseas with their husbands do not have separate cards because socially they present themselves together. A card reading *Mr. and Mrs. John Henry Brown* is sufficient. On the occasion when a woman might want to represent herself separately the "Mr." may politely be crossed out. Many women however find it convenient to have cards of their own in addition to the "Mr. and Mrs." card. A husband does need separate social cards with his full name, omitting the "Mr." Men's cards are smaller 2 x 3½ inches; women's are 2¼ x 3¼ if made separately; the "Mr. and Mrs." cards are 2½ x 3½ inches.

Social calls are never longer than fifteen minutes unless a guest is particularly urged to stay longer. If a maid or butler answers the door the cards should be sent ahead to the lady upon whom the call is made. If she herself opens the door then a visitor should give her name and lay the card on a table near the door. If the lady is not at home or is unable to see visitors, the cards are left with the corner turned down to indicate that they were brought in person and not sent by a driver, as is sometimes done. A wife leaves either a card of her own and two cards for her husband or most commonly one "Mr. and Mrs." card and one of her husband's cards. She calls only upon the lady of the house, her husband (in person or by proxy) calls upon both the lady and her husband, hence the reason for his leaving two cards while she only leaves one.

At a household where there is more than one adult lady (grown daughters or a mother-in-law, for instance), extra cards would be left to indicate that these ladies, too, are being recognized by the callers. Likewise in an American family where there is an adult woman member or relative in addition to the wife, she could either accompany the wife when she makes calls or send her cards along with those of the wife so that she too might be included in the diplomatic community's social activities.

A call may or may not be returned depending upon the position of the one who receives the call and the demands of her schedule. It is up to her to make the next move. Newcomers should in any case be registered at the American Embassy so that those who want to locate them to make calls or to issue invitations may inquire there for their address. A lady receiving a caller will sometimes ask the guest to write her address on a card or will record it herself.

Some people think it is stuffy to make calls and they avoid doing it overseas unless their jobs require it. A few make calls only because they feel it is a necessary price for getting ahead socially. But most Americans look forward to becoming acquainted with people of other countries and with those countrymen who are living in the same foreign city with them. I have always looked upon calling and receiving visitors as an interesting adventure in the realm of human relationships.

Protocol With Perspective

Within the diplomatic circle and at the official affairs for which it was prescribed, protocol makes sense. It provides an orderly way for doing things, and it is a guide for dissimilar people to know what to expect. But out of its place it may be just plain pompous!

I remember one morning in a foreign city the American Wives Group was gathered informally in a home to listen to a lecture by a woman professor at the University. She had just been introduced when the wife of the Counselor of the American Embassy (at that particular time the highest ranking member of our diplomatic mission in residence) slipped in late. The hostess opened the door quietly and indicated a chair at the back of the room. I am sure that the latecomer was relieved that an inconspicuous place was available and she was going towards it when one of the more junior embassy wives spotted her and, no doubt remembering her training that the senior woman should always be given the most favored seat, she stood and looked around expecting everyone else to stand. No one else stood, because no one else forgot the respect due at that moment to the speaker. Persistent in her *proper* behavior she called out, "Oh, Mrs. A., won't you sit here in front?"

"Thank you very much I shall be just fine right here," said Mrs. A. with embarrassment and then turning to the speaker she said, "I hope you will please excuse me for being late." The incident was thus smoothed over satisfactorily. But it was ridiculous that it should have occurred at all.

It is easy for those steeped in the processes of formal society to let these same processes guide their behavior in situations where the formalities are not required and may be out of place. When this happens then the onlooker can only conclude that the one who makes a show of formality is taking herself and her position in society too seriously, or else that she is an uncertain newcomer in social circles and is making too obvious an effort not to make a mistake.

It seemed funny and a little pathetic to me when a woman who had lived overseas with her husband who was in an official position told me that when she had once called together the American women under her in a foreign capital to let them know about something that was coming up she wrote the notes of invitation.

"Mrs. Thomas Smith requests ...." and the replies came: "Mrs. William Henry Brown accepts ...." These were women within her own organization whom she knew well and saw every day!

I heard of one foreign capital where a group of American women had a long and earnest discussion about whether they should have white gloves on or off when they greeted a prominent American woman who was going to be in their city. The visitor is a person so deeply concerned with vital matters that I am sure she would never notice whether a hand she shook was gloved or ungloved. But some of those in charge of a reception given for her were, months later, still remembering with chagrin that when the day arrived a few of the well briefed ladies made a glove mistake.

Appropriate dress and courteous behavior should be expected at a function where a distinguished fellow citizen is being honored. Americans abroad should be thoughtful in such matters both out of respect for the eminent person and in order to let it be known in the community that we recognize our distinguished people. But when Americans permit themselves to get agitated about the minute details of what constitutes proper dress for them in their appearances even with fellow Americans, it is time for them to make a serious reappraisal of themselves as persons. There is a grave danger that they are losing sight of the values of individuality and spontaneity which are so essentially a part of being an American.

One of the things that often happens on the fringes of diplomatic circles is that others who have no need to behave with undue formality become greatly impressed with the surface expressions of protocol and out-do the diplomats in the way they think and act. We see this in some foreign capitals. Americans who have always before done informal entertaining may make a great production out of a dinner just for friends, with formal service and with seating arrangements precisely calculated according to sex and age and rank.

Someone told me of a situation in an Eastern country where an American host and hostess got into a heated controversy with two American guests (of similar job status as theirs and in the same organization) who were visitors from another country as to who should properly escort the local dignitaries to dinner. By the time a compromise had been arrived at they discovered that the national guests had gotten tired of standing around and had just walked over to the table and seated themselves.

Some Americans who are accustomed at home to accepting people with no thought of rank begin to make discreet inquiries about who is senior to whom when they get overseas. Those who are thought of as "top brass" are sometimes sought after not so much because of themselves but so that the host or hostess may say, "The Helms are coming, you know he is the top man in Standard Oil" or "Won't you come meet some friends from the Embassy" as if that would be a special inducement regardless of who the embassy folks were.

The other side of this story is that some react with false modesty and dare not let themselves approach or give a first invitation to those who are senior or older or somehow more highly placed than they. I have known older people in prominent positions abroad who were lonely because the younger or junior people stood in awe of them.

I heard of two young American clerks in Vietnam who were innocent enough or wholesome enough not to be scared of an elderly office boss and his wife. They asked them for supper on the cook's night off, gave them simple but delicious food, let them help wash the dishes, and treated them as the couple's grown-up daughter in an apartment in New York City might have done. The older people loved it and remembered in turn to include the young women whenever they were planning the kind of an outing or party they thought they might enjoy.

One day when I was visiting in a foreign capital a young missionary wife whom I had met earlier came up to speak to me at a swimming club.

"How are things with you today?" I asked her. That seemed to be all she needed to enable her to talk about something that was bothering her.

"Oh, Mrs. Winfield," she said desperately, "I just don't know whether I have what it takes to be the First Lady." It so happened that there was a national election approaching back home but I knew that her husband, likeable and capable as he is, was most unlikely to be a candidate for the presidency of the United States. I asked her to tell me what she was talking about. Here is the situation. She and her husband were the newest and youngest of their particular mission group in that city. The vacation schedules had worked out in such a way that for one month all the other married couples were going to be away including the most senior couple who usually took charge when special visitors arrived or when the mission needed to be represented at some official gathering. This young woman, new to the ways of a diplomatic society, new to the rank consciousness which even a small group of missionaries had caught in the foreign capital was sick with anxiety.

I resisted the impulse to say, "Dear child, take it easy." I told her first that I was quite sure that she would be able to handle graciously any social responsibility that might come to her. I reminded her of a thing she would have known if the senior married women hadn't been so smug about being senior and about being married, that the two single missionary women who were there had been many years in the country and would know how to meet, or how to help her and her husband meet, any social emergency that might arise.

It is fortunate that those who must do all they can to keep the relationships between nations on a mutually respectful basis have a clear cut set of directions for their behavior in relation to representatives from other countries. It is reassuring that Americans overseas may demonstrate their loyalty to the principles of their government by the way they conduct themselves in relation to their ambassador who is the symbol of the United States of America. But let us hope that in spite of the pace set by a few social climbers and the example of the unimaginative social sticklers, most Americans will have the good sense and the good grace to recognize the limits within which the protocol of diplomacy needs to operate and will concentrate upon the opportunities for unfettered and undirected associations in foreign lands.

Chapter XII

FOOTLOOSE

For the most part Americans going overseas alone have the same kinds of adjustments to make, run into the same kind of difficulties, and receive the same kinds of satisfactions as those who go as families. With certain exceptions the preceding discussions have been directed as much to single people as to the married folks. There are, however, certain aspects of overseas living which are of special concern to the unattached people who go overseas, to those who employ and send them, and in the case of young people to the parents who wait and wonder at home.

Problems of the Unattached

I have asked many single people and many who have been responsible for them what seemed to be the most difficult thing about their living overseas. Loneliness is always mentioned first.

It is not that the journey to a foreign land is harder for a single man or woman (goodness knows it is hardest of all for mothers with little children) but that the single people frequently must make the journey alone. It is not that cultural shock upon arrival is any different for a lone woman or a single man, but one who feels shocked and has no one with whom to talk about it is more likely to be homesick.

I remember meeting a young woman who had traveled for the first time out of New York City and for the first time on an airplane to a country half way around the world. She hadn't eaten anything because she thought she might be airsick; she hadn't slept because she didn't feel safe in the air. She looked like a scared kitten by the time she got to us. We were able to take her to live with an American family who helped her through the adjustment period, but if she had been taken to a hotel room or directly to her own apartment she might have had a hard time.

The most obvious solution to this problem is that whenever possible young men or women moving abroad for the first time should be sent with a companion or with a group. This can't be done where a graduate student is going on his own to Nepal or when only one stenographer is needed as a replacement in Peru. In cases like this the traveler has to muster all the maturity he can for the journey and make sure that someone is expecting to meet him at the other end.

Young single people generally make a better adjustment to overseas living if they can be housed with someone else their own age. While tensions may develop when incompatible people are billeted together, personality clashes are easier to live with than loneliness.

The feeling of aloneness can be more acute for a woman than for a man because in almost any foreign country a man can get out into the community by himself while in many places a single woman can't go out alone at night and shouldn't go too far off the main thoroughfares by herself during the day.

Loneliness is not an experience unique for single people in foreign countries. It is a condition common to all men and is more particularly a burden for single people wherever they live. It is unrealistic for them to hope that they might escape from their human plight just by turning up in a new part of the world, and it is unfair to blame the new community itself if old and familiar feelings have followed them. Nevertheless, it is true that an unfamiliar setting and the restrictions of an alien society coupled with the absence of supporting friends and relatives may increase the tendency to feel desolate in those who are already inclined in that direction. If the circumstances are especially trying even a young person who has previously never minded seclusion may find it intolerable overseas.

One stenographer who lived alone in Korea said, "I didn't have a lot of beaux back home and I didn't expect to have many dates here, but at home I had my blouses to iron at night. With a maid to do my work here I haven't anything at all I have to do after I leave the office."

Support From Outside—Direction From Within

No one should be sent on an overseas assignment who is still so immature and dependent that he must have a nurse to look after him. Single people, unfairly perhaps, must be checked against an even more rigid emotional maturity scale than married people because they are not going to have the personality props which husbands and wives often supply for each other. Having demonstrated before they leave their homeland that they can measure up, they still need some help when they reach the foreign field.

I am not proposing that camp counsellors or deans of women should be scattered around the world to give aid and admonitions to all the bachelor men and women. I do suggest that overseas Americans who are married and have the good fortune to have their marriage partners with them in a foreign community should make a conscious effort to think about the unattached Americans more than they do.

Wives who frequently do such a helpful job of initiating new wives into the social customs and housekeeping procedures of a new area ought to extend that service to the single women and in many cases to single men who must run their own houses. Much of this kind of help is given during the day time when single people are working. Evening sessions could also be scheduled for the employed women. When a special daytime session is likely to be outstanding and cannot be duplicated at night, the wives who are planning the program should take the initiative in inviting the working homemakers and might go to their employers with the request that those who care to, be permitted to attend.

The bosses for their part are derelict in their duty if they do not see that young men and women on their staffs have help in getting households organized, and that they have access to transportation where it is needed, especially at night.

An administrator should make every effort to give even the lowest paid American on his staff a chance to study the local language. If he can't afford to let a new secretary take time off to join a language class which is held for more senior staff people during the day, he ought to find funds for a night class and encourage the typists and clerks to attend. Nothing will more quickly help them to feel at home in a community than the ability to talk with people.

Hostesses should forget the silly idea that the number of men and women at a dinner should always be balanced and should include single people more readily. Furthermore, married couples might discipline themselves to carry on conversation which doesn't begin and end with family interests so that the single people won't so often have to sit around feeling like fifth wheels. Not that the single people require a censored sort of conversation; it is just that they should not be reminded all evening that they are on the outside and must go home alone.

Families who share their children do a great deal to ease the pangs of loneliness for single people who may be wistful for nieces and nephews or younger brothers and sisters back home. The children like it too when a young man who enjoys playing baseball is invited along on a picnic or when a woman who knows just how to read stories is invited to come to dinner early enough to have time with the youngsters before they go to bed.

The grown up children in our family remember how much the "courtesy aunts" contributed to them during their early years in China. Dr. Annie Scott once spent a two-week holiday with us at Peitaiho Beach. She and Margaret combed the wooded areas for wild flowers, checked them for identification in *The Wild Flowers of North China.* Under Dr. Scott's patient guidance Margaret, not yet in kindergarten, learned how to press the flowers for future reference and how to print the labels on the notebook pages. Harriet was only three but she was not too young to go with "Dr. Annie" for long exploring trips among the big rocks and in the small coves of the beaches, responding with pride and pleasure to the grown-up who treated her always not as a *little* girl but as a person.

There were dozens of other single people in China who seemed to enjoy seeing our children and who meant a great deal to them. "Auntie Witham," from Kansas, was a brilliant biochemist who taught them many things which they still remember because her wisdom was sprinkled with such droll humor. "Auntie May K." was working on how to keep motherless babies alive with soybean milk, and she invited the children to come to her house and let them hold her white mice.

In Burma there were single people who joined us from time to time and seemed to like doing it, whose contributions to the family far outweighed any effort of ours on their behalf. The trip to Inle Lake would not have been nearly so much fun if Maurine Cavett who had been a missionary in the country for many years hadn't been along to give us background information and to help us bargain for the boat and the things we bought in the floating market.

Bill Greene is not a single man. He spoke often of his wife, of his children and especially of his grandchildren. But his wife hadn't been able to go to Burma with him; so he was alone then and it was our pleasure on many occasions to have him join us for dinner or parties. In fact, whenever we were planning any guest list one of the children was sure to say, "You're going to ask Mr. Greene, aren't you?" His genius as an after dinner storyteller is unsurpassed.

We won't ever again be able to serve shrimp without having someone in the family say, "Remember when Bill Greene told us about that time in China when he tried to whisper to his companion at a feast about how to eat the live shrimp, and the man didn't hear him say to just bite off the tail but put the whole crawly thing in his mouth head first?"

If I had only invited couples to dinner or only those who might have been able to ask us back (Bill lived at the hotel) we might have missed knowing a man who is remarkable not just as a storyteller but as a person who has made outstanding contributions to the development of better agriculture in a number of Asian and South American countries.

The married man or woman who is overseas alone can be just as lonely or in some cases more lonely than the bachelors, and it is helpful to them and can be rewarding to a family if they are included in gatherings from time to time.

Whatever families do with or for their single colleagues however must be done genuinely and with the focus on a regard for them as individuals. No unmarried girl wants a matron to be nice to her in a charitable sort of way. A single man doesn't want to be "adopted" and treated like a school boy by people who are his professional peers. Single people seldom enjoy being entertained collectively as if they were orphans being treated to a once-a-year excursion into the outside world.

In many cases the unattached people have busy and active lives of their own and aren't sitting around waiting for invitations. They should be as free as anyone else to send regrets or to ask for a rain check without a hostess getting huffy and saying, "No need trying to include the spinsters; I asked Mary Brown once and she wouldn't bother to come."

The important thing is to remember that there are single people who might have a special contribution to make to a social group and might appreciate being included. Another thing to remember is that a few of the younger and less resourceful single people may feel stranded unless the married people assume some responsibility for helping them learn how to be at home in a foreign land.

Single people can do a great deal to help themselves. They needn't wait to be asked to parties. They can take advantage of the newcomers' prerogative and go around and call on the people they would like to know. They needn't feel that they must do elaborate or expensive entertaining but can plan suppers or coffee and dessert evenings to which they invite people they think they are most likely to enjoy. They can look around overseas as they do at home to find clubs, cultural institutes, or church groups where they might find interesting and useful activities and where they might make friends. They can pursue creative hobbies and use free time to brush up on their skills.

The unattached person overseas has a good opportunity to perfect his sense of humor because he is going to have so many occasions to use it. A man who doesn't know much about cooking in the first place, who hires a mediocre cook because he hasn't any idea what qualifications he should look for, and who has to be away from the house all day, may come home and find meals that fall far short of the ones his mother used to fix. He could sit down and cry, of course, or he could get mad and rage unreasonably. But he had best see the situation with perspective and take steps to improve it.

He could suggest that the cook confine his efforts to simple dishes at first, scrambled eggs and such. He could scout around and find a friend who has an experienced cook and ask if the homemaker would arrange for his cook to be tutored. He could even write his mother and ask her to send him by air post the simplest illustrated cookbook she can find. Then he could hire a local person to write in translations if his own use of the cook's language is limited. (Of course there is a chance the cook will not know how to read!) All this time the hungry man must keep a good grip on his sense of humor.

A single woman who is assigned an apartment and is helped only to the point of having her baggage delivered is in an equally good position to practice being patient as well as being amused. She won't have a husband to rip the metal bands off boxes. Unless someone has warned her she won't even have a screw driver and a hammer to do it with. She may have a servant who has handled tools even less than she has. If one vital box of household equipment hasn't arrived she may have to wait for weeks until she can find some man at the school or in the office who will go (as a woman couldn't) down to the wharf or out to the airport baggage room to hunt for the missing piece.

If she needs to buy an extension cord or to find a plumber she may have to go out into a man's world and try to find someone who will take her seriously enough to let her state her business. If she has a service man arrive who knows less than she does about installing a piece of equipment she can't expect him to listen to a mere woman tell him how to do it. She can't even be excused for swearing like a man if she is furiously frustrated while she is trying single handedly to carry the responsibilities of both a man and a woman.

But she can learn to keep calm, to keep sweet, and to go on looking pretty and helpless even while she is managing to move mountains and to endure exasperating delays and inconveniences.

When a reasonable amount of outside support is given to single people and when they exert a fair effort themselves, there is every reason to expect that their overseas experience will be both productive and happy. In the vast majority of cases it is. But if adequate guidance is missing and if personal resources are limited then single people may seek to avoid loneliness or boredom or a feeling of failure in ways which are neither satisfying to them nor acceptable to the community.

A girl who feels lost and neglected is an easy mark for the first man who comes along and says, "Let's have some fun." She may be desperate enough to believe the irresponsible Beau Brummell who assures her that in her case it will be different. But she will be as left-lonesome as the last girl when the man moves on to another port or to another conquest and leaves her to solve her problems alone.

A single man overseas without guidance and without a sense of direction can have his own kind of problems with the opposite sex. A young North American in a Latin country reports he was stationed in a place where there were no single North American women his age. He wanted to meet the educated and attractive young women of the country but found that by custom they were carefully protected. The process by which a foreigner could get himself introduced to a young woman of a good family was so slow that he feared his tour of duty would be finished before he had a chance to meet the girls he wanted to know. Meanwhile, the kind of girls he wasn't interested in threw themselves at him from every direction. He said he was fortunate to be situated where he could indulge a love for good music and where he had older married friends who kept him from feeling too lonely and finally were able to facilitate his introduction into social life with cultured young men and women of the country.

A few single people have had an overseas assignment terminated because they turned from loneliness to liquor and let the habit get completely out of hand. We hear of a few others who withdraw and brood about their loneliness, becoming more and more careless about food and exercise, sleeping poorly, and ultimately having to be sent home with a bad health record which may involve both physical and emotional illness.

Unrealistic Expectations

Part of the problem for the small minority of single people who don't make the grade overseas is that they have gone abroad with serious misconceptions about the life they would be living. No one has meant to mislead them. Yet, they have sometimes conjured up, out of the references in recruitment literature to fascinating places and interesting people, a glamorous picture of exotic settings peopled with maharajas and dancing girls, with smartly dressed lieutenants asking for the next dance. They listen to the orientation lectures about cultural patterns and cultural changes, but they don't really hear because their minds are dreaming about something out of this world. They aren't prepared for the down-to-earth conditions which they find.

Some of them have been chafing under the restraints of the social conventions around them at home and think that the only way to escape from the hometown busybodies is to go to some far off place. They don't reckon with the fact that many foreign cities have within them a small clique made up of Westerners and the local elite close to them and that gossip and scandal travels around even quicker than it does at home. "So I flirted with her husband" one single woman reported, talking about a married woman in the foreign capital from which she had returned unhappily. "I was only having a little fun, did she have to start the whole community talking as if I were a woman of the street?"

Single girls sometimes think that there will be a better chance to find a husband overseas, and they are often disillusioned. One secretary stormed into a high-level staff meeting in a European city and announced her resignation. She left the room and then came back in with this post script: "I came to this job expecting champagne and proposals. I want you to know that it has been nothing but beer and propositions."

One of the reasons why highly trained professional women seldom have special problems overseas while the young single women and single men doing less skilled work may encounter some of the difficulties I have been describing, is that the professional people are more likely to be interested first of all in the job itself and in its relation to the country. They are not primarily attracted by the atmosphere of the community or by the possibilities of fringe benefits of living there even though both of those may provide certain added inducements.

They have the focus on a research project, an administrative responsibility, a class room, health problems of a community, or on any one of countless other full-time responsibilities which American women are carrying overseas. They take the community and their adjustments to it and the social life within it in stride just as the married people do. Some of them do it better than others just as is the case with the professional men and their wives. But what happens after work hours is not of primary importance to the women who have significant professional responsibilities as it may be for the younger single people who take an overseas job in order to get to a foreign country, not always having a realistic picture of what being there is going to be like.

The single people who go along on a job just for the ride and expect the situation to offer many plums and few demands are more and more the exception. Increasingly careful screening keeps most of them at home.

I talked with one young secretary who admits she applied for an overseas job primarily because it would give her transportation to a foreign country. "I have always wanted to see and to learn at first hand about people of other lands. I would have to work for years before I could save enough money to go to even one foreign place for a short visit." She went on to say that she worked very hard in her first office jobs in this country to demonstrate competence so she would have good recommendations.

I have learned that once she was overseas she made every effort to do her job well and that she proved to be outstanding in her ability to make a good adjustment in a community that was listed as a hardship post. On the side she took correspondence courses from an American college to keep on improving herself and to be qualified for other overseas jobs in the future. Here is the example of a young person who didn't have the advantage of a job motivation as such, but whose motivations otherwise were so good that any office any place in the world would be lucky to have her on the staff.

She had some of the other qualifications which the older professional people who work themselves up to a responsible position overseas usually have. She is personally resourceful. She has a good imagination and a sense of humor. And while she gives every evidence of being an attractive woman who isn't single by choice, she seems to have made peace with herself on that score and without appearing resigned to "single blessedness" she isn't letting her judgment of a foreign country depend upon whether or not she is given an engagement ring in that place.

A Full And Creative Life

As I have called single people who have lived overseas to ask them about special problems they have faced, I have frequently received a reply something like this, "Problems, oh yes, there are problems but you know when you are overseas there are certain ways in which there are real advantages to being unattached."

Housing is one example. Married people need to have room at least for the two of them and many need a larger house if they have a big family. A single person is not so limited in his or her choice, but may be able to take a small or inconspicuous place if that is what he likes. On the other hand a single person whose position requires that he do a fair amount of entertaining or who wants to keep open house for local friends may find that he is more able than he was at home to afford and maintain a suitable home.

Single people frequently take rooms in the homes of nationals and are in this way better able to acquire a use of the language and to learn about the people than a family or a couple who wouldn't as easily be able to find the space or the privacy they would want in a home with another family.

Single people also have certain advantages when it comes to travel. One person is a freer agent in choosing a time for a trip. A family must wait for a husband to get leave, for a wife to square away her community responsibilities, for children to be on a school holiday or for all to be finished with the measles. A once-a-year ceremony at some ancient ruins doesn't wait and it is the single man rather than the family man who is most likely to get there. A single woman in some places can't travel alone but she can take the initiative in finding a like minded national or fellow American who wants to go where she does and can arrange to be free when she is.

I have read in *The Newsletter* of the Inter-American Schools Service a report about three single North Americans, two women and a young man, all teachers on holiday, who drove a jeep from Cartazena, Colombia to Santiago, Chile—a distance of six thousand miles through the length of the Andes. The young man had to leave the party in Puna (Peru) but, undaunted, the young women did the last thousand miles alone. I'm sure that they will not come back home reporting that there was nothing to do when their classroom jobs were finished.

A young woman who has returned from teaching in an armed forces school in Germany says that on her trip over she met another single teacher going to a similar school in Spain. Because the schools operate on the same schedule the women were able to arrange to meet for holidays and during the two-year assignment managed to take trips to numerous places in Europe to which they were both attracted.

I have been told by a number of single people that a hobby can often be pursued more thoroughly overseas by them than by married people who may not be free to spend so much time or money on a personal project.

If I weren't for so many years so happily married, these single people I have been talking to might tempt me, with their descriptions of the advantages of being fancy free, to wish that I might join their ranks. They have at least convinced me that a single person abroad needs no special sympathy because he or she can have a chance in any foreign country to live a full and creative life.

Grass Roots

One thing the successful single people have stressed most frequently in our conversations is that the unattached Americans overseas have special opportunities to form deep and lasting friendships in the local communities and that many of them do. One woman said to me that she felt that if unattached men and women were wisely guided any of them would be able to put roots down in foreign countries and that their personal experiences would be richer and the American picture would be a better one because of this.

One single woman's close contact with the country began with an appreciation of some of the old Chinese porcelains she saw in small shops in Taipei. She bought one or two and then began to look at other pieces in other shops. She continued to buy from time to time but became a more discriminating collector and actually found herself more interested in learning about the beautiful pieces of porcelain than in owning them. Shopkeepers sent her to old families from the mainland who had managed to bring treasured items when they fled from the communists.

She stepped up the pace of her language study in order that she could more easily talk with these people. She went with them to see other Chinese who were artists or who had interesting samples of the old porcelains that intrigued her. She met both Chinese and Westerners who were art historians. She began to acquire a library. She found herself entertaining an interesting assortment of people and going with these new friends to see art exhibitions and to hear Chinese operas.

She asked for and was given a second term of service at that post. Back in this country now, she is known as an authority on a particular period and particular form of Chinese art. In addition to that, and probably of greater satisfaction to her, she maintains contacts with a circle of people in Taipei whom she will always cherish as friends.

Another single woman was able to increase her understanding of and to make close friendships with nationals through the social service work which she did after working hours. She was living in Teheran and became interested in the problems of the Iranian women who came into the city to find work. She was able to help organize and guide leaders among the local ladies as they established a hostel for the country women. In the course of this work she became well acquainted with the leaders who assumed responsibility for the project and also had interesting and helpful associations with the residents of the hostel.

Two young American secretaries in an African country were assigned to a small house. They found a man and his wife to look after the house and the garden as well as laundry and cooking so they had time on their hands after work. One night at some public function they met a couple of young men of the country who were recently returned from several years of study in the United States. They saw at once how happy the boys were to talk with Americans and sensed that they weren't having too easy a time getting used to being back in a less sophisticated place.

On the spur of the moment they said, "Come over on Friday night and we can talk." When Friday night came the boys brought a couple of other returned students with them. Then and there what came to be called the University Club was organized by the local boys and was sponsored by the two American girls who had each had but two years at a college before going to a secretarial school. The girls furnished the meeting place and the soft drinks and American cookies they had taught their cook to make. The boys rounded up a dozen others who had studied in American universities and they planned an agenda for discussions.

They and their girl friends who spoke English and cared to join the group appeared every Friday evening at eight o'clock. For one hour the discussion followed the fixed agenda and then for an hour or two the conversation was informal. Before the meetings had been going on long the young men decided that they would like to give other people in the community a better idea of what America is like. Once again the girls came to the rescue. They suggested that films and a projector could be borrowed from the United States Information Service Library. The boys scouted around town to find a place for outdoor shows. They found that the YMCA had a large courtyard with a white wall and that the directors were willing for the students to use it. Word was sent out that movies would be shown there every Wednesday evening. Large numbers of people turned up at the weekly showings. They saw two American girls assisting a dozen local men and three or four local girls to greet people and help them find spots on the ground where they could drop their cushions and sit comfortably for shows which gave them accurate glimpses of life in America.

In a Middle East city a young mail clerk at the U. S. Embassy thought it would be fun to go for a picnic on the Tigris. He asked the four young women clerks if they would like to go along. None of them knew how to go about renting a boat so they decided to ask one of the young nationals who worked in the office what to do about that. He said that he would pilot the group. They invited the other unmarried nationals to accompany them and arrangements were made about time and food. That was the beginning of regular outings planned and attended both by young American employees and the unmarried local employees. Every Friday a notice was posted as to where they were going, when to meet, and what food or money would be required.

The nationals who might never have felt able to entertain in their homes carried their part in this cooperative arrangement. Americans who would have been lonely saw the country and made friends with its people.

Volunteers for Peace

By the time this book appears the Peace Corps will have young—and for the most part unmarried—Americans working in Tanganyika and Nigeria. Other groups will follow them to Africa and still others will go to many countries on several continents.

These young people have advantages which some Americans who go abroad do not have. They are all well motivated. This has been checked and double checked. They will all be assigned to work which the leaders of the nations to which they go feel is urgent and which the young people themselves can see is important.

They are being given long and intensive periods of training so that they will know how to perform their tasks and so that they will speak the language and understand the customs of the people to which they are going. They will be supplied with books and learning materials basic to their undertaking. They will be given the appropriate innoculations and will be instructed in health and sanitary procedures. Their travel will be arranged for them. The need will be recognized for them to have a settling-in period.

They will be housed in unpretentious quarters and will have money only to live simply. Most of them will work side by side with local people. They will have to learn from the nationals how to operate in the local situation; the nationals will need to learn from them certain technical skills. Older and understanding Americans will be available to guide them. But in a very real sense each volunteer will be on his own as he does his share of work and as he moves in a foreign community mingling with the people and making friends.

I, for one, am rejoicing in this latest wave of American migrations. I have confidence that the Peace Corps members will represent well the best that is American and will in easily understood ways help other peoples to move towards their own high goals.

Over four hundred students from a great number of American colleges assembled at the American University in Washington, D. C. in March of 1961 for a conference sponsored by the United States National Student Association to learn about the Peace Corps and to make known their opinions about a youth service program abroad. The delegates had competed for the privilege of being representatives. They had used vacation time to make the trip and each had paid his own transportation, or had hitch-hiked as best he could.

Their enthusiasm and single minded attention was ample evidence that across our country there are large numbers of young people who believe in the humanitarian purposes for which the Corps was established.

There is evidence that many other citizens as well as college students are supporting in spirit not only the Peace Corps volunteers but all other Americans whether old or young, whether single or married who go abroad intent upon living usefully and considerately.

When Senator Hubert Humphrey spoke to the Youth Service Conference in Washington he was speaking for many of us and his words might well be extended even beyond the Peace Corps:

"I want to tell you that I'm thrilled to say just a word about this endeavor. It makes me feel that we are living again; that something is stirring in this nation of ours, something worthwhile and good; that the heart beats a little faster; that the muscle tone is a little better; that the spirit is a little brighter. This is what I think the world wants from this country more than it wants its money or even more than it wants its technology. It wants from America the reassurance that we believe in people."

Chapter XIII

HOME AGAIN

Most people have mixed feelings when a term of foreign service is over and they are packing to come home. They are anxious to bring the new baby back to grandparents; they want to see relatives and old friends. They want to feel the cold of snow if they have been in the tropics. They want to bask in the sun if they have lived through months of rain.

They want a chance to go off duty as conspicuous Americans and get themselves lost in a New York City crowd. They dream of hot showers, and imagine the smell of good rare beef. At the same time they wish they didn't have to leave the adopted country.

I remember watching a small child stand in an airplane as soon as he was permitted to unfasten his safety belt. He pushed backwards against his seat as hard as he could. I knew how he felt because I too felt the tug of the place we were leaving. I wished I could see for a little while longer the faces of all those at the airport who had come to be our friends. One twelve year old tried to put it in verse:

"Soaring through cloud mottled blue
We flew over pagoda's gold dome;
I puzzled on a thought not new,
Which way is my home?"

Shock In Reverse

Americans also have mixed feelings when they get back home from just a couple of years overseas. On the one hand everything looks wonderful; broad clean streets, touch control houses, raw celery and water from the tap. At the same time much seems strangely changed. Even those who have been aware of rapid change in a foreign community find themselves considerably surprised to discover that things at home hadn't remained static.

One friend says he was horrified when he came home the year the new cars had come out in pinks and purples and ten shades of yellow. He thought a circus was in town. A woman said she felt as if she had been away for ages when she saw at the homeside airport that women's skirts cut the knee cap while her year-before-last coat seemed to drag the ground.

A foreign service officer who claims California as his home says that it shocked him to discover that in what used to be a quiet rural community giant shopping centers had mushroomed all over the countryside. He was delighted that huge irrigation projects had brought water and prosperity to formerly hard pressed farmers, but he found something a little disquieting in the sight of a new two-thousand-dollar boat as well as a new three-thousand-dollar car in almost every yard. He had become used to seeing refugee camps where eager young men waited in line for a chance to borrow one book.

People who have been off where wheels turn slowly feel breathless when they get back into rush hour traffic or try to fit into the pace of rushing men. One young woman said it frightened her to see so many young men in a coffee shop in the nation's capital looking old and tired and so very much alike.

Mothers find themselves relieved that baby food is so easily available and that they needn't feel anxious if children play in what after being in germ infested communities they may call "good clean American dirt." But women who may have been yearning for the comforts of home have often forgotten, during the time they have had servants, how much work is involved in keeping even the most modern house picked-up, clean, and comfortable. They re-discover in shock who does most of that work. If little children have grown into Brownies and Cub Scouts and if high school age children stay after school for dramatics or sports, the mother turned *amah* and cook and houseboy finds the full time chauffeuring the most taxing part of all.

People who are on short home leave before a second tour overseas don't get the full impact, however, because frequently there are relatives or friends who step in and share the load of laundry, cooking, and babysitting. Most house guests are considerate in servantless households I'm sure, but occasionally one hears of those returned from abroad who are not.

One hostess was hurrying around getting breakfast when a friend just home from overseas and servants walked into the kitchen with an armload of dresses and said, "Blanche, would you please get these pressed today?"

Blanche has a sense of humor as well as a busy schedule so she said, "You're back in America now my friend and I'm sure your ironing arm is as good as mine." The guest was being perfectly honest when she said, "Oh, heavens, I just forgot."

A man also forgot when he was staying in a home with friends in

Washington during his de-briefing period after a two-year stint overseas. He left his bed unmade, his clothes on the floor, his suits to be sent to the cleaner, and he asked for personal services that a harried young mother could ill afford to provide, and she didn't quite know how to go about inducting her husband's college roommate into the self-help fraternity.

Women not only have to manage to get back into the swing of homemaking and a highly organized community life, they have to learn to do it without talking about how much easier it was to live overseas. People who normally care little about patriotism can get righteously indignant if someone who has lived abroad seems to be criticizing the good old U.S.A.

Children returned from overseas sense this prejudice against foreign countries and it is sometimes a source of disturbance to them. They may have loved the other country but they love America none the less. In fact, after being expatriates for a while they may be more conscious and proud of their national identity than youngsters who have never been away. But if a child comes back to an average American community and has much to say immediately about the places he has been and the things he has done overseas it isn't long until someone says, "He thinks he's so smart."

One boy whose heart had been set on getting back to this country so he could be on a baseball team came home from a Little League play ground in a gloomy mood one day. The next day at the usual hour he didn't go. His father tried to diagnose the trouble but had to wait until the boy confided sadly, "They said I was German and couldn't play."

He had lived four years in Germany with his family. He spoke German, had enjoyed his life in Germany and somehow it showed. "They," of course, were the boys his age whose opinion mattered more to him than any words of welcome or encouragement from a friendly coach.

The Old Home Town

The children, bless them, often have more than their share of the coming-home load. Even little children may feel it. People sometimes gush over them unpleasantly because they are much traveled. They want them to say something in a foreign language, to do a foreign dance, or sing a foreign song.

Ladies at a tea party caught a four-year-old daughter of ours some years ago. They asked her the usual embarrassing personal questions some people ask any child. Then they started telling her how marvelous it was that she had been so many places. "To think that such a little girl should have crossed the Pacific three times!"

The child took a deep breath and pulled away from her captor saying emphatically, "That's nothing—I have a baby sister and she crossed the ocean before she was even born!"

Teen-agers returned from a foreign land may not find it so easy to pull away and silence their tormentors with a last-word-on-the-subject reply. Adults may find them poised and interesting and engage them in serious conversation about their life and observations abroad. It is the peer group that makes them shy. Their contemporaries sometimes resent the newcomers' easy discourse with the grown ups. They miss in their conversation the current slang and popular small talk which they have been away from and so don't know. Their contemporaries have no idea how much those returning from abroad want to be accepted by the young people at home.

Like much cultural shock, the first encounters are the hardest. Given a little time and supported substantially by their parents the children who take the brunt of the attacks from isolationists, conformists, or the idly curious frequently show a remarkable ability to adapt to the home situation and at the same time hold on to the values of their foreign experience. The child who was a heckler yesterday may be a best friend tomorrow and the one most eager to hear about the places overseas.

Children can be unmerciful to a newcomer but given time they are generally more flexible than adults and more open to new ideas and information. More than one American child home from abroad has been responsible for a gradual change in a group's attitude towards foreign countries and for the establishment of a student exchange program or a drive to support an orphan in some foreign place.

Adults may find a lack of interest in foreign affairs more rigid and are sometimes less able than their youngsters to arouse interest in world issues in communities where only the world series seems to take people's attention far away from home town concerns.

One man who has worked overseas for a number of years says that when he gets back home he is always invited to make the rounds of the luncheon clubs and they ask him to talk about his work. He always wonders if the members have enough background information about the part of the world he works in and enough genuine interest in it for him to say anything subtly significant. He always gives them the benefit of the doubt, and who can say that he has not stimulated some of them to further reading and prompted others to think about a candidate's foreign policy when they go to the ballot box?

A couple of elderly people who have worked for many years on a university campus in India have retired in a small city which they both had called home. People are friendly but the adjustments haven't been easy for two people long accustomed to a stimulating intellectual life and a broad involvement in social problems and international affairs. They don't know where to begin to establish contact with people who read only a local-gossip newspaper, sit for hours before run-of-the-mill television shows, and seem to let their tastes be guided by commercials that often are childish if not crude.

In time these cultured people will likely find that these first impressions of an American community are not completely accurate. She will eventually find her way to the local branch of the League of Women Voters, the United Council of Church Women, and the Association of University Women. He will be found by the Human Relations Council and asked to help with a study on inter-racial housing. They will discover the small but well supported art museum and will be asked to loan some Indian paintings. Before long the local librarian will be asking them to suggest titles when she is ordering new books. They will discover that a Little Theatre group puts on good performances and that the local symphony orchestra concerts are good.

It will take time for the thoughtful people in the community to discover the new comers and it may take even more time for the new comers to discover that some of their neighbors are not as low brow, as provincial, or as gullible as they seemed to be at first. Their problem this year may be to find like-minded people. Their problem next year may be to keep to a reasonable number the engagements they make to speak and answer questions at churches, at schools, at clubs, and at back yard suppers where they will be sitting with friends.

The Inquiring Reporter

Those returning from overseas must face a great variety of questions. Many of the questions reveal a genuine desire for information and those who answer carefully and fully render a significant service because new knowledge obtained from a personal source is frequently valued and retained. It is not uncommon now to hear someone say, "A friend just back from Afghanistan told us that the movement to unveil the women there met with strong resistance from some fanatical groups but a government decree now permits women to put aside the veil" or "I met a man just home from Guatamala who says that the government is carrying out quite an extensive program of resettlement.

A good many people who used to be tenant farmers are now homesteading farms of their own."

It can be extremely helpful to the cause of international understanding when those who have lived abroad return and pass on to their friends and associates specific information about the countries they have lived in. It is even more helpful when the information is given within a framework of history and with a picture of present day changes and trends.

We recently heard a man who had returned from Pakistan give such a succinct statement about that country that those listening to him could follow his discussion with interest and understanding even though some of them had only a vague idea about the Muslim Country whose support is of significant importance to the United States. He began by giving the facts about the two parts of the country—East Pakistan and West Pakistan—which are separated by a thousand miles of territory belonging to India. He described the population, pointing out the fact that while in the two sections there is a common religious bond the people speak different languages and have different customs and consequently face problems of balance of political power between the two sections of the country.

He reviewed the origin of the country by partition from India following independence from Great Britain after World War II. Then he went on to talk about the internal problems. He described in detail some aspects of the problems of land ownership and showed how they are tied up both with the struggles for political power and the economic structure of the country.

This speaker did not assume on the part of his listeners a familiarity with background information about the country from which he had returned. He told about the newly organized system of "basic democracies" for local government and showed how the arrangement, which merges the processes of election and appointment, is in keeping with the Pakistani ways of thinking and working and is contributing to the stability of the country. He identified the principal leaders of the country, outlining their political relationships, and he summarized the major national goals.

After briefing listeners on the essential historical facts, he gave them up-to-date information and an analysis of current situations. Consequently, he was able in a short time to have a group of people prepared not only to question him about points of special interest but to go out on their own to find reading material and to listen to news reports with understanding and profit.

Those who have returned from living overseas are sometimes handicapped when they attempt to answer questions because those who pose the questions have preconceived ideas about a country or a situation and so do not at first hear with understanding what has been said.

A newspaper reporter who had learned some years ago that I was visiting in her community called me one day to ask if she might have a story about the work my husband had been doing as a missionary in China. I told her about his relationship to a university and about a research project in which he and his colleagues had been able to work out a way to compost human fecal material so that the fermentation heat would sterilize the night soil killing the parasitic organisms and even the resistant eggs of the intestinal round worm, thus providing a hygienically safe and economically reasonable fertilizer for the North China soil which had been depleted through countless years of intensive use in densely populated rural areas.

The reporter seemed fascinated, asked me for more details and thanked me as if she were in a big hurry to write a piece which had all the elements of a good feature story. In a few minutes the phone rang again and the same voice minus the enthusiasm said, "Mrs. Winfield, all the things you told me were so interesting. But I was supposed to get a story on your husband's missionary work. Could you tell me about that?"

Both the reporter and her editor had a stereotyped picture of a missionary as a solemn faced individual who stood on a soap box preaching to "convert the heathen." They had an idea that a missionary might heal people or feed them or perhaps teach them to read in order that they might more effectively persuade them to become believers, but they had no framework of reference into which they could fit a missionary who applied the processes of scientific research to the related problems of health-agriculture-education-economics and community development not as a sideline to but as an integral part of a helpful ministry in a depressed area.

There has been great improvement in popular knowledge about the rest of the world and about the ways in which Americans are working in foreign countries, but there is still to be found in any American community persistent and generally erroneous concepts which must be corrected before people are ready or able to accept new ideas or new information about the rest of the world.

When one speaks publicly or replies to the questions of newspaper reporters it is necessary to be careful that the information or the impression given is not misleading or is not likely to be embarrassing either to our government or to the foreign country involved if the report should be picked up and given national or world wide publicity. A man may think he is just popping off among friends, but news coverage being as widespread as it is today, a casual remark, if it has sensational overtones, may be racing around the world in a matter of hours.

When an American comes home from a foreign country and says without modification or without substantial evidence, "The government of—is rotten to the core" he is not only reporting irresponsibly, he is running the risk of having his statement quoted in the foreign capital where he has respected friends who are hard working and proud government officials.

It is important in reporting about another part of the world to avoid using the terms which the people of that region or country feel are disparaging. The followers of Islam, for instance, do not like to be referred to as Mohammedans because that seems to them to imply that they worship the prophet Mohammed and to them this would be idolatry because they worship only Allah ("The Lord our God is one God") and consider that Mohammed is the chief prophet of Allah. They prefer to be called Muslims.

People in many of the less developed countries of the world dislike being called "the natives." This is, of course, a perfectly good English term for those born in a certain area (a native Virginian) but it has come to people in many places to have overtones of primitiveness, and if a student from an Asian or African country were in the audience when an American spoke of "the natives" in the student's country, he might immediately conclude that the speaker had a colonial point of view and that he looked down upon the student's people. It is always safer to refer to people of another country by their national name such as Indians, Thais, Ethiopians, or Indonesians. In most countries the English word "nationals" is an accepted term referring in a dignified way to the people of a country as citizens.

Unless one is familiar with officially stated policies of the American government in relation to another country, it is unwise for him to make public statements about foreign policy. When a man says in a speech that it is the American policy to support a certain movement or to oppose a certain leader in another country he may be only giving his own impression of what he has observed, and he has every right to make a personal observation, but the reporter who covers his speech may not qualify the remarks, and if they happen to be startling they may receive undue attention both at home and abroad, with the result that Americans may be misled and foreign leaders may be unnecessarily agitated.

A government official home from overseas has to be doubly careful about this. Officers may avoid making public statements and some of them admonish their wives to be non-commital even about personal aspects of their lives overseas, because they dare not run the risk of inadvertently making comments which might create difficulties with a foreign government.

Those who have been abroad unofficially need not be so prudent, but all Americans should be deliberately responsible when they speak about things they have heard or observed in a foreign country.

Report In Pictures

Many people come back to this country with hundreds of still pictures or with dozens of rolls of movie film they have taken abroad. If used effectively pictures can be of tremendous help in bringing back to relatives and friends as well as public audiences a vivid account of far away lands and neighborly people.

In order that visual reports may come through to either a large or a living room size audience with clarity and impact some thought must be given to their selection. The attention of an audience will be lost and dinner guests will become bored if the amateur photographer hasn't done his homework before he starts running his projector.

In the first place he must accept the fact that people can absorb at one sitting only about forty or fifty still pictures and no more than an hour of carefully edited movie film. So he must discipline himself to select in advance the group of pictures most suitable for a given audience and then not let himself be tempted to push just one more and then one more reel or group of slides on a satiated audience.

The selection of pictures needs to be made according to subject matter with the baby's first steps placed with family high lights and the Prime Minister's appearance at the dedication of a cotton mill placed with a report on national development. Any picture used must have good quality from the point of view of exposure, color balance, and focus; but a picture should not be placed in a group just because it has technical merit. The emphasis must be on content. The whole group must say something in particular and each individual picture must contribute to what is being said.

A good picture story begins with a location shot or two so that people may know where the scene is laid. Then detailed close-up pictures should follow. Those who work with pictures professionally say that the amateur tends to use too many long or medium shots and not enough close-ups. One who is viewing pictures needs to feel that he is stepping close enough to a man to speak to him, that he is getting close enough to an operation to see in detail how it is performed, that he is seeing places and things in particular and not just views in general.

In order that he may give to those who see his pictures a sense of participation in the recorded event, a photographer needs to have two or three times the number of pictures that he can use so that he will have a wide range of choice available when he edits his material. When he makes the final selections he must be careful to use pictures which are not cluttered with too much detail that is not a part of his story.

An excellent example of the effective use of pictures was shown to my husband and me recently when friends who had lived in Greece gave us and a few other dinner guests a brief glimpse of the Greek countryside. They projected colored slides on to a neutral wall space and the very first shots had so much depth and naturalness that we felt as if we ourselves were standing where the photographer had stood when he took the panorama shots of fields and orchards and a road winding through a valley. We went close enough to a farmer to see the shape of his hoe. We were near enough a tree to reach out and pluck the fruit. As we passed a cottage I thought I could smell the white carnations and I actually saw a bee on a red hibiscus.

The group of pictures had a good balance between things as they are today and things as they used to be in ancient times. After we had seen a modern farmer working in his fields and modern students cycling along the road, we went into a restored amphitheatre and our hostess gave us a brief description of a Greek drama she once saw performed in that place. But when we looked at the theatre (as we watched the slides) we looked with a group of American tourists, and we saw with them the Greek guide who went down to the very center of the stage to whisper in order that the tourist might appreciate how perfect the theatre acoustics were. In one picture I saw the guide's lips open and in the next picture I saw the startled faces of the Americans who were sitting on the back row of that vast outdoor auditorium. I too caught my breath marveling that I could hear from such a distance.

After we left the amphitheatre we stopped to read a road sign, seeing in a close-up picture the English name of the town spelled out under the Greek script. It was interesting to see how our language looked in relation to another language but it was even more interesting to realize that an English speaking visitor in Greece would feel welcome and would be able to find his way around the Greek countryside.

Those who use movies as a medium of communication must be even more skilled than the reporters who use slides because the American public has become accustomed to such high quality films that jumpy, cloudy, and timorously edited movies are now appreciated only by indulgent relatives. But a good many people who live overseas have taught themselves how to shoot and how to edit movie film, and they are able to bring back visual reports which have the extra dimensions of movement and in some cases sound.

Not long ago we saw a home movie which was an outstanding demonstration of the power of the camera to record memorable events and the possibilities that exist for a photographer who has both imagination and discrimination. The movie had been made in Taipei. The subject was Chinese Festivals and Ceremonies. Over a period of two years a curious American with color film in his 16 mm. movie camera had followed wedding processions and funeral processions and had attended numerous ceremonies.

On one occasion he had slipped into an inconspicuous but well lighted corner of a pagoda where Buddhists celebrated the birthday of *Kwang Yin* (the goddess of mercy). As we looked at the film we saw crowds of people entering with fruits or flowers or incense. We saw apart from the crowd a father teaching his young son to go through the motions of obeisance before a small shrine.

In the courtyard of a Confucian temple we saw high ranking government officials in formal black silk jackets and young school girls in light blue cotton uniforms bow in respect to the revered sage. There were other ceremonies and festivals which were alive with color and action. In all of it we were able to feel that we were actually observing at first hand the traditions and practices which many people who now live in exile follow even as their ancestors on the mainland had observed these same ceremonies for countless generations.

Productive Americans

All of us who have lived overseas have at one time or another seen an individual or a group of Americans behaving in such a way that we have regretted their actions.

A friend just home from Africa tells us how mortified she was at an airport where a group of American tourists led by a genial but conniving tour director ignored the announcement given both in the local language and in English that transient passengers should re-enter the plane before newly embarking passengers. A group of local people were ready to go back to their seats and their belongings, but the minute the gate was opened, to the astonishment of everyone including the local airline official at the gate and the local stewardess who stood at the door of the plane, the white-skinned well-dressed tourists who had not previously been on that plane moved in what could only have been a well rehearsed and repeatedly practiced maneuver. With a quick thrust and a tight formation they forced their way ahead of the slow moving and naturally retiring local passengers and rushed on to the plane where they chose choice seats and settled themselves and their flight bags. By the time the local people came back to their former seats, the Americans comfortably grouped together had their seat belts fastened, and the little people could only retrieve their bags and parcels and find seats here and there as best they could.

Polite and shy as they were not a one of them protested vocally. "But how," our friend asked us as she concluded the story, "can we guess the depth of their resentment?"

It is inevitable that people who are as incensed as she was about this disgraceful episode should come home and report it with indignation. Perhaps such reports will serve to alert others who go overseas to the undeniable fact that unless good manners go with Americans ill will is sure to be directed against America.

But fortunately our friend had seen only this one instance of badly behaving Americans and she told us of several dozen outstanding Americans she saw during several months in Africa and the Mid-East. As she told us about different ones she had seen who are making significant contributions in the countries where they are working she said, "This man is *producing* educational television programs which will reach the public schools of Nigeria" or "That man is responsible for the *production* of improved rice seed in Liberia" or "That woman is teaching women in Kenya how to *produce* better balanced meals for their families."

All who have lived abroad have seen at first hand scores of Americans who are not only contributing to the rapid production of much needed goods and services but are at the same time producing in full measure a kind of good will which may be the most important product of all.

Other friends have told us that they have seen American bankers overseas providing banking services, including investments and loans, for the development of the countries. We get reports that the introduction of modern marketing techniques, such as those provided by Sears and Roebuck, in several countries in Latin America has resulted in the stimulating of new local production so that literally thousands of small businesses have been started to supply the mass sales outlets of the American firms.

We hear of American men who are members of medical research

teams, financed from the sale of surplus agricultural commodities, who are contributing to the study of a series of tropical diseases at overseas research centers. The Ford Foundation, the Rockefeller Foundation and others have programs through which Americans working with nationals are assisting schools, colleges, and universities in areas where educational needs are pressing.

The pages of a whole book would be insufficient to describe even briefly the productive activities of but a few overseas Americans. It is important that the American public should learn about those Americans overseas who are engaged so effectively in useful enterprises. Many of them are government employees and taxpayers deserve to know how much their tax dollars are buying in terms of helping people to help themselves to higher standards of living and to a fuller use of modern tools and modern knowledge. All of them whether working through government or business firms or churches or foundations represent the creative genius of America, and Americans at home ought to hear more about them.

Who is in a better position to inform the American public about their compatriots who are quietly at work on the frontiers of today's world than the ones who have seen them at their jobs? I hope that all who return from an overseas assignment will not only describe the people of the countries where they have lived and point out the development that is going on in other places, but that they also will find many opportunities to say: "Let me tell you what a man from Nebraska is doing in Nepal, what a woman from Oregon is doing in Libya, what a couple from Arizona are doing in Colombia."

The Welcome Mat

Many times I have heard Americans who have had a rewarding stay in a foreign country say, "What can we ever do to repay these people for their kindness?" Those who leave a foreign airport with their arms loaded with flowers and farewell gifts, and with memories of months of pleasant associations sometimes have an overwhelming sense of indebtedness. Americans are occasionally able to send back small presents to a few foreign friends and in special ways to be helpful to other people. Few of us are able to do as much as we would like to. Sometimes the needs exceed our economic capacity, and generally it is not easy to know what people might be needing when we are half a world away from them.

It seems to me that we must do all we can to be good neighbors and thoughtful friends wherever we are and then as we move to a new neighborhood accept the fact that we are not obliged to "pay back" directly the people who have done a great deal for us in the place we have left. We can, however, in an indirect way acknowledge our gratitude to people who have befriended us in one foreign country by extending friendship and hospitality to other people from that particular country or to those from any foreign place who live in or visit the American community where we reside after we return to America.

No need is greater than the need felt by a lonesome African student who finds himself in an American city surrounded by strange voices, strange food, and strange customs. If he makes a stop-over in a southern city he may find himself barred from a restaurant and turned away from a first-class hotel because of his black skin. Each of us who has lived abroad should not only try to find as many lonely students as we can and give them a personal welcome, but we should feel obliged to make certain that all the public facilities in our communities (waiting rooms, rest rooms, restaurants, hotels, YM and YWCA hostels, movies, parks, barber shops, libraries) are operating without discrimination so that there is not a chance that a foreign visitor seeking a bed, a meal, or an hour of relaxation will feel embarrassed or rejected.

It is not only the undergraduate or graduate student who may feel lonely or unwelcome in our country. There are large numbers of middle-age professional people now coming for special short term study tours. Many of them travel from place to place, and while living arrangements are provided for them at some scheduled stops there are overnight or week-end stops when they must look after themselves. In many ways their adjustments are more difficult than those of full time students who have the chance to become acquainted with other students and to join into campus activities.

In many large cities there are international centers where professional or volunteer staffs make efforts to provide information and hospitality for both transient and resident foreigners. Every community needs such a center and hundreds of people are needed who will sign up to provide transportation, to act as guides, and to keep open house for visitors from abroad.

Almost every college and university has foreign students in attendance. These students generally have no place to go during the holidays. It would be a splendid thing if a family returned from overseas would write or call the college nearest its home and ask to have the name of a foreign student whom they might invite to their home for Thanksgiving, Christmas, or a spring vacation.

Those who have lived abroad should be particularly sensitive to the needs and interests of people from other countries. No one should be better able to understand the loneliness of one who has left his family behind him than the American who has himself been a stranger in a foreign land and has seen how family-centered most foreign countries are. He can recognize the young student's need to feel he belongs to a family in this country. He can appreciate the family man's longing to play with little children and to show his own children's pictures to an interested audience. He can know how eager a woman from abroad is to see an American kitchen and to help prepare a meal.

The one who has lived overseas can realize how much it will mean to a foreigner to have a hostess prepare some food familiar to him. On many occasions I have seen unrestrained delight on the face of an Asian guest when I have carried a bowl of steaming rice to the table. The same thing has happened when we have placed a bowl of yogurt before a student from a Middle-East country.

The things we may do for those who are foreigners in our country are so simple and demand so little of us that we are likely to be unaware that we are rendering an important service when we open our doors and invite a Latin American, an Asian, an African, a European, or a Middle-Easterner to come in to live with us for a while, to spend a week-end with us, to share a meal, or just to have a cup of good hot tea.

Chapter XIV

TWENTIETH CENTURY PIONEERS

The astronaut with all of his paraphernalia and elaborate countdown is, without doubt, a conspicuous symbol of the second half of the twentieth century. Less conspicuously but no less significantly the peripatetic American with a foreign language dictionary and a bulging brief case in his hands, accompanied by his wife and children and an assortment of suitcases and packing boxes is just as surely a reminder of the fact that by the middle of the twentieth century man has achieved enough knowledge not only to go out into the vast reaches of space to see what space is like and how it might be used but also to go into the furthest outposts of the earth in order to make available to all men sources of knowledge about healthful and productive living.

The outpost pioneers like the outerspace explorers are drawing upon the same store of accumulated knowledge. Both rely upon what science has demonstrated about the universe and its component parts. Both must reckon with what is known about the nature of man—his physical needs and his emotional drives. Each group of pioneers proceeds from a known body of facts towards an unknown number and kind of variable factors.

In both enterprises the crewmen need to be selected for maturity and adaptability as well as for professional skill. Both those whose families wait out space flights at a home base and those whose families go along to establish a new home must have the kind of families who recognize the importance of the pioneer projects and can adjust to the kind of life that accompanies them.

Both groups require special training. Training for astronauts is more specialized, more exacting, and more rigorous. But the preparation of the men, women, and children who go from the United States to work and live in foreign countries needs to be broader and more comprehensive because their assignments may be of a more subtle nature, requiring of the individual a wider variety of skills and a greater degree of reliance upon personal insight and judgment.

The astronaut may not know exactly what he will find on the moon, but from objective evidence he has a pretty good idea what to expect.

When he gets there he will have a clearly defined set of objectives and plans of action. The globe-trotting pioneer, on the other hand, frequently finds that specific information about the place to which he is going may have changed by the time he arrives. Many of the operations he will perform will have to be determined on the spot by circumstances related to local regulations, to political pressures, to customs and cultural attitudes, as well as to the puzzling factors of personality encounters. Those who go overseas under government auspices may find also that their performance has to be related to the deliberations and vacillations of the American Congress!

Circumstances affecting the overseas Americans are dominated by the human factors. To build a dam is admittedly a physical feat. Details can be calculated. Results can be seen. But getting a plan for a dam accepted, acquiring the rights to flood a land area, training people to install and operate machinery, and teaching even greater numbers of people how to make the best use of the new water supply as well as the electrical power generated involve problems of human and social engineering that can't ever be worked out on a drafting board or reported on a chart.

There are no push-button controls for Americans who work overseas. There are only the slow and steady efforts to perform effectively and acceptably, maintaining a precarious balance between one's understanding of what needs to be done and one's understanding of what the people of a community are ready and willing to do.

In the last analysis the success of an American overseas is dependent upon his skill as a communicator. Diplomats, engineers, bankers, missionaries, doctors, military personnel, teachers, housewives, teenagers—whoever ventures out to other countries—must be able first of all to listen to the voices of the people of the countries and then must be able to speak understandably in words, in attitude, and in conduct.

To listen with understanding and to speak with clarity in a foreign environment is never an easy undertaking but it is a thoroughly natural kind of performance and those who let themselves be involved deeply in the experience of living overseas will discover that it is possible to achieve a personal interaction across barriers of language, culture, political ideologies, power struggles, and technological development stages. Most of them find themselves able to move beyond the self conscious period of feeling looked at by strangers or of being exposed to an alien culture and will arrive at the place where they are apprehending some ranges of the inner meanings of what the people around them think and do, coming finally not just to understand them but to understand with them some of the hopes and aspirations, the fears and apprehensions which are common to all men.

Those who communicate most successfully overseas seldom put the emphasis on any special techniques of "overseamanship" or even on the particular forms of communication. There is no one way for Americans to speak and no best way for Americans to work and live abroad. Each must speak the truth as he sees it and each must use the methods or tools of delivery most natural for him and most understandable for his audience. With due regard for the sensitivities of his neighbors, each man must live according to his own bent.

But there is a paramount emphasis that is needed by all Americans overseas. It is an emphasis on the content of the messages they are both consciously and unconsciously transmitting. There is an urgent need for each overseas American to keep his attention focused on life's deepest meanings and values whatever his daily work.

The peoples of the earth are all searching for material well being and with man's knowledge and resources as abundant as they are there is no excuse for anyone being denied his basic needs. But people long for meaning beyond bread and shelter and medicine. They want freedom—not just freedom from the fears of war and hunger and pestilence. They want also the freedom to live with dignity and self-respect, the freedom to enjoy opportunities for growth and creative activity. Americans who live abroad are involved in the processes of expanding the frontiers of freedom.

Our pioneers of a previous century set out to conquer a wilderness in the process of building a nation. The American pioneers of the nineteen sixties will in a very few cases climb into capsules and be hurled out to conquer space. In more than a million and a half cases the pioneers (including their wives and children) will find their way to down-to-earth places beyond our shores and their objective in one framework or another will be to build a world community in which there are cooperative efforts to improve the lot of all and in which there are congenial relationships between free people. If this kind of community begins to emerge in our time it will not be exclusively an American achievement, but it certainly will be in line with the American dream of universal prosperity and peace.

I would not be foolish enough to argue that those who go out to enrich and strengthen the community of man are doing a more noble or a more needful thing than those who go out beyond the known realms of men. I do assert that if those Americans who move around on the earth, slowly assisting people in their struggles to achieve a higher standard of living, steadily learning to understand and to identify with foreign cultures, dauntlessly believing in human freedom, and dynamically expounding the concept of free men working responsibly for the common good are not encouraged and assisted so that most of them succeed in their undertakings, then the sending of explorers into outer space may in the long run be of little importance.

The thing that is of importance is that America never cease being a country which produces pioneers, that we never abandon our traditional respect for the interrelatedness of material and spiritual goals, that we continue steadfast in our loyalty to the spirit of revolution which prompted us first to pioneer in representative government and prompts us three hundred years later to salute and to assist the revolution of rising expectations throughout the world.

Those Americans who go overseas and those at home who send or support them should feel no need to hide the altruistic aspects of an overseas assignment as if the homely virtues of helpfulness and hopefulness were out of date or represented the foolishness of our nation's youth. It was in hope and mutual help that our republic was born and it is only because there are still so many Americans who are willing to work for the general welfare and who dare to believe in goodness that our nation has health today and expectations of a happy future.

Our pioneers on the outposts of the modern world may be carrying a great many other things like plows, drills, hypodermic needles. filmstrip projectors—and they should—but the biggest percent of them are at the same time carrying the American ideals which are as valid and as essential today as they were three hundred years ago. Wherever an American business man is contributing to the greater production and flow of good quality commodities, wherever an exchange professor is participating in a search for new knowledge, wherever a nutrition expert is a member of a team working to provide a more balanced diet, wherever an educator is helping to develop a system of good schools, wherever a missionary is helping people in a rapidly changing community to find and live with enduring values, wherever a diplomat is maintaining good working relationships with the government of another country, wherever a member of our armed forces is helping to keep the peace, wherever a printer is showing people how to operate a modern press, an engineer is at work on a highway, an agricultural expert is working with farmers, an American youth is working beside a youth of another country, an American wife is rolling bandages with women of her host country, a white American child is smiling at a black African child or a black American child is sharing a toy with a brown Asian child—there is an example of the flowering of American ideals. Let us acknowledge it for what it is and be glad.

If Americans cherishing spiritual values were not actively involved in the problems of the rest of the world, our ideals would be dying at home and much that is most virile in our nation would be dying too, suffocating in isolation and a self-centered materialism.

To be sure, any overseas expedition is expensive. It takes money for an oil company to send men and machines and school teachers to Saudi-Arabia. It costs thousands of dollars for the Rockefeller Foundation to send a public health specialist and his family to India. It is expensive for the State Department to open embassies in all the new countries of Africa. It is a financial effort for a church in Arlington, Virginia to support a missionary in a literary center in Rhodesia. It is expensive for the American taxpayers to send Peace Corps volunteers to Ghana and public administration technicians to South America. To those who protest all such expenditures I would ask: Since when have Americans forgotten that our own high level economy is the result of economic investments and that our high standard of living is the result both of generous expenditures of money and a persistent faith in the rights of all the people to have the opportunities which money can provide? Surely no one can believe that either our standard of living or our freedom of opportunity can long endure if we try to keep our society alive in a vacuum.

If anyone is bothered about the cost which the pioneer himself must pay, let me say that in my thirty years of close association with Americans who live abroad I have known only a few who made any special sacrifice, and none of those few looked upon themselves as martyrs. What if carrying the fruits of modern knowledge and the leavens of freedom to the frontiers of the world should require sacrifice on the part of the couriers? Would we deny them the chance to live with courage or deny ourselves the chance to be a nation which honors the kind of level-headed and whole-hearted dedication which the twentieth century so desperately needs?

A member of our family needed to get to the doctor the other day. Our car was not at home. I called a neighbor to see if anyone there was going to be driving near the doctor's office. "We will pick you up right away" was the reply.

When we went out to get into the car I realized that the head of the household, dressed for his office which was in quite a different direction from the doctor, was our driver. "Are you sure it is convenient?" I asked him. "And if it weren't convenient?" he asked me. I was overwhelmed with the simplicity and the splendor of neighborliness.

I knew at that moment just what I had been trying to say about living overseas. It is important to do the things that need doing in the world. It is important to do them graciously as one neighbor to another. In general it is not difficult nor unduly costly. Most frequently it is interesting and rewarding. But if it weren't—could any of us who care about people refuse to suffer the inconvenience of responding to human needs wherever they exist?

INDEX

E

F

H

I

J

L

M

N

P

R

S

T

U

V

W

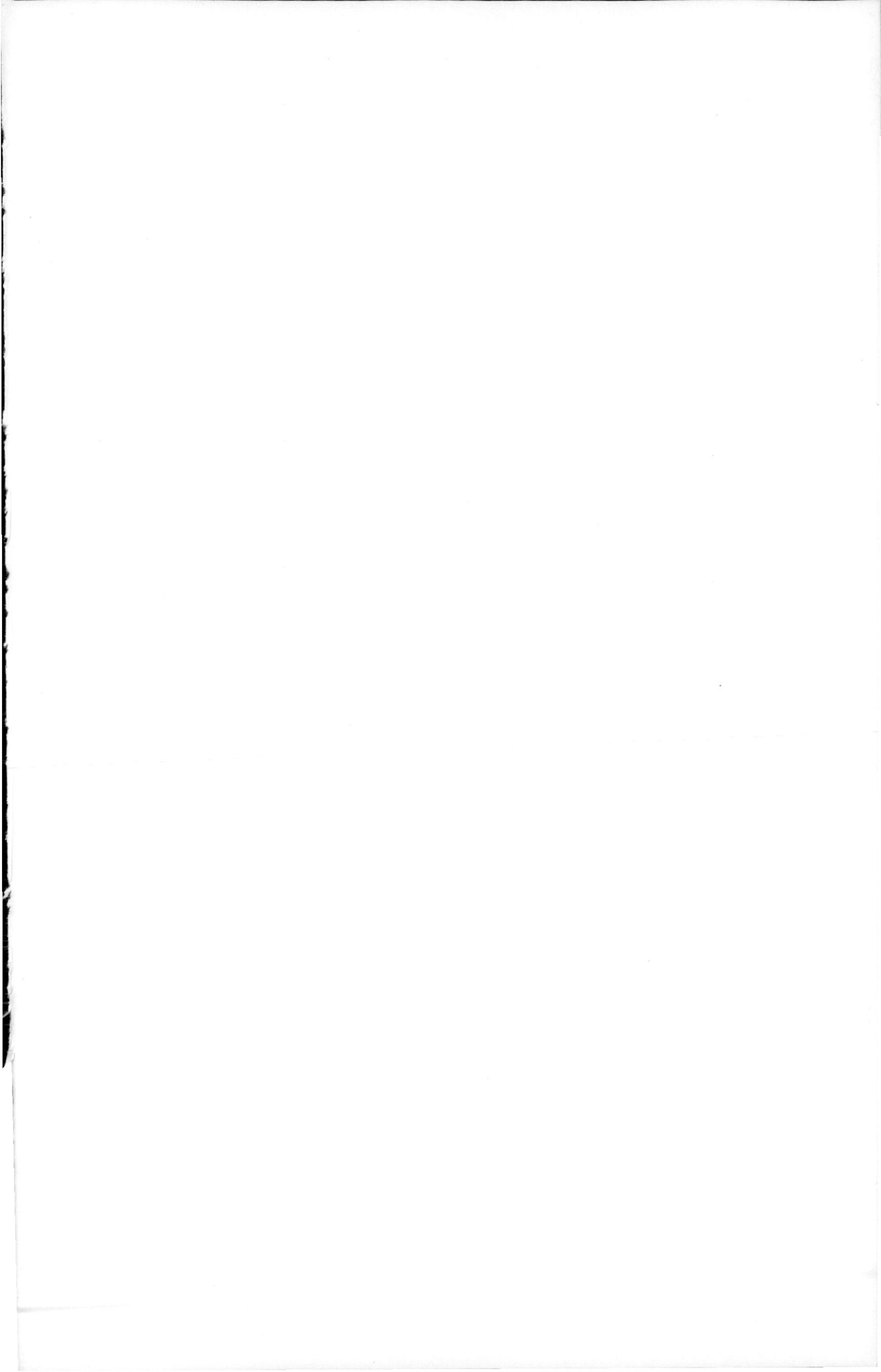